Curriculum and Policy in Irish
Post-Primary Education

Denis O' Driscoll

Kingston   June '82

For my wife Mary and our children

Curriculum and Policy in Irish Post-Primary Education

D. G. Mulcahy

Institute of Public Administration
Dublin

Published by the
Institute of Public Administration
59 Lansdowne Road
Dublin 4
Ireland

First Published 1981

British Library Cataloguing in Publication Data

Mulcahy, D.G.
   Curriculum and policy in Irish post-primary education.
   1. Curriculum planning 2. Education, Secondary — Ireland
   I. Title
   373.19'09417   LB1629.5.I/

ISBN 0-906980-02-X

Set in Baskerville by
Lagamage Company Limited.
Printed by Mount Salus Press Limited, Dublin

Contents

vi

List of Tables

Is the curriculum you've got in your secondary schools — which I find rather 'traditional' — is that really what you want for the future? I should think that a country with 50 per cent of its population under twenty-five would be having educational debates as to what you want your schools to be like by the year 2000.

Professor Jerome Bruner, RTE Radio, 7 October 1980

Preface

It is important to expose educational policy and practice to critical analysis and evaluation. It is especially important at the present time, for reasons which I hope to make clear in the following pages, that post-primary education in Ireland should enter a new period of debate and development and that the question of the curriculum should be central to that debate. What follows will, I hope, help to focus discussion on the curriculum, provide a framework within which debate may be conducted, and provoke further much-needed debate and research.

In any study of this kind one necessarily builds on the work of others. There are two people, however, to whom a special word of appreciation and thanks is due in bringing this work to completion. A very special word of appreciation is due to Dr Johnny Coolahan of University College, Dublin. Dr Coolahan has read the draft manuscript in its entirety and has made many valuable suggestions. As a result a number of important changes were made in both the structure and the balance of the work. To Professor Séamas Ó Súilleabháin of St Patrick's College, Maynooth, I am indebted for his encouragement and his incisive comments on a number of draft chapters. I need hardly add that the responsibility for errors of fact or viewpoint which may remain lie entirely with me.

I wish to express my gratitude for assistance given to me by the staffs of different libraries where I have worked and especially the libraries of University College, Cork and Trinity College, Dublin. I should also like to record my thanks to the Department of Education in Dublin for procuring for me copies of various documents from time to time and for making various facilities available to me.

Finally, I am greatly indebted to my secretary, Ita McEnnis, for her patience and skill in preparing the typescript and for her

ix

assistance with the bibliography. And I am indebted to Jim O'Donnell of the Institute of Public Administration for his support and for his seeing the study to publication.

D.G. Mulcahy

University College, Cork
January 1981

Introduction

The evaluation of post-primary education in Ireland

Attention in this study is focused on a problem which is as old as that of formal schooling itself; yet it is one which remains central to the concerns of educational policy-makers and practitioners in developed and developing systems of education alike. The subject of enquiry is the problem of a general education. More specifically, the study is concerned with the analysis and evaluation of present-day curriculum provision for the purpose of general education in post-primary education in the Republic of Ireland.

It can hardly be seriously questioned that some such analysis and evaluation is desirable at this time. Despite the changes of recent years, at no time during the past fifteen years or indeed at any time since the setting up of the Department of Education in 1924, has any sustained assessment and critical analysis been undertaken in regard to the overall purposes and programmes of post-primary education in Ireland. Yet the past decade has seen an unprecedented questioning and criticism of the role of formal schooling in many western societies, including Ireland. The optimism which marked the expansion of educational systems during the 1960s gave way in the 1970s to a mood of uncertainty regarding the value of education as a cure-all for social ills and shortcomings. For some, the school — and particularly the second-level school — has lost its way.

In a number of countries educational authorities and educational interest groups have begun to take up this new challenge. Thus in the United Kingdom there has been the so-called great debate initiated by the Prime Minister in 1976. In that debate much of the attention has been focused upon devising new forms of curriculum and examinations at post-primary level. In the United States the past decade has seen various educational commissions

1

re-assess the state of second-level education in particular,[1] and recommendations for reform have been made. In Ireland, hopefully, the publication of the recent government *White Paper on Educational Development* will mark the beginning of a period of sustained and wide-ranging debate of such matters.

The criticisms of post-primary education in Ireland are wideranging in character. Much of the criticism is levelled against the programmes on offer and the examinations. Criticisms offered by the public at large, and not necessarily by those who are professionally involved in education, frequently take the form of charging the schools with being too academic in emphasis; with being insufficiently geared to preparing pupils for life and the world of work; of catering primarily for the few, the university-bound, rather than the many; and, increasingly, of being out of touch with the needs and demands of modern-day youth. The strain and weight of the public examinations provoke incessant complaint.

This study will examine these criticisms, for although such criticisms are not always well articulated they do seem to be deeply rooted in the public's consciousness of post-primary schooling. It is one thing, however, to take up and apply criticisms. It is quite another to try to interweave such criticisms with analytical and critical perspectives in a systematic way in order to throw light on the system under examination. Yet unless this can be done valid criticism may be both ineffectual and at the same time run the risk of being merely sporadic, carping and superficial. Accordingly, this study will establish perspectives which will provide a conceptual framework for the analysis of post-primary education in Ireland, for the assessment of its strengths and weaknesses, and for the consideration of alternatives.

It was encouraging, as this study was nearing completion, to read in the *White Paper* that one of the aims of the Curriculum Unit, which was set up in 1977, in the Department of Education, is 'to develop a conceptual framework for curriculum by analysis and evaluation of the existing curriculum (rationale, institutional structure, modes of operation) and, as an ancillary process, to construct and evaluate alternative models.'[2] Analysis and evaluation are necessary first steps in the consideration of reform measures.

This study will also be of interest to comparative educationists and curriculum theorists, for an approach to the evaluation of school programmes of a broad and general scope has also been developed.

To criticise schools on the grounds that they fail to prepare pupils for life or for work, that they concentrate too much on academic or literary studies at the expense of more practical pursuits, or that, in general, they are irrelevant in preparing pupils to meet the various social, economic, moral and personal demands of the world in which they live, is to imply that it is the responsibility of the schools to seek to achieve these various objectives. If the attainment of such objectives is espoused by the schools, then the criticisms are valid. But do the schools, or more specifically, does post-primary education in Ireland espouse these goals? Is it accountable to such charges?

It will be argued here that it is an espoused aim of post-primary education in Ireland to prepare pupils for life and the implications for the curriculum of the post-primary school will be considered. The question, however, is not quite as simple and straightforward as it might seem. To begin with, although post-primary education in Ireland does aspire to provide a general education as a preparation for life and has done so for many years, its commitment to this goal has not always been expressed very clearly or very forcefully. It is arguable, moreover, that the curricular and other measures taken were, at times, either misguided in their intent or dictated by a too narrow and, again, a not very explicit concept of what was needed. Secondly, although post-primary education in Ireland does seek to provide a general education as a preparation for life, it is not entirely clear what this goal includes. Other goals appear to be the provision of a suitably qualified and adequate supply of manpower and the preparation of pupils to enter institutions of higher education. It is quite unclear what relationships exist, or are intended to exist, between the various aims and goals.

If it is granted that one of the aims to which post-primary education in Ireland is committed is the preparation of pupils for life, the question arises what constitutes general education for life. Although a certain orthodoxy has prevailed in school programmes when it comes to action on this question, the question is nonetheless a vexed one. It has, moreover, an important dimension which is usually overlooked: this is a dimension which I shall refer to as the pedagogy (as distinct from the public content) of the curriculum.

In this study, in addition to a consideration of the public content of the curriculum, four aspects of the pedagogy of the curriculum are touched upon with a view to identifying some of the ways in which aspects of curriculum practice actually influence or shape the learning which takes place. Recent years have seen a growth of interest in the phenomenon known as the hidden curriculum and the 'hidden' ways in which it can influence learning. As yet little thought has been given to how this phenomenon might operate in post-primary education in Ireland. However, it is important. To take one example it is important to study the pedagogical impact of the public examinations and their probable influence on pupils' conceptions of schooling and learning in this 'hidden' way.

Aims and philosophy, curriculum content and pedagogy constitute the chief aspects of existing curriculum provision in Irish post-primary education which will be considered in this study. The historical background to curriculum provision, however, will also be taken into account. It would be unrealistic to undertake any examination of current provision without looking at the reform attempts of the mid-sixties. The impact on schooling of these efforts has been considerable, and it is still being felt. Likewise, it will be helpful to bear in mind the course of development of post-primary education in Ireland since the establishment of the intermediate system in 1878. In this way it will be possible to identify those elements in the Irish tradition which have long been a source of dissatisfaction.

An approach to the qualitative evaluation of curriculum

As a study in curriculum evaluation rather than in the evaluation of pupil achievement or learning, what is at issue here is the adequacy of curriculum content and pedagogy for the attainment of sought-after ends or goals. There are different ways of measuring or assessing the adequacy of a curriculum; two chief types can be identified. The first one is quantitative or empirical in character. A study of this kind might, for example, base its assessment of the curriculum on a sample of the opinions and attitudes of employers, parents, teachers and pupils in regard to various aspects of the curriculum.[3] Or it might make a comparison between Ireland and other countries on the basis of range of subjects studied, number of years required to complete the programme, financing, resources, equipment, and pupil performance on standardised tests.[4]

It is more difficult to get an agreed name for the second chief approach to evaluation. It might be described broadly as employing philosophy, history and literary criticism as modes of analysis and discussion. The present study adopts this second approach. It is an approach suited to a consideration of conceptual issues and issues of principle affecting curriculum, and it is with such matters that the present study is largely concerned.[5]

Basic to the evaluation of curriculum carried out here is the notion of education as a means-ends activity in which various measures are taken by educational authorities which are considered appropriate to the attainment of sought-after goals or ends. This general approach has been well recognised in education, being central to the so-called classical model of curriculum development.[6] Accordingly, while education, as understood here, promotes values in the form of growth and development of persons, it does not of itself pick out any particular value or values which ought to be sought. The selection of ends or values to be sought, that is the adoption of aims, is considered to be the responsibility of those who choose to educate or to whom is assigned the responsibility for its furtherance. And the role of aims in the educational enterprise is seen to be one of prime importance. It is from aims, or ends to be sought, that the entire educational enterprise takes its shape and character, indeed its entire *raison d'être*.

Believing that educational practice ought to be shaped by educational aims, philosophers of education have always accorded special attention in their discussions to aims in education. Notwithstanding this, however, in Ireland as elsewhere, the importance attached to the question of aims in discussing educational matters has not always resulted in the careful setting forth of statements of aims and the drawing up of educational programmes in line with them. It is for this reason that a central concern in this study is the attempt to clarify and establish what are considered to be the aims of post-primary education in Ireland.

But what constitutes an adequate statement of aims in education? Certain basic conditions need to be met in setting forth statements of aims, otherwise it may be difficult to see what measures are needed to achieve the ends in view, or even to know whether the ends have been achieved or are achievable. Whatever criticisms may be levelled at the behavioural objectives movement of recent times, by calling for the setting forth of objectives in terms of pupil behaviour it did have a salutary effect. It focused attention on the need for educators to become more clear in their own minds what it was that education was being expected to do for pupils. In its quest for definitiveness the behavioural objectives movement insisted on statements of aims which perhaps attempted to be too specific. Nonetheless, the principle of encapsulating in a statement of aims, even if only a general statement, the kind of development which is sought in terms of how it will be manifest in pupils is an important one.

What is the relationship between aims and curriculum? What is the importance of aims for curriculum? The general view of the relationship between aims in education and the curriculum which is envisaged here is broadly as follows. Aims specify the ends or kinds of development in pupils which are to be sought. Curriculum, in its broadest sense, is seen as the means to promote this development, to achieve the ends or values in view. Accordingly, it is necessary that there be a fundamental consistency between the aims posited and the curriculum or the means employed. Once the question of aims has been attended to, the next question is how consistent with, how suitable for the attainment of the ends in view, is the curriculum. Where no statement or satisfactory statement of aims exists, it is difficult to see what basis there is for drawing up, justifying or even evaluating a curriculum.

Having attempted to establish what appear to be the aims of post-primary education in Ireland, major attention in this study focuses on an examination of the extent to which the curriculum of post-primary education in Ireland is suited to achieving its goal of a general education as a preparation for life. It is necessary, first of all, to clarify what is understood by a general education and it is concluded that a general education as a preparation for life entails the preparation of pupils to cope with a number of major demands of living. These include the vocational, the recreational, the philosophical and various practical demands of living. The present-day curriculum of post-primary education in Ireland is then examined to see how suitable it is as a preparation for meeting these demands of living. This examination is carried out in terms of the content and pedagogy of the curriculum.

While the emphasis in this study is on analysis and evaluation, some consideration is also given to possible alternative courses of policy and practice which might be part of a new approach to the reform of post-primary education in Ireland. This discussion of alternatives, which of its nature can only be broad and tentative, is itself rooted in the analysis which runs throughout the entire study. Accordingly, it focuses largely on the areas of aims and philosophy, curriculum content and pedagogy. It is an attempt to apply critical and analytical perspectives to the challenge of educational reform. And it is based on the belief that analysis and critical appraisal not only constitute a necessary first step in forward planning and policy-making but that they constitute one of the important sources of recommendations as to the eventual scope and shape of reform.

Chapter 1

Facing the Challenge

The post-primary inheritance

Though he might have wished to do so in some respects, when Dr Patrick Hillery, the then Minister for Education, announced his plans for the future of post-primary education in Ireland in May 1963, he was not turning his back on what had gone before. He was not and he could not, for a legacy had been bestowed and it could not be ignored. It was a legacy which contained two strong but distinct traditions, the secondary or intermediate tradition and the vocational tradition.

The secondary or intermediate tradition

Whilst secondary education existed in Ireland in one form or another long before 1878, it was to enter a new phase with the passing of the Intermediate Education (Ireland) Act of that year. The 1878 Act established a system of public examinations which has been from that time a central element and a controlling mechanism in secondary and, more recently, in all of post-primary education in Ireland. Born out of a compromise between the authorities of the Catholic Church and the state, a compromise which evolved during the hotly contested battles of the preceding fifty years over primary and university education rather than intermediate education itself, and welded into uniformity and given vital support through its system of examinations, the intermediate and later secondary education system was to remain viable despite neglect down through the years.

It was through the offices of the Intermediate Education Board for Ireland, established by the terms of the Act of 1878, that intermediate education was administered. It was the function of the Board to provide secular intermediate education for the country by instituting and implementing a system of public examinations,

8

by providing prizes and exhibitions, and by awarding certificates to successful candidates in the examinations. It also paid fees, to become widely known as 'results fees', to school managers. These fees were based on the successful performance by pupils in the examinations and they were subject to the school's compliance with prescribed regulations. There was, however, an important qualification to the effect that no subject of religious instruction could be offered for examination.

Despite the limitations of the Act itself, its financial provisions were welcome at the time. During the penal era Catholic education in all forms had suffered a severe set-back. With the gradual relaxation of the penal laws in the second half of the eighteenth century, and especially under the Relief Act of 1782, there was an expansion of facilities for secondary education for Catholics. But while Catholic secondary schools had been allowed to develop in the 100 years before the Act of 1878, they were still unwilling to make use of the monies which were available for secondary education. The effect of the Act of 1878, whilst not interfering with existing endowments, was to enable Catholics to avail of monies made available for intermediate education.[1]

In quite a different respect also secondary education in Ireland was ready for the provisions of the Act of 1878. During the second half of the nineteenth century external examinations and examining bodies became a feature of secondary education in Europe. London University was one such body to which a number of Irish secondary schools became affiliated at the time. In 1857 the Catholic University of Ireland adopted a system of affiliation, and in the following years a number of Irish schools became affiliated to it. Through such affiliation pupils could sit for external examinations of the body to which their school was affiliated.[2]

Although the external examination had its attractions it also brought with it its own share of questionable educational practices. Not least of these was the decline of school autonomy in curriculum affairs; and under the levelling force of the external examination the distinctive character of a school was also threatened. Yet it was difficult to argue with the appeal of the external examination, for success in the examination conferred a benefit of sorts on all concerned. It provided the successful pupil with a recognised certificate of educational achievement and possibly a university scholarship; and it greatly enhanced his employment prospects. It provided the school with a measure of its own standing. And it kept universities and employers supplied. Thus, both the growing participation in second-level education and the search for affiliation to some recognised external examining body, particularly during the second half of the nineteenth century, invited further state participation in Irish intermediate education. Such participation was achieved through the Act of 1878 and the system of public external examinations which it created.

From its very beginnings intermediate education in Ireland assumed a highly academic and literary character along with a strong sense of subservience to the dictates of the external examination. The literary bias of the subjects recognised for examination was further accentuated by the fact that more generous results fees were made available for English, Latin and Greek than for other subjects in the examinations, thereby making them more attractive to pupils seeking prizes and exhibitions. Indeed the Intermediate Board itself frequently expressed dissatisfaction with many aspects of the system, including the inadequate funding available; and it felt that the curriculum was not always as well suited to Irish schools as it might have been. Clearly, the situation encouraged only an academic or grammar school type of education and one which reflected, in many ways, the practice in secondary education in England at the time. Indeed one teaching order which had been offering courses with a commercial and industrial orientation in a number of its schools found it necessary to change to a more academic type of course since that alone was found to pay its way. Not surprisingly one of the charges against the system was that it catered almost exclusively for a university preparatory education to the neglect of commercial, industrial, agricultural and other forms of education. Science education and, even in the literary field, Irish language and literature were also badly neglected.

Arising out of the discontent regarding such matters a number of attempts were made to improve things. These led to minor curriculum reforms in 1902 and 1903 and to a comprehensive educational reform bill which was introduced in 1919 and again in 1920. Little came of these efforts, however, and it was left to the Provisional Government, which assumed responsibility for the administration of Irish education on 1 February 1922, to take up the cause of educational reform. Without delay the new government set about dismantling the old set-up and reorganising the educational administration of the country.[3] In 1924 it abolished the results fees system of payment in favour of a method of capitation grants and direct payment of teachers. And in general a certain urgency marked the approach taken to the reform of secondary education.

As early as 1921 the Dáil Commission on Secondary Education was set up to investigate the kind of secondary education considered desirable. Largely on the basis of the recommendations of this commission a new programme for secondary schools was drawn up and it came into operation on 1 August 1924. In the report of the Department of Education for the year 1924/5, this programme was hailed as constituting the culmination of the 'sweeping' reforms of secondary education under the new government which saw a 'revision of the educational basis' of the system and a 'complete reform of the secondary programme'.[4] Under the new programme one of the conditions for the recognition of a school was that it should offer instruction in an approved programme of stipulated subjects. For the year 1924/5 these were: Irish or English; a language other than that offered already; history and geography; mathematics; and science, or Latin and Greek, or commerce. Irish was to become an essential subject in 1927/8, and science was proposed as an essential subject for 1929/30. In concept, though to a lesser extent in practice, this idea of a required core of subjects which a school must offer, was a novel feature of the programme introduced in 1924.

Changes in the examinations were also made. In place of the old grade examinations, the junior, middle and senior grades, two examinations were introduced, namely the Intermediate and Leaving Certificate examinations. The purpose of the Intermediate Certificate was stated as being 'to testify to the completion of a well-balanced course of general education suitable for pupils who leave school at about 16 years of age, and alternatively, to the fitness of the pupils for entry on more advanced courses of study in a Secondary or Technical School'. The aim of the Leaving Certificate was 'to testify to the completion of a good secondary education and the fitness of a pupil to enter on a course of study at a University or an educational institution of similar standing'.[5] Along with the abolition of the grade examinations of the old intermediate system, the prizes and exhibitions of that system were also abolished. They were replaced with a scholarships scheme which gave assistance to financially needy pupils of outstanding ability.

Although the extent of the changes in the curriculum of secondary education introduced under the new government in its early years may be a matter for debate, a definite change of policy and practice emerged in relation to the study of Irish. In the intermediate system, secondary education in Ireland was clearly un-Irish: the study of the Irish language and culture had been neglected. This was soon to change under the native government as it adopted a policy of encouraging Irish studies with particular reference to the language. This was reflected in practical terms in the conditions laid down for the recognition of secondary schools, for recognised pupils status, and for the passing of the Intermediate and Leaving Certificate examinations. It has been seen already that in the *Rules* for the year 1924/5 Irish or English was a required subject in the school curriculum for the years 1924-7; and from 1927 onwards Irish became a required subject in the school curriculum and from 1928 onwards an essential subject for the Intermediate Certificate examination. In 1932 Irish became a required subject for all recognised pupils in secondary schools, and from 1934 up until 1973 it was to remain a required subject for passing the Leaving Certificate as well as the Intermediate Certificate examinations. In 1934 Irish also became an essential requirement for entry to secondary school. And in 1942 a certain proficiency in oral Irish became a requirement for registration as a secondary school teacher, a regulation which still obtains.

In other respects also the early years of the new Department of Education were years of minor experimentation. Between 1928 and 1938 in particular a number of proposals for alterations in the curriculum of the secondary school, and especially in the Intermediate Certificate course, were put forward by the Department. The intent of these proposals was to alleviate particular difficulties encountered by small numbers of schools as a result of the one general set of rules and regulations being applied on a national scale. In many of these attempts the Department met with opposition and for the most part little came of their efforts. Nevertheless, some changes in the rules and programmes and in provisions for examinations laid down in 1924 were made, and these were to be contained in a revised programme which came into operation in 1939. According to the new programme prescribed texts were to be reintroduced for English, Latin, Greek and modern languages. This was a reversal of the much vaunted policy of abolishing prescribed texts which had been introduced in 1924. Within two years the same regulation was adopted regarding Irish. Lower courses, which had been introduced in a number of subjects at both junior and senior level between 1932 and 1934, were abolished in all cases except in the Intermediate courses in English and Irish. In the Intermediate Certificate course, the Irish courses were re-named 'Gaedhilge' and 'Litríocht na Gaedhilge' and the English courses were re-named 'English' and 'English Literature'. Elementary mathematics, which had also been introduced in 1932 as an alternative mathematics course for girls only in the Intermediate Certificate course, was retained for girls only. In each of the lower courses, Gaedhilge, English and elementary mathematics, honours could not be obtained in the examination. Finally, all junior pupils were now required to study at least six subjects. Irish, a second language, and history and geography were required of all pupils; mathematics was also required of boys. As before, senior pupils were required to study at least five subjects, one of which had to be Irish.[6] In all other essential respects, however, the rules and programmes governing secondary schools remained the same as those laid down in 1924, even though some minor differences had existed in the intervening period.

To some extent it is probably correct to see in the revised programme of 1939 the actual completion of the reforms of the 1922-4 period in secondary education. Thereafter there was to follow a period of calm and inactivity for a full quarter of a century before any further noteworthy developments in the system took place. This is brought out clearly in *The Report of the Council of Education: the Curriculum of the Secondary School* which appeared in 1962. In the words of the report itself, the curriculum then prescribed by the Department of Education for recognised secondary schools was 'still on the lines of that adopted in 1924 following the recommendations of the Dáil Commission on Secondary Education'. Developments and changes there had been but 'no departure from the fundamental principle that each school must provide a certain basic core of general education for all recognized pupils'.[7] But perhaps the most striking indication that the curriculum of secondary education in Ireland had changed little over the years was in the general thrust of the report of the Council of Education. Not only did it show that the curriculum and examinations had changed only in details since 1924 but through its highly defensive and conservative tone, as exemplified both in its assessment of the status quo and in its recommendations, the report clearly demonstrated that the Council did not consider that there was any great need for change. In the recommendations of the report on the questions of curriculum and examinations, and other related matters, there was general acceptance of matters as they stood. Thus, although the most significant changes in post-primary education since the foundation of the state were to take place following the publication of the report, the Council itself clearly advocated no break with the past. Paradoxically, the report, which one might reasonably have expected to chart the future course of secondary education in Ireland, marked what has by now come to be seen as the end of an era. Scarcely was the report published than its views on many of the questions on which it pronounced with authority were ignored in the face of growing demands for profound changes in post-primary education.

The vocational tradition
Whereas intermediate education in Ireland was largely an out-growth of the tradition of grammar school or liberal education, technical and later vocational education grew more in response to a need to provide those engaging in a variety of occupations of a practical nature — in agriculture, industry, commerce and else-where — with the necessary practical skills to do so satisfactorily. From its beginnings various social and economic needs had greatly influenced the course of its expansion and development. It also assumed a mixed theoretical and practical character in the course of its development. And, although it was never to attain the prestige of the secondary sector, it suffered less by comparison with it on the grounds of its ideals and general method of pro-cedure than on grounds of status.

State involvement came to technical education in Ireland later than it did to intermediate education. As in the case of inter-mediate education, however, though to a lesser extent, isolated institutions of a private or corporate nature which had grown up around the country had attempted to provide some forms of technical education prior to the participation of the state. It was not until the turn of the century, however, following developments in England, that the state began to provide for technical education in Ireland.

During the second half of the nineteenth century it had become a matter of some concern in England that she appeared to be lagging behind other countries in her provisions for technical education. The first concrete steps to rectify the matter came in the form of the Technical Instruction Act of 1889. Partly for financial and partly for administrative reasons this Act, while it applied in Ireland also, had little immediate impact on the state of technical education in the country. The first significant state involvement in technical education in Ireland did not come about until the passing of the Agricultural and Technical Instruction (Ireland) Act of 1899, which made way for the establishment of the Department of Agriculture and Technical Instruction in 1900. To this Department was given responsibility to develop and administer a state system of technical instruction. And for thirty years, up until the passing of the Vocational Education Act of 1930, the system of technical education in the twenty-six counties — and in all of Ireland until the 1920s — existed along the lines laid down by the Act of 1899.

The Vocational Education Act of 1930 provided for the establishment of a system of post-primary education of a literary and practical nature to prepare pupils for employment in trades and occupations in industry, commerce, agriculture and elsewhere which required technical and manual skills. In doing so, it was making provision largely for the fourteen to sixteen-year-old age group which had completed primary education and wished to enter employment. The type of mixed general and technical education to be provided for this purpose was designated 'continuation education'. It was much broader in concept than was technical education which was also to be provided in vocational schools, both as part of continuation education and as specialised education for more advanced students.

Continuation education is defined in the Act of 1930 as 'education to continue and supplement education provided in elementary schools and includes general and practical training in preparation for employment in trades, manufactures, agriculture, commerce, and other industrial pursuits, and also general and practical training for improvement of young persons in the early stages of such employment'. As an alternative to secondary education, the content of continuation education de-emphasised subjects of an academic and literary kind while giving greater attention to those of a practical and vocational nature, such as woodwork and metalwork. Fourteen was the normal age of entry, though pupils who had completed sixth class in primary school could enter at thirteen years of age.

Technical education was defined in the Act as 'education pertaining to trades, manufactures, commerce, and other industrial pursuits (including the occupation of girls and women connected with the household) and in subjects bearing thereon or relating thereto and includes education in science and art (including, in the county boroughs of Dublin and Cork, music) and also includes physical training'.

Continuation and technical education, the one more of a general character, the other more specialised, were to constitute the substance or content of vocational education as conceived in the Vocational Education Act of 1930.

In matters of curriculum and organisation, throughout the 1930s continuation education became established and definite patterns began to emerge. In 1942 a document of considerable significance for continuation education, one which was to shape its general course for up to twenty years, was issued by the Department of Education. The Document, known as *Memo V. 40*,[8] set out the main principles for the conduct of continuation education and in doing so it drew heavily on the experience gained since the passing of the 1930 Act. The memorandum attempted to draw up outline courses suited to the different needs of county borough, urban and rural areas. Central to the approach adopted was the identification of the distribution of occupations in the different areas. Depending on the types of prevailing occupations in an area, course outlines were suggested which were geared to preparing pupils to meet the occupational needs of the areas in question. Thus quite different course outlines were drawn up for county borough, urban and rural areas. In all, four major different course outlines similar to those already referred to were suggested. A day preparatory course for boys and one for girls was suggested for county borough areas along with a junior technical course and a junior commercial course. There would be separate courses for boys and girls in each case. More or less the same range of courses would be made use of in urban areas, but there could be quite some variation in the actual courses offered by the different urban centres. A junior rural course, in which there would be a considerable difference between the course for boys and the course for girls, was suggested for rural areas. Common to nearly all post-preparatory courses, however, was a fairly common first year, a mix of general literary, business and practical subjects, a school week of about twenty-eight hours instruction, provision for religious instruction, and separate courses for boys and girls.

Table 1: **The junior technical course for boys proposed
in Memo V. 40**[9]

Subject	1st Year	2nd Year
Manual instruction		
(wood and metal)	8 hours	10 hours
Drawing	3 hours	2 hours
Science	3 hours	3 hours
Mathematics	4 hours	4 hours
Irish	3 hours	3 hours
English	3 hours	2 hours
Physical Training	1 hour	1 hour
Religious instruction)		
Other subjects)	3 hours	3 hours
Total hours	28 hours	28 hours

Note: This course is illustrative of the types of courses proposed
by *Memo V. 40*.

The guidelines set forth in *Memo V. 40* were applied throughout the country, but there were variations in practice from one
area to another, with Dublin, and to a lesser extent Cork, offering
a greater variety of continuation courses than those laid down in
the memorandum. Furthermore, new developments and pressure
for changes were continual. In particular, approaches were made
to the Department of Education by the Irish Technical Education
Association to have the question of holding public national
examinations in vocational education looked into as a means of
providing certification to pupils seeking employment. The outcome was the institution of the Day Group Certificate examination
which was held for the first time in 1947. The general reaction to
the new examinations was favourable. Subsequent to a review in
1951/2 some changes in regulations were introduced. These were
to become effective in the examination in 1954.[10] This development was also to mark the last major event in the evolution of
continuation education prior to the new plan for the development
of post-primary education in Ireland announced by the Minister in
1963.

The initiation of reforms

The inheritance of the 1960s in the matter of post-primary education in Ireland was one of mixed blessings. In the place of a unified post-primary sector there existed two separate, almost segregated, systems. The one, secondary education, was highly academic, examination-oriented and inflexible in character. Tradition-bound and enjoying a higher status than its vocational counterpart, it attracted the generally brighter pupil and controlled the main access routes to the professions, the universities, the civil service and the church. Vocational education, on the other hand, was highly employment-oriented in outlook. It took its bearings and starting point from a consideration of social and community needs of a local and national kind and of the interests and aptitudes of a large and somewhat neglected section of the post-primary school-going population. It shaped programmes accordingly to be flexible, motivating, outward-looking, and of a mixed literary and practical nature. Cooperation, or more correctly, interaction between the secondary and vocational sectors was almost non-existent, with virtually no interchange between pupils, teachers and programmes. And for many in the early 1960s this course must have appeared set to continue for the foreseeable future. For this, in effect, was the recommendation of the Council of Education. But it was not to be.

Unlike the Council of Education there were others in educational circles who were concerned about the need for reform of secondary education. Intermittently from 1924 onwards the case for reform had been argued,[11] notably by Seán Ó Catháin and J.J. O'Meara in the 1950s. It had much to support it. Since 1878 secondary education had been subjected to constant and wide-ranging criticisms; yet it had remained largely unchanged in its essential character ever since then. At the same time, other countries, even those with educational systems less bound by the past than was Ireland's, were engaged in major attempts at organisational and curriculum reform of second-level education.

If the Council of Education had somehow managed to remain untouched by all of this, other forces were emerging within the country which were not quite so complacent. If the Council of Education had thought it unnecessary or was simply unwilling to redirect the future course of secondary education, there was a growing concern in government circles regarding the matter. The concern was that the traditional pattern of post-primary education in Ireland was not sufficiently well articulated with emerging national needs and with possibilities in the economic sphere in particular. It was a concern which was to result in a bold attempt to set post-primary education in Ireland on a new course.

The attitude embodied in this new approach was itself a reflection of a pronounced change in Ireland. Most writers on the subject agree that such a change became apparent in the late 1950s.[12] Whatever the overall character of this change, a growing realisation of and confidence in the possibilities for economic growth and development were a major part of it. Post-primary education was to become one of those aspects of national life where this new consciousness would have a considerable impact. Thus for over a decade the Department of Education under successive Ministers for Education and within the context of the *Second Programme for Economic Expansion*, was to expend a major effort in attempting to bring post-primary education into line with the dictates of this new way of thinking.

Economic considerations were to affect thinking regarding the future development of post-primary education in Ireland in a number of ways.[13] To an extent unknown in earlier times expenditure on education came to be seen as investment. At a time of growing economic buoyancy it made sense to argue that the economic and industrial development of the country was dependent on a labour force which enjoyed a good level of education; conversely, an under-educated work force could be seen as a wastage of manpower capacity. And so the greater education of the greater number became a desideratum. Secondly, and related to this view, although increased participation in post-primary education itself was considered desirable, greater participation in forms of education directly related to economic and industrial growth came to be viewed as necessary. Vocational education, of course, had always attempted to cater for needs of this kind. As matters stood, however, the vocational sector was not considered to be in a position to produce either the numbers or the levels of education envisaged if the technological and industrial potential of the country was to be fully exploited. Finally, economic considerations began to assume a new importance in respect of building and running costs of post-primary education.

In discussing the response made to the challenge facing post-primary education in Ireland in the 1960s it is important to realise that Ireland was not alone in facing such a challenge. And the task ahead was not dissimilar from what it was in other developed and developing countries. In many countries the period was marked by an air of optimism regarding the benefits which could be derived in both human and economic terms from greater investment in education and, as a consequence, the 1960s saw exceptional expansion and change in education. As in Ireland, the principle of investment in education was basic to this expansion and change; and with this went an increased emphasis on manpower planning and on attempting to make second-level schooling in particular more responsive to the needs of industry and commerce.

Alongside the principle of investment in education, and working hand-in-hand with it, was the principle of equality of educational opportunity. Ever since World War II educational systems had been attempting to give effect to this principle; during the 1960s these attempts were to find expression in quite enormous increases in enrolments. Increases in enrolments were also accompanied, and to a certain extent brought about, by a raising of the minimum school-leaving age in many countries.

The initiation of curriculum development projects was also to become a distinctive feature of educational change in the 1960s. Much of the impetus for this came from the United States where developments of this kind – the new maths programmes introduced into Ireland in the 1960s are an example – were underway from about the mid 1950s. These developments got an unexpected boost from a most unlikely quarter. The launching of the Russian satellite, Sputnik, in 1957 was seen as a serious threat to American technological superiority, and a huge effort was put into the strengthening of science and mathematics curricula to combat this. The curriculum development movement soon spread to other subjects and to other countries. In England it was promoted initially by the Nuffield Foundation. More recently the Schools' Council has been active in this area. Curriculum development began to make its appearance in Ireland with the setting up of a number of curriculum projects in the early 1970s.

It was against this international background that educational reform in Ireland commenced in the early 1960s. As Dr Patrick Hillery, who was Minister for Education at the time, and indeed as the government of the day saw it the task facing post-primary education in Ireland was very largely one of developing the post-primary resources of the country to meet social needs – notably economic and industrial needs on a scale not envisaged before –

as well as individual needs in the emerging Ireland. Taking Ireland's own tradition in second-level education into account, this was a task which would necessitate a challenge to conventional attitudes, structures and approaches. It would call for a reassessment of the relative merits of secondary and vocational education and the advisability of their continued separation. Above all it would call for an open-mindedness and greater willingness in the secondary sector, and as it turned out in the university sector as well, to see education in terms of meeting social and even material needs, as well as individual and spiritual ones.

Prime among the objectives sought by Dr Hillery was the expansion of facilities to cater for the increased participation in technical and other forms of applied education, especially commercial and business studies. Dr Hillery himself put it bluntly:

> Secondary education with us is only one stream. What we really need in this country is the other stream, the technical, the scientific. We need to develop these but the argument goes that we need free secondary education for everybody. Now if you were to give secondary grammar, academic type education to everybody you would be wasting your money in two ways: you would be getting too many people taking a course which is no use to most of them — we haven't jobs for them, we haven't need for them! And these people who are so trained and cannot get employment have lost the chance of being trained in skills, whereas we need people with skills and we need them very much.[14]

While a more modified version of this view had been a guiding principle in the development and conduct of vocational education from its beginnings, it was tantamount to heresy in the secondary sector. Yet, if the vocational sector alone was not in a position to cope with the numbers of students and the levels and variety of technical education envisaged to meet the emergent needs of a growing economy, or if to do so by expanding the vocational sector alone was not considered desirable or practicable, how was it to be done?

The course chosen by the Minister was both sophisticated and simple. To increase the rate of participation in post-primary education he would introduce a greater diversity into the post-primary school curriculum, thereby providing pupils with a wider range of choice while at the same time catering for pupils of academic ability and for pupils of practical ability.[15] To increase the rate of post-primary participation in technical and other applied studies, the Minister would attempt to make these studies attractive in their own right and to place them on a par in status with the traditional secondary school subjects. Both of these objectives he would attempt to achieve by introducing a comprehensive post-primary school curriculum which would include academic and practical subjects, by making available facilities for technical and applied education, and by holding out reasonable prospects for advanced technical and technological education to promising pupils. In his major and important statement on 20 May 1963,[16] Dr Hillery announced the outline plan which, as well as directly achieving these objectives, would also constitute the first steps towards creating a more unified system of post-primary education. In matters of detail, the plan was altered as time went on, and it was also substantially developed; nevertheless it did contain the essential elements of official policy in post-primary education for the subsequent decade and beyond.

Central to the plan was the notion of a unified system of post-primary education. Measures to be taken in this direction would include the introduction of a largely common curriculum and common examinations in the vocational and secondary schools up to the Intermediate Certificate level. Hitherto only secondary school pupils were eligible to sit the Intermediate Certificate examination; now pupils from all kinds of post-primary schools would be entitled to do so. The common curriculum would be made up of subjects drawn from both the secondary curriculum and the vocational school curriculum, though some coordination and modification of existing courses would take place. A Technical Leaving Certificate examination was to be introduced which, it was intended, would be on a par with the existing Leaving Certificate examination. It would provide encouragement and prospects for pupils to engage in technical studies to a level beyond that catered for in the existing post-primary arrangements. To facilitate both of these developments, two new types of institutions were to be created and built. In areas where post-primary facilities did not exist, but where there was a need for them, a new type of 'post-primary day school' was to be built. It would receive direct state financing and it would be the physical embodiment of the concept of a unified post-primary system. These schools would be known as comprehensive schools. They would offer a combination of vocational and secondary school subjects and they would prepare pupils for the Intermediate Certificate examination. Secondly, a number of regional technical colleges designed to offer courses for the proposed Technical Leaving Certificate courses would be built in selected centres around the country.[17]

By implementing such a plan the Minister was hoping to achieve a number of related objectives. Firstly, by building comprehensive schools rather than separate vocational and secondary schools he was hoping to cut down on building and running costs. Secondly, since the comprehensive curriculum was intended to cater for a wider range of pupils than either the secondary or vocational curriculum, it was hoped that it would prove helpful in promoting greater participation in post-primary education. Thirdly, vocational and technical education had always suffered in status by comparison with secondary education; by opening up the Intermediate Certificate examination to all post-primary schools, by the introduction of the Technical Leaving Certificate, and by attempting to put qualifications in technical and applied forms of education on a par with those in the secondary sector, it was hoped to alleviate this problem and to encourage and facilitate increased participation in technical and applied studies at post-primary level. It was hoped that these courses, and especially those at senior-cycle level, would open up employment prospects as well as the prospect of under-graduate studies in certain university faculties and in colleges of technology. The absence of provisions for upward mobility of this kind in technical education had acted as an impediment to greater participation in such studies in the past.

The aspect of Dr Hillery's plans which caught the public imagination most forcibly, however, was not his designs for the promotion of technical and applied education at second level. It was, rather, the notion of the comprehensive school. Although the idea of a comprehensive curriculum may have been a more fundamental one in subsequent discussions and attempts at development in post-primary education than was the idea of a comprehensive school, the comprehensive school itself had powerful symbolic value — and, very likely, political value besides. This was hardly surprising. Interwoven with the economic arguments and justifications for a new line of development in post-primary education were a number of other considerations to which reference was made in Dr Hillery's statement of 20 May 1963, and which would be given extensive airing in the years that followed. From the outset statements and justifications of official policy were couched in terms of social and individual concerns which became crystallised in the rallying cry of equality of educational opportunity for all. And if the comprehensive school was to be the physical embodiment of the aspiration to a unified system of post-primary education, it was also to become the symbol of official commitment to equality of educational opportunity.

Undoubtedly such a view of the comprehensive school was justified at the time. The earliest of these schools were all to be located in reasonably remote areas of the country where adequate post-primary educational facilities had not been previously provided. They were to be non-selective in pupil intake, and by offering a wide range of vocational and secondary subjects they not only attempted to cater for the various needs and aptitudes of pupils but they provided pupils with the opportunity to sample a wider than usual range of subjects before making a final commitment to any. It may well be the case that the comprehensive schools, and indeed the entire range of post-primary educational policy itself, included provisions designed to achieve greater equality of educational opportunity for all. And they may well have provided at least some measure of it. But they also represented one of the first steps, as well as some of the earliest thinking, in furthering the government's new economic objectives in post-primary education. The comprehensive school introduced one further element to which little attention was given at the time; it marked the beginning of an entirely new degree of involvement by the state in post-primary education. As the years passed, this would assume even greater proportions as costs and financial considerations loomed larger and as the state continued to be the main innovator and leader in many areas of educational development.

From the time of Dr Hillery's statement of 1963, it was a full three years before any of his plans materialised, but when implementation did commence it was achieved with impressive punctuality and many further developments followed rapidly. In 1965 a survey team, which had been set up by Dr Hillery in 1962 to inquire into the long-term requirements of Irish education, produced its report *Investment in Education*. With this available, plans could be drawn up more firmly and the direction of needed developments could be seen more clearly. Besides, with the thinking behind the report available to the Department of Education before its publication, the plans for future development were drawn up in anticipation of the findings of the survey team. Likewise, steps were being taken before Dr Hillery's statement of 1963 to facilitate the implementation of his proposals.[18]

Late in 1962 a Vocational Amendment Act was passed enabling vocational educational authorities to receive a substantial increase in income from local rates and from state funds. As a result, the vocational sector was to enter a period of considerable and rapid expansion. This expansion was aided by the fact that the new regulations for entry to apprentice training announced earlier by An Cheárd Chomhairle were to be implemented from 1963 onwards. These regulations called for higher levels of education at entry and further services to be provided by the vocational schools. The implementation of the plans announced by the Minister in 1963, however, was to constitute the major source of demand for expansion.

The year 1964 marked a significant year for expansion in the secondary sector. In that year a long-standing policy of the Department of Education in relation to the provision of capital funds for secondary schools was terminated; henceforth, building grants would be made available to secondary schools. In the same year the sites for the first four comprehensive schools were announced, a regional technical college for Carlow was in the planning stage, and draft syllabuses for the Technical Leaving Certificate were given to the vocational education authorities and to teachers. Sometime before the end of 1965 another important development took place, enabling the Department to exert greater control in respect of physical planning and development. A new policy was adopted whereby the sanctioning of all funds for new buildings was to be subject to an overall review of post-primary building needs.[19]

The year 1966, however, saw the first concrete developments in the implementation of the new plans for post-primary education. In that year the first of the comprehensive schools was opened. Common Intermediate Certificate courses and, as it turned out, common Day Group Certificate courses commenced in vocational, secondary and comprehensive schools. But even as the central elements in Dr Hillery's original plans were being implemented, modifications and extensions were being and would continue to be adopted by Dr Hillery himself and by his successors. There was no change of overall policy, however, and for the most part whatever modifications and extensions were made were introduced probably in the light of experience and as more precise data on numbers, needs and costs became available.

Essential to the attainment of the government's objectives in post-primary education, including that of equal educational opportunity for all, was, in the eyes of the policymakers, the notion of the comprehensive curriculum. The notion of the comprehensive curriculum itself and, for that matter, any of the objectives — economic, social or educational — being sought, generated little or no opposition. The measures proposed and taken to implement the comprehensive curriculum, however, while cutting down costs, did provoke controversy and opposition in many quarters. Early in 1965, shortly before the end of his term as Minister for Education, Dr Hillery spoke of the idea of the comprehensive curriculum as being more important than the comprehensive school itself. This view was to be taken up by Dr Hillery's successor as Minister for Education, George Colley, and subsequent Ministers. The comprehensive curriculum was to become the vehicle through which attempts would be made to cut down on costs while at the same time providing a comprehensive education and the benefits which were to accompany it, namely equal educational opportunity for all and the attainment of the government's economic objectives through education. Thus, the notion of the comprehensive curriculum was to provide the educational justification for policies of 'sharing of facilities', 'amalgamation of schools' and 'post-primary centres', policies adopted during George Colley's term of office. These policies were in line with such findings as those of the county surveys of post-primary education initiated by the *Investment in Education* team, and they were suggested by economic considerations as much as by the aspiration to comprehensive curricula and equality of educational opportunity for all.[20]

Concrete steps toward the implementation of the policy of sharing facilities were taken by George Colley early in 1966. At that time he wrote to vocational and secondary school authorities asking them to come together with one another to investigate the possibilities for co-operation and sharing of facilities in their localities.[21] While many such meetings did take place, and while some progress towards a sharing of teachers was made in some areas, it became evident early on that progress, if there was to be any, would be slow and troublesome. As a follow-up to the Minister's initiative on this question, later in the same year post-primary schools in a number of counties received copies of the county surveys of post-primary education. These surveys had been conducted by the Department of Education from 1963 onwards.

In these surveys, which were to have a major impact on post-primary planning at the time, and one of the purposes of which was to seek a pooling of facilities, the notion of shared facilities was spelled out more fully than it had been before. The surveys sought to identify throughout the country 'post-primary centres', by which was understood places having one or more of a boys' secondary school, a girls' secondary school, or a vocational school. To each such centre was assigned a 'catchment area' covering an area of six miles' radius from the centre. A notable feature of the surveys was the provisions made for cost-cutting and amalgamation of schools. Since the size of enrolment needed to support a comprehensive curriculum would be larger than that found in most post-primary schools in Ireland, it was proposed that where the annual intake of pupils in a post-primary centre was no more than about fifty, a centre would be designated a 'junior centre'; it would offer courses up to Intermediate Certificate level only. A centre where intake was in the region of eighty to 100 pupils would be designed a 'major centre'; pupils from junior centres would be transported to a major centre at senior level. And areas which could not support a junior centre would be served by transport to a nearby centre.[22]

Clearly the sharing of facilities policy was a cost-saving strategy aimed at cutting down on costs while at the same time aiming to ensure that every post-primary centre would provide, in an economical manner, a comprehensive curriculum. Where separate vocational and secondary schools existed in an area, it made good sense, it was suggested, to pool or to share facilities so as to provide comprehensive facilities.[23] This view, however, was not always shared by the school authorities whom it affected directly, and from the beginning the scheme ran into serious difficulties. While the policy might not be said to have been a complete failure at the time — some forms of co-operation and amalgamation did take place in a number of areas — it was far from being a success.[24] And while the policy was never formally dropped it did appear to give way to the idea of the community school which, as it turned out, was intended to incorporate a number of aspects of the sharing of facilities policy. These aspects, such as the community orientation envisaged for post-primary education, had not been highlighted earlier on. Government policy on these matters today appears to remain substantially what it has been over the past fifteen years or so, though it has, perhaps, become somewhat more flexible.[25]

If the policy of rationalisation of schools and with it the reduction of operating costs was at best to become a long-drawn-out matter of mixed success, there can be little doubt that in respect of achieving an increase in pupil enrolments the objective of bringing about greater participation in post-primary education was an overnight success in itself. Indeed, so successful were the efforts in this direction, at least in so far as enrolments were concerned, that inadvertently they may have been a contributory factor in hindering greater success in other areas, including the sharing of facilities policy initiated by George Colley. When George Colley's successor as Minister for Education, Donogh O'Malley, announced the introduction of a scheme for free post-primary education in 1966, he was quite within the bounds of overall government policy in relation to increased participation in post-primary education. Ever since Dr Hillery's statement of 1963, and even earlier, the goal of increased participation in post-primary education had clearly been sought. Regarding details, however, 1970 had been seen as the year in which the first major and direct steps in this direction, namely the raising of the school-leaving age from fourteen to fifteen and, most likely, the introduction of free education up until that age, would be taken. And there was good reason for this.

Speaking in the Dáil in October 1959 on a motion related to raising the school-leaving age to fifteen, the Taoiseach, Seán Lemass, stated that the government favoured the idea in principle and was working towards it;[26] it was necessary, however, first to create the facilities and capacity at post-primary level before raising the school-leaving age. Under Dr Hillery as Minister for Education the kind of facilities considered most in need were those which would promote greater participation in technical and applied education; increased pupil participation in the existing pattern of secondary and vocational education alone was considered wasteful. Attention was given, therefore, to developing the facilities and structures necessary to support and promote technical and applied education; there was also some broadening of the post-primary curriculum to cater for a wider range of pupils' interests and aptitudes. Both of these objectives were given priority over the immediate one of increasing the school-leaving age. Moreover, it was on the assumption that 1970 would be the year for raising the school-leaving age

that the projections for post-primary enrolments, teacher recruit-
ment, space and facilities requirements and cost projections in
Investment in Education and the county surveys of post-primary
education released in 1966 had been based.[27]

The introduction of free education in 1967 was to invalidate
these projections and surveys and the plans based on them —
notably planning in regard to the designation of post-primary
centres contained in the county surveys — because it led to an
unanticipated increase in numbers as against expectations based on
increases arising out of raising the school-leaving age to fifteen in
1970. Arguably it proved disruptive in other areas of emerging
departmental planning and initiatives also. The introduction of a
comprehensive curriculum, through means of co-operation and the
amalgamation of schools, depended to some extent upon the
implementation of the findings of the county surveys; so also did
the implementation of a scheme to be suggested in 1967 for the
grouping of subjects at senior cycle and upon which, in turn,
depended in part both the promotion of technical and applied
studies at senior cycle and a degree of subject concentration, if
not quite specialisation, by all pupils. But the applicability of the
county surveys had now been undermined. Besides, the crisis
created in the schools by the absence of the necessary facilities —
sufficient pupil spaces, teacher numbers, curriculum options and
other facilities already alluded to by the Taoiseach in 1959 and all
of which were needed to support a substantially increased enrolment in the early years of free education — made it virtually
impossible for schools to participate in yet other innovatory
schemes.[28]

In brief, 1970 was the year in which the first direct steps to
increase post-primary enrolments by means of raising the school-
leaving age to fifteen were to be taken. In 1967, when free education
was introduced by Donogh O'Malley, and with it a relatively huge
increase in post-primary school enrolments, the necessary groundwork needed to support it had not been completed. Neither had the
necessary groundwork been completed — and this is an important
point — to attain the objectives of a comprehensive curriculum for
all post-primary pupils, the encouragement of proportionately
greater participation in technical and applied studies, and the
cutting of operational costs.

The failure to gain the acceptance of the policy of compulsory
grouping of subjects at senior level suggested in 1967 was a setback

to plans for subject concentration at senior level and the promotion of senior-cycle studies in technical and commercial studies in particular.[29] The schools were not alone in their opposition to the idea, however. The universities also objected.[30] But by this time the rejection of these proposals by the universities was not the only obstacle which the universities presented to the implementation of post-primary policy. By virtue of the matriculation requirements of the National University of Ireland in particular, along with the conditions under which higher education grants to students were awarded, the third-level sector was seen as posing a distinct threat to plans for the expanded post-primary curriculum, and particularly the promotion of technical and applied subjects at senior level.

In a wide-ranging article which touched on many of the developments under way in post-primary education, and which bared many a sensitive issue without ceremony, Seán O'Connor, then Assistant Secretary of the Department of Education and head of the Development Branch in the Department, drew attention to these points.[31] In the first place he expressed the fear that the requirement of four honours in the Leaving Certificate examination for entitlement to a higher education grant would force pupils to forego a broad curriculum in order to concentrate on a narrow range of subjects; as a result non-examination subjects and activities, which he considered to be of greater value in adult life than the examination subjects, would be neglected. Secondly, and this may have been his main point, the matriculation requirements of the National University of Ireland exercised a strong influence on the subjects which a pupil took in post-primary school, owing to the prestige of the university and the aspirations of many to enter the university. To avoid a narrowing effect on the range of subjects studied at post-primary level he suggested that, contrary to existing practice, all Leaving Certificate subjects should have equal value for purposes of matriculation. 'There is little point,' he argued, 'in encouraging a potential university student to develop his interests and aptitudes if the subjects of his interests do not tally with university requirements.'[32]

At the beginning of his short discussion of the influence of university entrance requirements in post-primary education, Seán O'Connor wrote that he had 'no intention of discussing higher education' in his article.[33] Like it or not, however, the restrictions imposed by the university sector on official plans for post-primary education may well have dictated direct entry into the higher education sphere as the next stage in the implementation of these plans. Seán O'Connor's article was widely considered to foreshadow a number of subsequent developments in post-primary education, notably the community school idea. Could it be that it was also hinting at novel developments in higher education? Not only were the universities actually stifling the implementation of a broader curriculum at post-primary level, but neither did they recognise for matriculation purposes those very subjects which had been introduced in the technical line which needed both encouragement at second level and outlets to higher study at third level. Dr Hillery's original expressed wish that such studies should lead a pupil to gain entrance to a university faculty was not being fulfilled. Dare the state enter the third-level educational scene by introducing new structures and new institutions, just as it had done at post-primary level? Within six months of Seán O'Connor's article[34] the decision to do so was public knowledge and plans were well advanced. If the universities were not co-operating they would be circumvented and without apology.[35]

On 12 December 1968 the Minister for Education announced that 'the Government have decided to allocate the capital funds necessary to establish a third-level educational institution in Limerick'. It had also asked the Higher Education Authority (HEA) to look into the question of establishing 'a body which would award national qualifications at technician and technological levels'.[36] By March 1969 the HEA having considered both of these matters reported on how these plans should be implemented. In its report the HEA noted that there was a distinct need for third-level education of a technological kind in the country and it considered that the work of the proposed college in Limerick 'should be based primarily on a technological content'.[37] It also recommended the establishment of a council for national awards, later to become known as the National Council for Educational Awards (NCEA), to grant academic awards in the non-university third-level sector.[38]

The report of the HEA was accepted and planning went ahead for the establishment of the NCEA and the National Institute for Higher Education (NIHE) in Limerick. The NIHE had admission requirements somewhat comparable to but more flexible and inclusive of a greater variety of subjects than those allowed by the National University of Ireland for matriculation purposes. Its curriculum was intended to emphasise technological and commercial and business studies and it would, therefore, be considered more supportive of developments underway and objectives being sought regarding technical and applied education at post-primary level. It commenced courses in 1972. This was one year later than the year in which pupils who entered post-primary education in 1966, the year in which the first of Dr Hillery's plans was implemented, would normally have qualified for the Leaving Certificate. In 1972 also the NCEA was established on an ad hoc basis, and by this time a number of regional technical colleges had also commenced operations.

In the years since Dr Hillery's statement of 1963, much had been done to create institutions and structures, to provide facilities for achieving the objective of greater participation in post-primary education, and to encourage greater participation in technical and applied education at post-primary level than ever before. At post-primary level these efforts culminated in the emergence of the community school idea in the early 1970s along with its implementation or planned implementation in more than thirty centres throughout the country. While considerable controversy surrounded the introduction of the idea, and indeed its implementation in some cases, in terms of post-primary curriculum and examinations it followed closely on the comprehensive school which it was to replace. The significance of the community school, however, is not confined to these courses and examinations, possessing as it does the potential and facilities for a far greater degree of community participation in its affairs than has been traditionally the case in Irish post-primary education.

When the promotion of technical and applied education was thought to necessitate direct entry by the state into third-level education this too was done. It was done in the form of creating new institutions and structures of higher education designed to cater for advanced technical, technological and other forms of applied studies in the belief that the existing ones did not provide the openings or the encouragement for official programmes at post-primary level. And while a change of government in 1973 was to result in new proposals for the organisation of higher education[39] these were to have no lasting effect. In any event, sufficient had been done by then to further something of the kind of articulation of post-primary and higher education that had been sought in the interests of promoting technical and applied education at both post-primary level and third level. Aside from this, however, nothing that has been said or done in recent years suggests any significant alteration in the course of post-primary development charted by Dr Hillery and his immediate successors in the early and middle 1960s. Thus, it would appear that by the mid-1970s a period of consolidation had been reached in which the objective was to extend the implementation of established policy throughout the entire post-primary sector insofar as this was consistent with the increasingly restrictive financial circumstances which were to follow.

The effects of the reform measures

It was primarily economic and social considerations which led to the attempts at organisational and curriculum reform of post-primary education which characterise the post-1963 era. From an economic standpoint the task on hand was largely one of achieving the maximum economic potential from the available human and manpower resources and from an educational viewpoint the task was fundamentally one of curriculum reform. New institutions and structures were also created as they were necessitated by curriculum reforms. These reforms in turn were regulated by financial considerations. The curriculum reform which was sought was chiefly of two kinds: firstly, a widening of the range of subjects available to all post-primary pupils with a view to meeting a wider range of aptitudes and interests; and secondly, an increased emphasis on technical and other applied studies, that is those studies most directly related to meeting the emerging manpower needs of an expanding and changing economy.

As we have seen already, although the reforms in vocational education introduced in 1930 were substantial and effective, most attempts at reform of secondary education had never met with great success at any time after 1878. As would become apparent in the years following Dr Hillery's original statement of plans in 1963, the reform of post-primary education being sought in the early 1960s was the most thoroughgoing and fundamental ever and great energies were spent on the task. It was a task which was taken seriously not only by the Department of Education; it constituted a central element in government economic policy. It led to a greater public awareness of educational issues, the establishment of new structures, institutions and approaches to post-primary education, and the emergence of at least a notionally unified and comprehensive post-primary sector.

Impressive as the developments of the time may have been, the question remains exactly what they have meant in terms of the actual subjects, courses, examinations and day-to-day activities in the post-primary school. Bared of the intense activity, the plans, the public interest and the actual drama of it all, what precisely was achieved by way of changing the essentially intermediate character of secondary education, the relatively low rate of participation in technical and applied or vocational studies, and the essentially binary character of post-primary education of the early 1960s? What has it meant to have an expanded and integrated curriculum of secondary and vocational education, a more unified and comprehensive post-primary educational system?

The major change affecting the curriculum and examinations of post-primary education was the introduction of common courses and common examinations in all post-primary schools. This had the effect of providing a wider range and choice of subjects, enabling pupils to study both traditional secondary academic subjects and traditional vocational practical subjects if they wished. Other changes affecting the curriculum have also taken place: new subjects have been introduced, some have undergone change, and others have been eliminated. As with the changes in regulations governing post-primary examinations, however, changes of this kind have been of a rather minor nature for the most part.

The list of approved subjects for secondary schools expanded at junior or Intermediate Certificate level from fifteen to twenty-two and at senior or Leaving Certificate level from twenty-one to twenty-five between 1924/5 and 1962/3. In the period since 1962/3 the list of approved subjects at junior level has grown to twenty-six and at senior level to thirty-one.[40] In neither case has the increase in subjects since 1962/3 been due to the addition of entirely new subjects alone: thus, subjects appearing on the lists for 1962/3 have in some cases been retained and in other cases either omitted, substantially altered or expanded into more than one subject.[41]

There have been changes also in the list of subjects for the Day Group Certificate examination since 1962/3. Today there are twenty-six subjects on the list, as opposed to twenty-five subjects in 1962/3. Commercial geography, retail practice, business methods, household science, mechanics and heat, magnetism and electricity as full subjects in themselves have been removed from the list; French, German, history, geography, Italian, science (syllabus A) and Spanish have been added.[42] Civics has also been introduced as a compulsory non-examination subject for all pupils studying for the Day Group Certificate examination. The subject groupings, as well as the compulsory subjects within the groups, have remained more or less unchanged since the examination came into existence in 1947. And since the introduction of the common Intermediate Certificate examination course in 1966, and the co-ordination of vocational and secondary school syllabuses which accompanied it, quite a number of subjects have become common to the Intermediate Certificate and Day Group Certificate examination lists of subjects.[43]

Changes in the lists of subjects since 1962/3 appear to reflect the Hillery proposals of 1963 in many respects. In the period since 1962/3 substantial content of a technical and applied kind has been introduced into the one-time secondary sector. This has been achieved by introducing subjects like building construction, engineering workshop theory and practice, accounting, and business organisation into the Leaving Certificate examinations list of subjects and subjects such as metalwork and woodwork into the Intermediate Certificate list. At the same time substantial additional content of an academic nature has been introduced into the one-time vocational sector through the introduction into the vocational schools programmes of Intermediate and Leaving Certificate subjects like history, geography and modern languages. Further changes reflecting the Hillery plan have also been achieved through reorganising or extending the number of subjects in a particular area of study. Thus, whereas commerce was the only business studies subject for the Leaving Certificate examination in 1962/3, at present there are at least four business studies subjects available.

The most extensive changes were in the introduction of multi-syllabus subjects which offered alternatives in terms of content and, to some extent, in terms of approach to the subject. Thus, at the present time, science, history and geography, and music and musicianship for the Intermediate Certificate, and music and and musicianship and home economics for the Leaving Certificate examination each offer a choice of syllabuses which differ from one another in content and in some cases in approach. Since the mid-1960s changes, usually of a lesser degree than those already noted, also took place in almost all subjects at post-primary level not directly affected by attempts to increase participation in technical and other applied studies.[44] Many of these changes were brought about by the need to co-ordinate subject syllabuses at the

Day Group Certificate and Intermediate Certificate levels, the need to update subject matter in various subjects, and the introduction of different emphases in subjects and approaches to teaching them. Regarding curriculum change at the Day Group Certificate level other than that already referred to, it is difficult to ascertain the amount of change that has taken place in individual subjects since 1963. Information on courses and syllabuses for the early 1960s is scant,[45] and comparisons with present-day work are not easy to make.

In looking at the changes affecting curriculum and examinations since the mid-1960s one cannot fail to be struck by the extent to which the secondary tradition remained intact. That is to say that while the 1960s ushered in new policies, new institutions and structures and, in some cases, new courses and revised curriculum content, the attempted reforms were introduced almost entirely within the existing framework of the secondary school curriculum and examination system. From the beginning this was to exercise an inhibiting influence on actual reform. Thus, while the rules governing the curricula and examinations in post-primary schools have undergone changes in recent years in keeping with the aspiration towards a unified and comprehensive post-primary system, this latter notion still sits uneasily on the existing rules and programmes. And so, in place of a set of rules and regulations governing curricula and programmes in all post-primary schools derived from considerations of the nature of a unified and comprehensive post-primary system, what exists now, through alterations and extensions of the long-standing rules and programmes for secondary schools, is an adaptation of these rules to the vocational, comprehensive, and community schools, as well as to the common Intermediate and Leaving Certificate courses and examinations.[46] As a consequence reforms involving the vocational, comprehensive and community schools have had to conform very largely to the original rules governing secondary schools and programmes.

How this adaptation restricts programmes in non-secondary post-primary schools can be seen in relation to the rules governing examinations. In 1967/8 a rule was introduced that pupils who would be sitting the Intermediate Certificate examination in 1969 and subsequent years should be either recognised junior pupils (of a secondary school or secondary top) and have followed an approved Intermediate Certificate course of not less than three years duration or they should have followed such a course as would be approved for vocational, comprehensive or community school pupils.[47] Similarly, in the case of Leaving Certificate pupils from vocational, comprehensive and community schools, they were required to have completed an Intermediate Certificate course of not less than three years duration — thereby complying with regulations similar to those which obtain for recognised junior pupils in secondary schools — before being eligible to enter on a Leaving Certificate course. They were then required to follow a Leaving Certificate course, which is defined in identical terms to the approved course for recognised senior pupils in secondary schools, for two years in order to be eligible to sit for the Leaving Certificate examination.[48] Thus, by simply extending to the non-secondary post-primary schools the traditional rules and programmes designed originally for the secondary schools, pressure was, and still is, brought on post-primary schools of all kinds to comply with the more or less traditional secondary school mould in the matter of regulations governing both curricula and examinations. There may have been good reasons for adopting this approach at the time of introducing technical studies into the Intermediate and Leaving Certificate courses; to continue with it, however, may hinder the emergence of innovative and more flexible practices and forms of post-primary education.[49]

Recent changes in examination regulations have introduced some good features. Entry requirements to all post-primary examinations are of the one general kind. It has just been seen what these regulations are in respect of the Intermediate and Leaving Certificate examinations. Regulations governing entry to the Day Group Certificate examination have not changed greatly from what they were when originally introduced; to be eligible to be admitted to the examination a pupil must 'have followed an approved course for at least two years as a recognized pupil in a post-primary school'.[50] An approved course consists of the obligatory subjects of at least one of the groups of subjects as well as Irish, English and civics. Furthermore, a pupil must enter for examination in the subjects of at least one of the groups available.[51] In the case of each of the certificate examinations, a minimum age requirement for entry still stands. Fourteen and a half is the minimum age for the Intermediate and sixteen and a half for the Leaving Certificate examination. The minimum age for entry to the Day Group Certificate examination is thirteen and a half.[52]

Aside from the fact that vocational school pupils are now

permitted to take the Intermediate and Leaving Certificate examinations, and secondary school pupils the Day Group Certificate examination, the most notable development in the examinations in recent years is the official elimination of the pass/fail distinction of earlier years. Whereas formerly candidates were required to pass in five subjects – including Irish and, in the case of boys, mathematics as well – in order to pass the Intermediate Certificate examination, this rule no longer obtains. Neither does the rule obtain any longer whereby a candidate has to pass in five subjects, including Irish, in order to pass the Leaving Certificate examination. Likewise, a candidate in the Day Group Certificate is now awarded a Certificate as long as he sits for examination in the required subjects of examination. The move in this direction began, perhaps, with the introduction of a new marking system in 1968/9. In place of grades being stated in percentages, a letter grade was introduced with each letter grade corresponding to a percentage range (see Table 2).[53]

Table 2: **System of grades and percentage ranges introduced for Certificate examinations in 1968/9**

Grade	Percentage Range
A	85 or over
B	70 but less than 85
C	55 but less than 70
D	40 but less than 55
E	25 but less than 40
F	10 but less than 25
No Grade	Less than 10

At that time also it was decided to 'award' a certificate to pupils who obtained a grade of D or higher in at least five subjects, including Irish, from the approved lists. A 'statement of results' indicating the grades obtained at the examinations would be 'issued' to all who sat the examinations. The implicit distinction between pass and fail in this arrangement was eliminated in 1975/6 in the case of the Intermediate and Leaving Certificate, and in 1977 in the case of the Group Certificate examinations, with the decision that each candidate at the examinations would be 'given' a certificate of the grades obtained by him at the examination.[54] In 1968/9 the distinction introduced in 1924/5 between pass and honours at the Intermediate Certificate examination was abolished. This same distinction between pass and honours in the examination, along with the distinction between pass and honours papers in the Leaving Certificate examination, was eliminated in 1970/1. In place of pass and honours papers in the Leaving Certificate examination, ordinary-level, higher-level and common-level papers were introduced. Ordinary-level and higher-level papers were made available in most subjects, and common-level papers were made available in the remainder.[55] The one letter-grade system of marking is now common to all the post-primary examinations.

Other minor alterations in the rules governing the examinations have also been introduced in recent years. Persons over seventeen years of age are now permitted to sit for one or more subjects in the Leaving Certificate examination. In the case of some subjects at the Intermediate Certificate examinations, it is proposed that a percentage of the marks may be earned for work completed during the course of the school year and be awarded by the class teacher.[56] Likewise, oral examinations may supplement written work to a somewhat greater extent than before.[57] Recent years have also seen changes in the form of questions asked in some papers. Thus, for example, short-answer questions have become a feature of the papers in history at both Intermediate and Leaving Certificate levels.

While many of the changes in subjects, courses and examinations which took place after 1963 were undoubtedly aimed at implementing the policies enunciated by Dr Hillery and successive Ministers, and while such changes must be taken into account in attempting to assess the extent of educational reform accomplished as a result of government policy, one critical factor remains to be considered in assessing the effectiveness of the educational planning of the early 1960s. I am referring to the actual degree of pupil enrolment and participation in the new possibilities opened up by changes introduced since 1963. Consideration of changes already discussed indicates some progress. On the question of participation rates in more comprehensive forms of post-primary education, however, and particularly in regard to increased enrolments in the areas of technical and applied studies where it was sought most, progress has proved more difficult to achieve.

Possibly the best way of looking at enrolments in various subjects at post-primary level is through the numbers of candidates sitting for the Day Group, Intermediate and Leaving Certificate examinations.[58] Figures for the Leaving Certificate examination are of particular interest not only because the Leaving Certificate is taken to represent the apex of the post-primary programme but because pupils are required to take only one specified subject, namely Irish, as part of their course. Altogether pupils must study at least five subjects at senior level if they are to be eligible to sit for the examination and they are recommended to sit for no more than seven subjects in the examination.[59] Any other limitations which may be put on pupil-choice is determined not by regulations governing the public examinations but by the entry requirements of institutions such as the universities, the colleges of education, and other third-level or training institutions such as AnCO.

In 1979, the latest date for which figures are available, a total of 35,510 candidates sat for the Leaving Certificate examination.[60] The numbers of candidates sitting the most heavily-subscribed subjects contrasted very sharply with those for the newer technical subjects, and in general business studies subjects fared much better than the technical subjects (see Table 3).[61]

Table 3: **Number of candidates sitting various subjects in Leaving Certificate examination, 1979**

Subjects	Numbers of Candidates
Most heavily-subscribed subjects	
English	34,143
Mathematics	32,981
Irish	32,146
French	21,542
Biology	18,227
Geography	18,148
History	12,352
Business studies subjects	
Business organisation	9,898
Accounting	7,616
Economics	7,435
Technical subjects	
Technical drawing	2,540
Engineering workshop theory and practice	1,370
Building construction	1,357
Mechanics	14

The figures given in Table 3 are those for the 1979 examination only, but the trend whereby the newer technical subjects are poorly subscribed and the traditional and more literary subjects are the most heavily subscribed occurs in all years dating back to the introduction of the technical subjects into the Leaving Certificate examination in 1971. A similar trend, though much less pronounced, is noticeable also in the Intermediate Certificate examination in recent years which, in 1979, was taken by 49,980 candidates (see Table 4).[62]

Table 4: **Number of candidates sitting the most heavily-subscribed subjects in Intermediate Certificate examination, 1979**

Subject	Number of Candidates
Mathematics	49,541
English	49,229
Irish	47,163
Geography	46,478
History	46,369
Science	35,687
French	34,938

Subjects which were introduced into the Intermediate Certificate examination in 1969 as a result of the common course fared relatively better than those introduced at Leaving Certificate level. Thus mechanical drawing was taken by 10,684 candidates, woodwork by 8,788 candidates, and metalwork by 5,491 candidates. Other practical subjects fared even better; thus, after commerce, the eighth most highly subscribed subject, came art which was taken by 19,204 candidates and home economics which was taken by 18,170 candidates.

In the Day Group Certificate examination of 1979, which was sat by 19,050 candidates,[63] the five most highly subscribed subjects were ones which, with the exception of mathematics, did not belong to any of the compulsory groups (see Table 5).

Table 5: **Numbers of candidates sitting most heavily-subscribed subjects in Day Group Certificate examination, 1979**

Subject	Number of Candidates
English	16,898
Mathematics	15,667
Irish	12,422
Geography	10,895
History	10,263
Mechanical drawing	9,413
Woodwork	9,073

Note: Spanish with 224 candidates and German with 142 candidates were the two least heavily subscribed subjects in the examination.

The figures just presented for each of the examinations in 1979 cannot be dismissed lightly, for they are a fairly accurate guide to the number of pupils actually completing their studies in the different post-primary school subjects. Several points emerge from an examination of the figures. In the first place, the aspiration towards greater participation in technical subjects in particular at the post-primary level remains largely unfulfilled as yet; this is particularly true at the Leaving Certificate level where the technical subjects introduced for examination in 1971 fared very badly relative to the more established literary and academic subjects. Indeed, while the numbers of candidates taking the technical subjects which official policy was trying desperately to promote were very low, subjects representing the academic kind of education from which Dr Hillery was professedly trying to break away were benefiting handsomely from the increased enrolments and higher levels of education being pursued since the middle 1960s. As against this, of course, there are instances of traditional academic or secondary school subjects such as Latin and history losing ground in relation to business studies subjects, for example, at Leaving Certificate level; likewise, at Intermediate Certificate level subjects like commerce, art and mechanical drawing have made headway. Arguably, too, a trend towards greater enrolments in the technical and other applied subjects even at Leaving Certificate level might still emerge, now that the structures and diploma and degree-granting institutions and arrangements in these areas are established. As yet, however, there are no signs of any such development. Thus, while there was a considerably higher entry rate in technical subjects at the Intermediate Certificate examination than at the Leaving Certificate examination in 1979, this was also the case in 1977, the year in which students taking the Leaving Certificate examination in 1979 would normally have taken the Intermediate Certificate examination. By the time the 1977 Intermediate Certificate cohort reached the Leaving Certificate examination in 1979, however, the entry rate in technical subjects in the Leaving Certificate examination had dropped greatly by comparison with what it had been in the Intermediate Certificate examination in 1977. And it seems unlikely that the policy of encouragement of scientific subjects by means of special grants announced in the *White Paper* will improve matters substantially.[64]

A second point emerging from these figures is that the high rate of entry in the traditional academic and literary subjects at the Intermediate and Leaving Certificate examinations, and the very low rate of entry in the technical subjects at the Leaving Certificate examination in particular, is also to be found to some extent in the figures for the Day Group Certificate examination in 1979. Thus the three most highly subscribed subjects in the Day Group Certificate examination for 1979 are the same as those for the Intermediate and Leaving Certificate examinations. Moreover, in the Day Group Certificate examination for 1979 the most heavily subscribed technical subject — mechanical drawing — was taken by fewer than half of all candidates. At the same time history and geography were each taken by just more than half of all candidates. In the Day Group Certificate examination in 1963, the order of preference among the most highly subscribed subjects was English, Irish, woodwork, mechanical drawing, metal-work and mathematics.[65] And while it might not be very helpful to compare the 1963 figures with those for 1979 in some respects, the comparison does tend to support the view that, for whatever reasons, the technical or vocational subjects would appear to have lost rather than made up ground in relation to the more academic or secondary subjects, even in the Day Group Certificate examination.

It might be objected that the failure to increase the level of participation in technical and applied studies at the post-primary stage is less attributable to the Department of Education than to social and parental attitudes and to institutions of further education and the like, who set entry requirements which may favour the more traditional subjects. This may be so, but it does nothing to change the figures. It does, however, suggest avenues to be pursued in tackling the problem. Meanwhile it must be borne in mind that, in the final analysis, the success of the policy of increased participation in technical and applied studies at post-primary level will not be found in the provision of greatly improved structures and facilities but in the numbers of pupils taking and benefiting from these studies.

If the measures taken to achieve greater participation in technical and applied education at second level have been somewhat of a disappointment to date, neither can one afford to be sanguine regarding the policy of increased participation in post-primary education in general. It is indisputable that there has been a very considerable increase in enrolments. But an increase in enrolments, in mere attendance figures, can hardly be equated with participation in any worthwhile sense. To make adequate provision for increased participation and meeting the ideal of equality of educational opportunity for all pupils, it is necessary to take account of the various needs, interests, aptitudes, and home and socio-economic background of all pupils. And in this regard the attempts of the 1960s were very limited. The effect of government initiatives in post-primary education saw enrolments almost doubling from 132,407 to 231,093 between 1963 and 1973 alone.[66] But with an increase in enrolments came also an increase in background, variety, abilities, interests and educational achievements of pupils. The raising of the school-leaving age to fifteen in 1972, the full-scale phasing in of the new primary school curriculum in 1971 and the subsequent entry to post-primary schools of pupils who had studied the new curriculum, made very great and novel demands on the post-primary system. These developments called for new and varied types of programmes, different in many ways from those already in existence. Yet, notwithstanding the widening of the post-primary curriculum which resulted from the introduction of the common Intermediate Certificate course in 1966 and the common Leaving Certificate course in 1968, insufficient provision was made in the post-primary schools to cope with these new and varied needs.

This limited response was related to the fact that the concept of a comprehensive curriculum upon which the reforms were to be based was deficient in an important way. It was a deficiency which is to be found in Dr Hillery's original distinction between pupils of academic ability and those of practical ability.[67] As a consequence of this distinction, the task of the comprehensive curriculum came to be seen largely in terms of devising a curriculum which would be made up of the sum of the practical subjects of the vocational school and the academic subjects of the secondary school. Some new technical subjects and business studies subjects were also added on. It is questionable how adequate such an approach is to the question of a curriculum intended to provide for the participation of all pupils, and for equality of educational opportunity. Problems of motivation, aptitude, educational background and achievement cannot be resolved simply by a widening out of the range of subjects on offer.

While the 1970s saw a number of attempts on a rather small scale to face up to this aspect of the challenge of post-primary education in the form of curriculum and examinations projects, these measures, which were primarily pedagogical in intent, did seem to go beyond what was originally understood to be the challenge. Attention will be given to these developments in a later chapter. At this point it is sufficient to note that, alongside the specifically government-sponsored reforms of a largely organisational and structural nature, the force of events during the post-1963 period has, of itself, necessitated further changes of curriculum and examinations. Such changes, it would appear, were not fully anticipated or provided for in the Hillery reforms. To that extent it must be said that the goal of increased participation in post-primary education fell short of the success achieved in the matter of increased enrolments. It is a difference between enabling pupils to gain reasonable benefit from post-primary education and merely being in attendance at it.

Assessing the attempts at reform
In his statement of May 1963, and in the general thrust of developments that followed, Dr Hillery and subsequent Ministers for Education were attempting to develop post-primary education in Ireland to meet what they saw to be the challenge of the times. The challenge was seen very much in terms of economic objectives; throughout the period, however, measures taken to achieve these objectives were frequently defended on the grounds that they promoted equality of educational opportunity for all. And while

there is no reason for thinking that these measures were not motivated by such considerations, it happened that this objective as well as the economic objectives could be served through one and the same measures, or so it was thought at the time.

Whilst the more glamorous events of the 1960s captured the headlines and sustained public interest in the enterprise of educational change, from the time of Dr Hillery's statement of 1963 onwards the efforts of the Department of Education constituted an enormously heavy burden on the resources of the Department and involved it in an almost unending series of battles, conflicts and compromises with educational interest groups of all sorts. It is arguable, moreover, that the glamorous events also had the effect of distorting the reality of actual reform. For, whatever gains may have been made by the implementation of official policy, they were not achieved without creating new difficulties and ignoring or failing to resolve some existing ones.

The government of the day can hardly be faulted in the matter of bringing about increased participation in post-primary education, viewed from the point of view of enrolments. Much the same can be said regarding its efforts to introduce institutions and structures at both second and third levels to encourage and promote technical and applied studies. But although considerable effort was expended in attempting to attract greater participation in technical and applied forms of education, the enrolment figures in these areas are disappointing. Indeed, they suggest that the reality of technical and applied studies at post-primary level is far less promising than one might be led to believe from a selective consideration of recent developments.[68] For, as yet, little has been done to break the stranglehold of the traditionally 'popular' academic subjects at post-primary level. The adaptation and remodelling of existing arrangements for curriculum and examinations necessitated by the relatively huge increase in enrolments also fell short of what was required.

In introducing the comprehensive idea and in proposing common courses and examinations for all post-primary schools in 1963, Dr Hillery looked forward to achieving a 'parity of standard' in the vocational and secondary sectors.[69] On the basis of the figures at which we have looked, and the investigations reported in the *ICE Report*, however, commonality of courses and examinations would appear to have worked very largely to the detriment of vocational or continuation education, at least as continuation education had been conceived and developed originally. The co-ordination of Day Group Certificate and Intermediate Certificate courses in the mid-1960s involved the widening of the curriculum of vocational schools to include many of the traditional secondary school subjects, notably history and geography and modern European languages. This led to a lessening of time devoted to practical subjects and vocational school subjects which could not be taken in the Intermediate Certificate examination fell into disfavour, and in some cases they were dropped altogether. As the *ICE Report* puts it:

> A broadening of the curriculum brought about a lessening of the time devoted to practical subjects. The 'vocational' factor decreased; a phasing-in with the Intermediate course developed; rigidity set in; there was little time or opportunity for innovation and the system tended to become, in the main, a second-year exercise in the path towards the more prestigious 'Inter'...
> In the main, however, it may be stated that the continuation courses, designed at their initiation to suit pupils over fourteen years of age, are now embarked upon by young people of 12 years lacking in maturity and basic education. A curriculum planned at first as pre-employment is now virtually pre-Intermediate. Examinations which were terminal and taken by students of 16-17 years of age are now taken en passant by pupils of 14 years plus. The short tail of general subjects which was originally attached to the requisite Groups, has now grown to such an extent that it is assuming the greater significance.[70]

The implementation of official policy at post-primary level, therefore, and particularly the introduction of common courses and examinations, seems to have worked more to the benefit of secondary education than vocational and technical education; and whatever changes were implemented can be said to have been somewhat counter-productive. The policy of making a more comprehensive post-primary curriculum available to all pupils, and with it the cost-saving objective, also ran into great difficulty with the failure to gain satisfactory implementation of the sharing of facilities proposal and other similar proposals on the scale originally intended. The failure experienced in this connection also partially affected the aspiration to equality of educational opportunity for all, for this depended, to some extent, upon a more comprehensive curriculum being made available. Undoubtedly measures such as free post-primary education, the introduction of common courses and examinations, the comprehensive and community schools, the sharing of facilities, and the introduction of comprehensive facilities where this was achieved, went some way towards achieving greater equality of educational opportunity. But as has been suggested, the attainment of this objective – insofar as it is attainable[71] – necessitates the school taking other measures as well, measures which received little or no attention.

The attempts of the mid-1960s to meet the challenge facing post-primary education mark the beginning of a period of courageous leadership in post-primary education by the state and by the Department of Education in particular, and one can only applaud their efforts. It was only to be expected that there would be a mixture of success and failure in such an enterprise and it would have been a much greater failure not to have initiated any change at all. Before leaving this matter, however, two important areas in which the reform attempts of the 1960s were deficient, and to which little reference has been made, must now be taken up.

It is one thing to fail to achieve objectives which were sought, to leave certain difficulties unattended, and even to create additional ones. But in facing the challenge to post-primary education a failure of a more serious kind was also experienced. It was a failure to assess the full extent of that challenge. That the creation of a unified post-primary system of education, the provision of equality of educational opportunity for all, and the articulation of post-primary education in Ireland with the economic, technological and employment needs of the country constituted important elements in the challenge are not in question. Considerations other than those enumerated, however, must also be borne in mind in the adoption of educational goals and the formulation of educational policy. Economic and social considerations must be taken into account in arriving at decisions of this kind to be sure, but they must be broad in character and not confined solely to questions of manpower preparation and social equity. Relevant philosophical, moral, religious and other culture-related considerations which reflect the values and the cultural ideals of society also have an important claim to be represented both in the determination of educational policy and in regulating the weight to be given to specific economic and social considerations. Likewise, educational and psychological considerations are necessary in the determination of what is educationally possible and desirable and in safeguarding what may be of lasting value in the inherited educational tradition. The implications of changes of policy or practice in one sector of education for other sectors must also be understood and acted upon.

Although it may be true that broad philosophical, sociological, psychological and educational considerations of the type I have in mind were represented to a greater or less extent in the existing traditions of both secondary and vocational education in Ireland, their importance in relation to those considerations which seemed pre-eminent in determining post-primary educational policy during the 1960s is far from clear. This is not to say that undue consideration was given to economic questions in themselves — on the contrary *Investment in Education*, which carried much of the burden of the economic arguments, was a very balanced study in which there was a distinct awareness of its limited economic perspective — but it is to say that due consideration was not given to other matters important in the development and implementation of educational policy. Thus, it is quite clear that the broader social, psychological and educational implications of a massive increase in numbers and variety of pupils, and what this demanded by way of alternative and innovative forms of post-primary education, were never recognised and investigated at the time. And, as events such as the growing demand for new forms of curricula at post-primary level have shown, attention to these matters was as essential as attention to the questions of increased post-primary participation in general as well as an increased rate of participation in technical and applied studies. For if equality of educational opportunity was to be achieved, even in so far as the school can contribute to the attainment of this ideal, and if resources in terms of buildings, facilities and personnel were to be most fruitfully deployed, other matters called for attention just as much as did the promotion of technical education, for example. These matters included the development of new curricula and methods of evaluation and teaching suited to meeting the interests, needs and abilities of those for whom the more conventional forms of post-primary education — vocational or secondary — were unsuited. And, beyond this, in a time of considerable social change, and one in which attempts were being made to introduce a distinctly new vocational orientation into post-primary education in Ireland, a re-examination of the extent to which the conventional forms of post-primary schooling were suited to what was thought to be their function with regard to all pupils, namely general education, was called for. For, as matters stood and as will be argued in the next chapter, what general education stood for was anybody's guess. Yet if it was a major aspect of government policy to raise participation levels and to raise the school-leaving age so as to ensure a better education for all, this surely was a question of central importance. And all the more so as it is one which had never been settled satisfactorily since the foundation of the state.

Of no less importance than these considerations, from the point of view of achieving educational reform, is the question of broadly-based participation in the development, formulation and implementation of educational policy.[72] And in this respect the procedures employed from the early 1960s onwards were not characterised by the broadly-based involvement of educational personnel and other interested parties which might have been most effective. In its general thrust official policy-formulation had been the prerogative of the very few; and in the matter of its implementation, the involvement of educational personnel and others with interests in the matters in question was kept to a minimum, confined as it was largely to matters of management and organisation of schools. It is arguable, however, that many of the failures experienced during the period are partly attributable to the absence of adequate discussion and the consequent inability of interested parties to understand what was going on, notably the secondary school authorities and the universities. Curriculum committees, it is true, had been established in the different subject areas and although they did speak their own mind on matters, the Department viewed their role as a limited one, and the scope of their areas of responsibility was rather narrow.[73] With the exclusion of broadly-based professional participation in the reform attempts of the 1960s, it is hardly surprising that less than complete success was met with in the reform attempts of the period. And while there was to be greater teacher involvement in curriculum and other projects from the early 1970s onwards, by then the major policy decisions had long since been taken.

Chapter 2

Disregard for Aims

A lack of attention to aims

In his statement of 1963 Dr Hillery summed up by saying of his plan that it 'would solve in a practical way and within a reasonable time the main problems of our post-primary education'.[1] I have shown already how his plan and those elaborations of it which followed did not live up fully to the expectations of them. But before any final judgment can be made regarding the plan and the activities of the 1960s and 1970s, some further considerations are necessary.

One point which emerged forcefully from a consideration of the main events and pronouncements in post-primary education dating back to 1963 is the way in which post-primary education came to be viewed, in official circles at least, as an agent of economic development. To an extent unknown in earlier times, the post-primary school came to be seen as having a major role to play in providing forms of education which were considered to be closely related to the emerging economic needs and potential of the country, with an emphasis on technical and other applied skills of a vocational kind. And specific measures were taken to ensure that this would be achieved. What did not emerge, and still has not, is a clear view of the overall purpose or aims of post-primary education and how the more specific purpose of serving the economic needs of the country are related to it. Before one is in any position to evaluate fully the suitability and effectiveness of changes initiated since 1963, and the quality of post-primary education at the present time, it is necessary to have at least some idea of what the overall aims of post-primary education in the country are and have been, and how adequate they are as a basis for its conduct and development.

Little sustained attention has been given to identifying and evaluating the aims of post-primary education in Ireland, particularly at official level. Over the years a number of individual writers have addressed the question in varying degrees of generality. Under the intermediate system Patrick Pearse did so in a rather dramatic way in the *Murder Machine*. Since the setting up of the Department of Education in 1924 educational associations, such as the Irish National Teachers' Organisation in their publication of 1947 *A Plan for Education*, and educators such as Fr Ó Catháin in *Secondary Education in Ireland* published in 1958, and John Raven in *Education, Values and Society* published in 1977, have also given some attention to the question.[2] To find official views of any substance at all on the matter one must go back quite some time.

Since the setting up of the Department of Education official views on the aims of post-primary education in Ireland have been confined largely to two documents to which I have made reference already. The first of these was *Memo V. 40* which was published in 1942. While setting out to treat of a number of matters in the vocational education system it addressed itself also to defining 'the fundamental aims of continuation education' as carried on in vocational schools. The second of these publications was the *Report of the Council of Education: The Curriculum of the Secondary School* which was made available in 1962.[3] The report devoted one short chapter to a consideration of the nature and aims of secondary education. It would not be true to say that anything like a thorough or exhaustive treatment of the question of aims was undertaken in either document, however. At no point in either publication is there any consideration of the joint aims of vocational and secondary education; less still does any concept of a comprehensive or unified form of post-primary education emerge in either document — nor did one expect it to.

In the absence of any serious official attention to the identification and formulation of aims and derivative guiding principles for the conduct and development of a unified form of post-primary education or indeed for any form of post-primary education in the final quarter of the twentieth century, one is forced back almost entirely on one's own resources in attempting to establish what these aims might be. This can be done best, perhaps, by taking a look at what have been set forth as the aims or purposes of the various post-primary school programmes over the years, by examining in some detail the officially stated views on the aims of secondary and vocational education where these are available, and by a consideration of the impact of social and economic considerations on the development of post-primary education in Ireland in recent years.

The aims of the present-day programmes

As was pointed out in the foregoing chapter, each kind of post-primary school in Ireland today, be it secondary, vocational, comprehensive or community school, has been empowered by recent developments to share one common pursuit, namely the offering of courses towards one or all of the public state examinations at post-primary level. Enormous energy always has been and still is devoted to the pursuit of such courses and examinations, and the public examinations in turn exert powerful influences on the conduct of schooling. It is appropriate to inquire, then, whether the common pursuit of public examination courses by the post-primary schools indicate any useful overall or integrating set of aims for post-primary education in general.

As set forth in the *Rules and Programme for Secondary Schools*, the stated purposes of the Intermediate and Leaving Certificate courses give little precise information. They are given in the forms of notes in parenthesis before setting forth the various regulations governing each course and the stated purpose of each course is clearly derived from what was introduced in 1924 as a statement of the purpose of the Intermediate Certificate and the aims of the Leaving Certificate.[4] In the case of the Day Group Certificate course, however, no statement of purpose is given in the current rules and programmes which govern this course and the examinations in it. Discussion of the aims of this course is best left until considering the aims of continuation education as set forth in *Memo V. 40*, at a later stage in this chapter.

The stated purpose of the Intermediate Certificate course reads as follows:

> to provide a well-balanced, general education suitable for pupils who leave full-time education at about 16 years of age or, alternatively, who wish to enter on more advanced courses of study.[5]

Regarding the Leaving Certificate course, the statement reads:

> The aim and purpose of the Leaving Certificate course is to

prepare pupils for immediate entry into open society or for proceeding to further education.[6]

These are summary statements and as such they cannot be expected to provide detailed information. Lack of detail is not their only or most serious shortcoming, however. It is one thing to have a statement of aims, however brief, for a course or educational programme; it is quite another to have such a statement of aims actually function as such, that is to say as an end-point on the basis of which courses and programmes are drawn up, taught and evaluated.

There is no reason to believe that the statements of purpose or aims introduced in connection with the Intermediate and Leaving Certificate courses in 1924 were ever intended to serve as genuine objectives or end-points against which to draw up curricula and programmes. What evidence does exist suggests, in fact, that these statements were not drawn up with this in mind at all. Arguably, they were never intended to serve as anything more than a justification of sorts for what was already being done, or as an expression of confidence that what was being done was suitable as a preparation for life and for further studies. The original wording of the statements reveals, in fact, that they were not statements of aims for the Intermediate and Leaving Certificate courses at all but statements of aims or purpose of the actual certificates. Thus the original wording reads as follows:

> The purpose of the Intermediate Certificate is to testify to the completion of a well-balanced course of general education suitable for pupils who leave school at about 16 years of age, and, alternatively, to the fitness of the pupils for entry on more advanced courses of study in a Secondary or Technical school.[7]

Regarding the Leaving Certificate, the wording was:

> The aim of the Leaving Certificate is to testify to the completion of a good secondary education and the fitness of a pupil to enter on a course of study at a University or an educational institution of similar standing.[8]

Whatever else these statements may be or were intended to be, they certainly are not statements of the aims of the Intermediate

Certificate and Leaving Certificate courses or statements of aims of education of any sort. They simply state that the Intermediate Certificate and Leaving Certificate each testify or certify that students who have earned them have completed a 'good education' and can be considered fit for further studies of any kind and, by implication, for life. Moreover, the fact that alterations of phrasing have been introduced into these basic formulations from time to time since 1924 does not necessarily elevate subsequent formulations to the level of genuine statements of aims, even if these modifications were introduced in the light of a growing awareness of the need to state aims clearly.

What, then, can be said of the statements of aims as they stand at the present time? Do they give any indication of the kind of development in pupils which is sought in Irish post-primary education and which can provide a basis for drawing up school programmes and for assessing pupils' attainment of the kind of development which is sought? In the final analysis they do, but there are considerable shortcomings. Thus, for example, what does the statement of purpose of the Intermediate Certificate course say? It says that the purpose of the course is to provide a general education for sixteen-year-olds. But what are we to understand by a general education? What does it mean in terms of the development of the pupils? There is, perhaps, a suggestion that what is intended is some preparation for life on leaving school and for further studies, but there is no elaboration in terms of values, skills and attitudes to be developed. Yet some elaboration, if only in general terms, of what is intended by way of pupil learning and development is needed if one is to be in any position to draw up a suitable course for teaching purposes.

The statement of purpose for the Leaving Certificate course is scarcely any better. It does admittedly state clearly that the purpose and aim of the course is to prepare pupils for 'immediate entry into open society or for proceeding to further education'. One cannot be quite sure, however, what is meant by this or what it might entail in a course of studies. For example, what is entailed in a preparation for 'immediate entry into open society'? What is meant by 'open society'? Furthermore, this statement does not appear to be very different from the stated purpose of the Intermediate Certificate course. That course also seeks to provide an education suited to those who are about to leave school or engage in further studies. Indeed, so empty or unspecific is the statement of purpose for the Leaving Certificate course that it appears equally applicable to an almost endless range of courses from primary-school level – at least up until recent times in Ireland – right up to and including under-graduate university and college courses. Many of these may be said to aspire to provide an education which is considered suitable as a preparation for immediate entry into 'open society' or for proceeding to further education. That is, an education which is considered suitable for those who are about to leave a full-time education or remain in it!

The brevity with which the aims of the Intermediate and Leaving Certificate courses are stated, and their lack of elaboration or philosophical explication, leave a number of questions unanswered. Despite this, it might be said that the idea of a broad preparation for living, including further studies, emerges as a recurring theme. Yet this, on its own, provides only a shaky basis for programme development. By no means can it be taken to be the expression of a clear underlying philosophy or concept of a unified and com-prehensive post-primary school system. It is a position, however, which, as we shall see, is reiterated in a number of other places.

It might be objected that I have taken too narrow a view of the stated aims of the Intermediate Certificate and Leaving Certificate courses, discussing them as I have in dissociation from the stated aims and content of various Intermediate and Leaving Certificate subjects as spelled out in the *Rules*. On closer examination, how-ever, it will be seen that the position regarding the aims and content of the various Intermediate Certificate and Leaving Certificate subjects tends to support rather than reject my argument that insufficient attention has been given to the matter of aims as a basis for course development and content selection.

Quite a number of Intermediate Certificate and Leaving Certifi-cate subjects for which a syllabus is offered in the *Rules* are not accompanied by any statement of aims whatever. This is true of science (syllabus A), home economics, art and commerce at Inter-mediate Certificate level. In the case of the Leaving Certificate subjects, as many as half of the thirty-one subjects appear without any reference to aims, and this includes 'popular' subjects such as history, biology, home economics and chemistry. Furthermore, while honours courses in many subjects are considerably more extensive, and purport to be quite a development on the pass courses, only the one statement of aims is normally provided for both pass and honours courses. The same holds true of subjects where different syllabuses exist.

In the same vein, mechanics is chosen over and above other subjects although it seems that the aims set for it could equally well be attained through the use of other content. As set out in the *Rules*, the aims of the course in mechanics is 'to develop in the student the ability to apply basic principles to a wide range of problems which require deductive and logical analysis for their solutions'.[9] Surely the application of 'basic principles to a wide range of problems which require deductive and logical analysis for their solutions' is not the monopoly of mechanics! Other oddities also exist. Thus, in the case of Intermediate Certificate history a relatively substantial statement of aims has been introduced where none previously existed but without any equally substantial change in content.[10] And if this statement of aims represents an attempt to be more explicit on the question of educational objectives, it stands in sharp contrast to the situation in respect of Leaving Certificate history which sets forth each of the courses to be covered in a few skimpy phrases and without any reference whatsoever to the question of aims.[11]

It is noteworthy that rarely is any attempt made to show how the aims of a particular subject tie up with the overall aims of the Intermediate and Leaving Certificate courses respectively.[12] This being so, one must seriously question whether statements of aims for individual subjects are anything more than statements of intended outcomes from subject content already chosen on grounds that have not been made very clear at all. In some cases one is led to ask if the statements of aims are anything more than window-dressing.[13] Indeed the general impression one gains from an examination of the aims of many subjects is that it appears to be taken for granted that there is a necessary connection between the study of them and a preparation for life and further studies. How the aims are stated, and whether they are stated at all, seemingly, is considered a matter of little importance very often.

These factors taken together suggest that many subjects on the Intermediate Certificate and Leaving Certificate courses might have found their way into these courses on some grounds other than a thorough consideration of what these subjects have to offer as a preparation for life, whatever various combinations of them might have to offer as a preparation for further studies. Less still does their inclusion appear to have been justified by reference to any serious consideration of the post-primary educational needs in the country and the aims and curriculum content which these needs suggest.

Returning to the question of whether the statements of aims for the Intermediate and Leaving Certificate courses provide any useful and overall or integrating set of aims for post-primary education in Ireland, the answer can only be a qualified yes. It is intimated that the Intermediate and Leaving Certificate courses are concerned to provide an education or preparation for life and for further studies. Yet nothing is said at all about what is aimed at in terms of the development of pupils in virtue of which they may be considered to have had a preparation for life.

At their worst, such statements are so empty as to be almost meaningless; at their best, they suggest that the courses in question are concerned in some way to provide a general education or preparation for life and further studies.

Traditional aims in the secondary sector
I have already had reason to make reference to the idea of a general education in the context of post-primary education in Ireland. It is a notion which has had a strong association with secondary education in particular. This is clearly evident in the discussion of the aims of secondary education in the *Report of the Council of Education*. In turning now to a consideration of the stated aims of secondary education in Ireland which have been set forth in this report, it will be necessary to examine how the idea of a general education has been understood in relation to these aims.

Straightaway it must be said that the position of the Council of Education on the question of a general education is somewhat confused. It is a confusion which arises from the fact that for the Council a general education seems to have two rather different meanings. And the confusion runs throughout the discussion of aims in the report. Thus while a general education is sometimes understood in terms of the educational aims or objectives which it is supposed to achieve, that is all-round formation for life, at other times it is understood in terms of the curriculum of a general education, that is humanistic and general subjects. Both of these uses of the notion are employed interchangeably in the discussion of a general education in the *Report of the Council of Education*. This results in a confusion of means and ends, of curriculum and aims, in the discussion of a general education.

Referring to secondary education as being traditionally of a grammar school type, the Council points out that as such it is synonymous, in the early years at any rate, with general education. This, in turn, is understood as being 'humanistic and intellectual in character; providing classical and modern languages, mathematics and science . . .'.[14] That is to say, general education is understood in terms of the curriculum of a general education — classical and modern languages, mathematics and science. A little later on, one reads that 'traditionally, a liberal or general education has been assigned as the role of the secondary as distinct from the vocational or professional school'.[15] Depending on how the term 'role' is understood here, that is whether in terms of aims or curriculum, this entire sentence takes on a different meaning. Either way, however, the point is made that the vocational school does not have a general education as its 'role', and this is a point which must be raised again later in discussing the aims of vocational education.

In a paragraph immediately following on this, a general education is clearly conceived in terms of aims or objectives: 'a general or liberal education is an all-round formation, aimed at the development and enrichment of the faculties of the human person rather than his specialised preparation for a particular skill or profession'. The report continues almost immediately to say that the graduate of a secondary or general education would 'popularly be regarded as "educated" — a person of character and knowledge capable of taking a responsible place in the society of which he is a member'.[16] Here there is no mention of subjects or curriculum content; attention is focused on how the person of a general education behaves in life.

General education is conceived in a novel and interesting way when it is referred to next. The question is asked, 'what in practice constitutes a "general" education?' From the answer, it will be clear that a general education is understood here in terms of curriculum. The answer, the Council believes, can best be gained from looking at what has been the accepted practice in the traditional schools of Europe: 'religious and/or moral instruction; command of the native language in speech, writing, literature; a reasonable outline of history and geography; elementary mathematics; drawing, singing and some initiation into science'.[17] Besides providing an extended range of subjects which apparently qualify for inclusion in the curriculum of a general education, the notion that a general education is 'in practice' the curriculum of a general education raises an important question. It suggests that the criterion by which a school should be judged to be offering a general education or not is simply the subjects that are being offered, presumably in the belief that they are the ones which best prepare pupils for life and further studies. But surely the question of whether a school is providing a general education, understood as a preparation for life, is to be decided not so much by the subjects on offer but by whether in fact the pupils acquire the knowledge, attitudes and skills which actually constitute a preparation for life. The curriculum, moreover, as envisaged by the Council, was drawn up primarily on the basis of traditional practice and the belief that such a curriculum constituted the best possible preparation for life, the only curriculum of a general education.

While it is counter-productive ultimately to allow two different meanings of a general education to be used interchangeably, it does have its short-term attractions. It enables one to forego the difficult task of identifying and justifying what a general education aims to achieve in terms of knowledge and skills. It enables one to do this since what should constitute such a curriculum is 'known'. It is 'known' as long as a general education, understood in terms of the aims of a general education can be identified with general education understood in terms of the curriculum of a general education, that is what 'in practice' constitutes general education. As long as a general education is understood in this loose way, the aims of a general education are by definition achievable by the 'known' curriculum of a general education, that is a classical or grammar school type of curriculum. This, of course, begs the question of what should constitute the curriculum of a general education but, rather than answering the question, it simply evades it.

If this is so, it may well explain why the question of the aims of Irish secondary education has rarely been considered to be anything more than a matter for token discussion. For as long as the curriculum of a general education is 'known', the need for fundamental discussion of the aims of secondary education does not arise. Hence, perhaps, the eagerness with which the Council of Education shunned 'meticulous analysis' or 'abstract theorising' on fundamental issues in their discussion of the nature and aims of secondary education.[18]

Be this as it may, however, it does not account for the entire

curriculum of the secondary school today or even at the time of
the Council's report. While the curriculum of the secondary school
today is, and always has been, composed in large part of those
studies which have long been considered suitable in a curriculum
of general education – subjects such as classical and modern
languages, mathematics, the sciences, and humanistic studies such
as history, music and art – some other subjects have also been
included. Thus, a number of subjects traditionally not considered
very suitable, subjects such as business and commercial studies,
engineering workshop theory and practice, technical drawing,
building construction, woodwork and metalwork, and home
economics, are all official subjects on the present-day curriculum
of the secondary school. Moreover, while it is true that much of
the expansion in subjects traditionally not included in the general
education curriculum of the secondary school has taken place
since the publication of the *Report of the Council of Education*,
nonetheless a number of subjects of this kind, such as manual
instruction or woodwork, domestic science and commerce, were
considered suitable by the Council for inclusion in the curriculum
of the secondary school.[19] But one might well ask, on what grounds
were these subjects considered suitable if, according to the Council,
they were not normally included, in the European tradition, in the
curriculum of a general education, the criterion for inclusion
which the Council itself seemed to adopt?

To understand why it is possible to include such subjects it will
help if we return to the distinction which I made earlier between a
general education conceived in terms of aims and a general education
conceived in terms of curriculum. Commercial or technical subjects
of the kind in question were not normally highlighted as part of
the traditional curriculum of a general education, a point recognised
by the Council.[20] It is noteworthy that when justifying the
retention of manual instruction or woodwork – a subject actually
included in the intermediate system – the Council sought to justify
its inclusion not by reference to what it understood to be the
traditional curriculum of a general education. Rather it did so by
pointing to what manual instruction can do for the general education – understood now in terms of aims – of those who take it.
Thus, borrowing a quotation from the *Rules* of the day, it made
the point: 'the aim of manual instruction in secondary schools,
however, is "primarily an educational one, and the teacher's efforts
should be directed not only to the training of the pupil in the use

of tools and materials, but also to the development in him of self-reliance, resourcefulness, and initiative".'[21] In its argument for the inclusion of domestic science in the curriculum of the secondary school the Council again shifted its grounds away from considerations of the traditional curriculum of a general education and appealed again, indirectly, to what the study of domestic science does for the pupil. Thus, it continued: 'the desirability of providing instruction in domestic science for girls following a secondary school course is so obvious that it does not require to be stressed'.[22] And the case made for the inclusion of commerce is a mixture of appeal to tradition — it was included in the programme of the old intermediate schools ever since the 1890s — and the belief that commerce 'does, in fact, contribute to the pupils' general education'![23]

The inclusion of a number of subjects normally not considered suitable for inclusion in the traditional curriculum of a general education was, therefore, permitted by the Council of Education. Despite this, the secondary school could still be said to be true in practice to its 'role' of providing a general education as opposed to a vocational or professional education. This is so because the inclusion of these subjects was justified not by reference to the curriculum of a general education but, at best, by reference to the aims or objectives of a general education. Clearly one cannot condone this ambiguous and twofold use of the notion of a general education. Yet, when the traditional curriculum of a general education proved too narrow to cater for curriculum content which seemed reasonable or necessary on other grounds, this ambiguity of meaning and usage allowed an escape route.

Once this is seen as the way in which the aims of secondary education in Ireland have been thought about, it makes sense of much of what has been claimed in its regard. It explains, for example, why the secondary school could claim to give a pupil a general education, even though it may be evident to one and all that the pupil, far from being prepared for life, had received little genuine all-round development for life or preparation for further studies. Such a claim could be made because secondary education, it was maintained, offered the curriculum of a general education. It also explains why discussions of the aims of secondary education could remain so abstract, idealistic and esoteric, for, as was pointed out, once you 'know' what has to be the curriculum of the secondary school, how you state the aims is a matter of little consequence. Finally, it probably goes some way to explain the general scepticism one finds among many practising educators on the question of aims. For when the curriculum of the schools has been decided upon even before serious attention has been given to the question of aims, such discussions of aims as take place are nothing more than wishful thinking at best and, perhaps, more often than not, merely lip-service. The pity is that, thereby, the exhortations of those who call for genuine attention to aims of education as a basis for developing new curricula are discredited.

Where does this consideration of the aims of secondary education as discussed in the *Report of the Council of Education* leave us in our attempt to identify what have been understood as aims of second-level education in Ireland? The answer, it seems, is not very different from that suggested by a consideration of the aims of the Intermediate and Leaving Certificate courses. For while there is a confusion of aims and curriculum in the report of the Council, the point is made that the aim of the secondary school is seen as one of providing pupils with an all-round development and broad preparation for life.

Before leaving the *Report of the Council of Education*, two further related and important points are in order. Firstly, the general theological context within which education is placed in the mind of the Council: this is mentioned throughout the report and it received explicit mention in the discussion of aims. The Council of Education began its discussion of the nature and aims of secondary education in Ireland by setting forth what it considered to be the aims of education in general. It saw the school, be it primary or secondary, as an agent of cultural preservation and transmission as well as one of organised formation of the young. As a social institution, however, the school, in the view of the Council, was 'of its very nature subsidiary and complementary to the family and the Church'. And the 'sacredness' and 'ultimate worth' of the individual was to be highly valued and recognised: 'The purpose of school education, then, is the organized development and equipment of all the powers of the individual person — religious, moral, intellectual, physical — so that, by making the fullest use of his talents, he may responsibly discharge his duties to God and to his fellowmen in society.' In a word, the school was to prepare pupils 'to be God-fearing and responsible citizens'.[24]

This is an important stance to adopt and it is disappointing that little attention is given to drawing out its implications. Thus, little is said of the relationship between 'religious' aims and other aims. Likewise, there is little or no discussion of how various subjects or programmes might be thought to contribute to the attainment of the religious aim. Yet perhaps this should not blind us from acknowledging that in their day-to-day activities over the years secondary schools, and indeed vocational schools, were guided by considerations which have not been made fully explicit in the report of the Council. This was manifested by the attention given to promoting general education within a religious context, which in turn reflected a commitment to the values and ideals of the Christian way of life. It was manifest, moreover, not necessarily by reference to the formal curriculum of the school but through the broader religious atmosphere of the schools, which in most cases were owned by religious orders and in which daily prayer and religious education had a conspicuous place.

The second point is related to this, and again it refers to something which is touched upon in the *Report of the Council of Education* in its discussion of the nature and aims of secondary education. I refer to the broad concept of the educated man which was traditionally associated with the ideal of a liberal education. In this ideal there was highlighted a commitment to the development of the intellect, but it did include also a strong commitment to developing in pupils the social values and graces proper to those who would attain positions of leadership within society. This commitment was possibly more prominent in the English tradition of grammar school education but it was undoubtedly present in very many Irish secondary schools as well. It is a commitment which is well-illustrated, for example, in Cardinal Newman's celebrated passage depicting the 'gentleman', a passage which has remained on the English Leaving Certificate course for many years now. And while the commitment to the intellectual goal of a general education could always be visibly demonstrated by the array of subjects and examinations which were pursued in secondary education, the broader social education of the pupil was being attended to by the less visible protocols, games and authority structures which prevailed.

Accordingly, although the Council of Education in its discussion of the nature and aims of secondary education does not elaborate on these aspects of the secondary school, it is appropriate to make reference to them here. And while these ideals might not always have been fully realised in practice, they did form an important dimension of the traditional European concept of secondary education by which the Council was guided in its own thinking.

Aims in the vocational sector

In turning to a consideration of the officially stated aims of vocational or continuation education,[25] the situation is as unsatisfactory in some respects as it is in the case of secondary education. Since the appearance of *Memo V. 40* in 1942, no serious attention has been given to the question of the aims of vocational education. In the *Rules and Programme for the Day Vocational Certificate Examinations*, moreover, no statement of aims of vocational education or even of the Day Vocational or Group Certificate examination course is given.[26] Accordingly, in discussing the officially stated aims of vocational education in Ireland one must depend almost exclusively on *Memo V. 40*.

Vocational education in Ireland has always been practical and career-oriented in practice, and in this it has been quite distinguishable from secondary education in its overall character. Nonetheless, essentially the same general aims have been set forth in *Memo V. 40* for vocational or continuation education as have been set forth for secondary education in the *Report of the Council of Education*. Thus, although the Council of Education was of the view that its commitment to general education distinguished the secondary school from the vocational school, this view was not shared by *Memo V. 40* twenty years earlier. For there it was claimed that the general aim of continuation or vocational education was to provide a general education understood in the sense of all-round development. Thus it is stated that the 'general purpose' of continuation or vocational education, as opposed to its 'immediate purpose', was 'to develop, with the assistance of God's grace, the whole man with all his faculties, natural and supernatural, so that he may realise his duties and responsibilities as a member of society, that he may contribute effectively to the welfare of his fellow man, and by so doing, attain the end destined for him by his Creator'.[27] Such a view could be said to be in line with what the Council of Education considered to be the aim of any form of education. Yet it also expresses basically the same view on what constitutes a general education as was set forth in the *Report of the Council of Education*; or, more correctly perhaps, it could be said to express the same view as that set forth in the *Report of the Council of Education* when the idea of a general education was there understood, in terms of the aims of a general education, to mean all-round development of the person and preparation for life. With general education understood in this sense, then, the aspiration to provide a general education, contrary to what is said in the *Report of the Council of Education*, would not appear to provide a basis for distinguishing between secondary education and vocational or continuation education.

What does distinguish continuation education from secondary education, however, is the 'immediate aim' to which it aspires, along with the curriculum which it offers in pursuit of its immediate aim. And both in the identification of the immediate aims of vocational or continuation education as well as in the procedure employed in adopting them, the position is somewhat more satisfactory than it is in regard to secondary education. To begin with, the immediate aim was identified or presented in less vague terms. As set forth in *Memo V. 40*, the 'immediate purpose of day continuation education as organised under the Vocational Education Act, is to prepare boys and girls, who have to start early in life, for the occupations which are open to them'. Or, more specifically, the subjects of continuation education 'are taught with the immediate object of enabling boys and girls to make themselves useful as soon as possible in the economic and household spheres'.[28]

The procedure by which the immediate aims of vocational education were adopted, and by which programmes were developed in accordance with them, has no parallel in secondary education. They were adopted on the basis of an analysis of job-opportunities and needs in borough, urban and rural areas, and the kinds of skills which they required. Typically these opportunities and needs were found in agriculture, maintenance and manufacture, transport and communication, personal and domestic service, and commerce and clerical work. Based on the kind of preparation required for these different forms of employment, along with a consideration of the requirements of a more general preparation for life, a number of different programmes were then drawn up. What these programmes were we have seen already in an earlier chapter. Additionally, provision was made for adapting and developing the basic programmes in accordance with the inevitable variety of local conditions.[29] It was these programmes also which were later to form the courses of study leading to the Day Group or Day Vocational Certificate examinations which were introduced in 1947. This being so, it is, perhaps, reasonable to conclude that the aims of the Day Group

Certificate course were at one with those of continuation education. In light of the major changes which this course has undergone in recent years, however, it would be too much to expect that the course is as closely aligned with the original aims of continuation education today as it was originally.[30]

Through the identification of social or economic needs and the employment needs of individuals as the basis on which the immediate aims and, subsequently, the curricula and programmes of continuation education were to be drawn up, continuation education became markedly practical and vocational in character. And if it sought to provide a general education in the sense of a general preparation for life, and by way of context for a more specific vocational preparation, it did not allow itself to be bound by the highly academic and classical tradition of grammar school education. In its approach to the identification of more specific educational objectives, and in drawing up appropriate programmes, continuation education employed a much more explicit rationale for educational and curriculum development than was true of secondary education. It was an approach, moreover, which shows up many of the critical weaknesses of attempts at curriculum development and educational expansion in Irish post-primary education since the early 1960s.

The statement of aims of vocational or continuation education as set forth in *Memo V. 40* served as a basis for the successful development and conduct of continuation education throughout the 1940s and the 1950s. The events of the 1960s and 1970s, however, were to mark the decline of its influence. But if they did, nothing by way of a clearly worked-out and well-formulated over-all rationale or philosophy for the development of vocational, or for that matter any aspect of post-primary education, was presented in its place.

Unresolved questions

While a realisation of the implications of economic factors for post-primary education may have been the immediate cause of the major developments which have taken place since 1963, these developments were implemented largely without any systematic approach to educational or curriculum development. No clear concept of what a unified system of post-primary education would involve ever emerged; no worthwhile attempt was made clearly to identify and enunciate the educational aims and objectives of this unified form of post-primary education; no attempt was made to assess the extent to which the demands of economic and techno-logical growth should influence or determine the overall aims and philosophy or orientation of post-primary education; and less still were any attempts made to assess the relative merits of education for economic and technological growth and those of education for personal growth of the individual and his preparation for life, the traditional aims of secondary, and to a somewhat lesser extent of continuation education. Consequently, such attempts at educational and curriculum reform as took place at post-primary level were conducted largely within a philosophical or moral vacuum.

It may be objected that this is not so, that in fact ever since Dr Hillery's time as Minister for Education there has been a clear conception, at official level, of the aims of post-primary education. This, in any event, is the view of none other than Seán O'Connor to whose article 'Post-primary education: now and in the future', I have already made reference. Thus in addressing himself to the question of the aim or purpose of recent developments in post-primary education, he wrote that they were 'directed to the achieving of two fundamental purposes which each of the last four Ministers for Education has stressed from time to time. These are (1) equality of educational opportunity for all and (2) the fashion-ing of education so that it is responsive to the aptitudes and interests of the individual pupil'.[31] Two years later a document on community schools issuing from the Department of Education[32] referred to these two points, along with others, as aspects of the government's policy in relation to post-primary schools. On this occasion the issues were referred to not as educational aims or purposes but aspects of policy. And correctly so. Laudable as it might be to seek equality of educational opportunity for all or to fashion education to respond to the aptitudes of individual pupils, such objectives do not constitute educational aims or purposes. They are not concerned in any way to establish what it is that pupils are supposed to learn or know. They are, as was stated in the community schools document, aspects of government policy in relation to post-primary education. What we have in the first instance is an aspect of social policy, namely to provide all pupils with equal educational opportunity; in the second instance what is in question is a matter of educational method or procedural policy, not of aims, aimed at ensuring that the curriculum of the school would take into account the natural aptitudes of the child.

To say that there was no clearly developed and comprehensive position regarding the aims of post-primary education from the time that the idea of a unified system of post-primary education was introduced in the early 1960s and attempts made to implement it, is not to say, however, that no guiding principles at all existed to direct the course of the developments of the 1960s. I have already pointed out that economic considerations largely, along with social and educational considerations of the kind Seán O'Connor mentioned, played a significant role in determining the shape of post-primary education in these years. Throughout the period in question, in Ireland as elsewhere, the resources of post-primary education were being re-channelled to meet the emerging manpower needs of the economy. That this was so is best seen in the actual practical developments of the period, for instance the impetus given to practical forms of education through the introduction of common post-primary courses and examinations and the building of regional technical colleges.[33]

Indeed it is only by reference to developments such as these that one can discern, partly with hindsight, what appear to have become newly espoused 'aims' for the entire post-primary sector during the post-1963 period. Thus one outcome of economic considerations was, apparently, the official acceptance of the view that the preparation of pupils in technical and other applied knowledge and skills which were considered necessary to meet the emerging needs of an expanding and increasingly technological economy should become an aim of post-primary education in Ireland. Another aim, it would appear, which was espoused at the time, and again in the light of economic considerations, was the provision of a higher level of general education, as represented, for example, by raising the school-leaving age to fifteen and the provision of a more comprehensive curriculum to meet different pupils' aptitudes. But just as the social considerations of the time, notably the ideal of equality of educational opportunity for all, did not appear to issue in any specific educational aims, economic considerations did not issue in prescriptions of this kind in all cases either. Thus, one of the practical effects of these economic considerations was the policy of cutting educational costs through the building of larger and comprehensive schools and the adoption of policies of sharing facilities, amalgamation of schools, and so on. These, in themselves, would not be described as aims of education any more than the notion of equality of educational opportunity or the making of education more responsive to the aptitudes of pupils should be.

With hindsight, then, an increased level of general education and a higher level of preparation for technical and other forms of work would appear to have become newly espoused aims of post-primary education, at least in official circles, during the 1960s. But without any clear detailing of what was intended in both of these respects, and how they relate to the traditional aims of secondary and vocational education, one is left without any proper basis on which to conduct and develop post-primary education or to engage in the evaluation of present practice.

This being the case, the business of discussing the actual aims of post-primary education in Ireland today becomes a more speculative enterprise than one would wish it to be. A number of important issues have arisen, however, and it is necessary to identify here what these are. As I have argued, during the 1960s and possibly right up to the present day, a distinct effort was made to shape post-primary education in Ireland to meet the manpower needs of the economy. I do not wish to reject the view that the post-primary school ought to be shaped to some extent by such considerations. But it must be pointed out that before national economic growth, or the preparation of school leavers in the knowledge and skills directly linked to such growth, can be welcomed as a newly espoused aim of post-primary education, its ramifications should first be fully understood. Thus, the question must be asked is this to be considered the sole aim of post-primary education in Ireland, a major aim, or simply one other aim of post-primary education in Ireland? Furthermore, and without prejudice to either the secondary or vocational education traditions, one must ask what value is to be put on general education understood as all-round development of personality and general preparation for life as opposed to preparation in a range of knowledge and skills directly related to their immediate economic and technological applicability? What importance is to be attached to the achievement of personal growth *vis-à-vis* the prosperity of the larger social group?

These are important questions which need to be asked and answered before one can fully understand what it means to say that preparing pupils in the knowledge and skills necessary for economic and technological growth on a much larger scale than before is a new aim of post-primary education, let alone before one can feel that there is any justification for its adoption and implementation as official policy. And in this respect the approach taken towards the aims of post-primary education since 1963 leaves much to be desired, compared to the approach originally taken in relation to vocational education and as set forth in *Memo V. 40*, for example. There, the immediate or more vocationally oriented aims were set forth within a fairly definite context of general, social and religious education in which some attempt was made to relate these various forms of education to one another. This was done in the belief that more than economic considerations alone should dictate the aims or direction of continuation education.

There is a further aspect to this question and it has to do again with the idea of a general education. Insofar as it has become an aim of post-primary education in Ireland, or so it would appear, to prepare school leavers to be of direct economic and technological value to society, the question of the value which is to be put on technical and applied forms of education in itself arises. And it arises in acute form in view of the very rapid rate of obsolescence in technical and applied knowledge and skills. Thus at the present time, when vocational adaptability and job retraining are becoming more or less permanent characteristics of many forms of employment, the question arises as to how specific or how general should such education be at post-primary school level. To what extent is it a matter of physical skill, and how far is it a matter of general intellectual development and emotional orientation? Or, to extend the question a little, to what extent is this problem to be seen as a re-emergence of the perennial problem of a general education understood as all-round development and preparation for life?

Whatever aims are adopted for post-primary education they should not be adopted without giving due consideration to these sorts of questions. Yet as I have been arguing, this has not been the case in the attempts at the reform of post-primary education in Ireland since 1963. And, unless this is the case, no valid basis for the selection and organisation of curriculum content and for the adoption of evaluation procedures or organisational arrangements exists. To proceed in these matters as was done in the Ireland of the 1960s and 1970s, without any clear and comprehensive view of what post-primary education is intended to achieve, without any clear statement of aims and objectives, is, I have suggested, both illicit in terms of a proper procedure for educational development and non-productive in the matter of bringing about educational change. When such principles and procedures are ignored and violated, it is hardly surprising that there should be misunderstandings concerning efforts at reform or, more specifically, that there should be signs that traditional academic secondary education is making more headway than are those forms of technical and applied education which it was the intention to boost.

In this chapter I have attempted to look critically at the position regarding the aims of post-primary education in Ireland and I have argued that there was a serious breach of proper procedure. Thus, in the absence of a clear position on aims, no basis was established to ensure that proper procedures for the development of the curriculum would be employed. Accordingly, there has been a serious failure both to recognise the role of the aims of education in educational development and a consequent failure to spell out clearly, and at some length, the aims of post-primary education in Ireland. In virtue of this failure it has been necessary to attempt to establish or construct from on-going practice and developments what might be the actual overall 'aims' of post-primary education at the present time. In doing so, an attempt was made to identify the aims of the Intermediate and Leaving Certificate courses. Reference was made also to the traditional aims of secondary education and vocational education. And finally, from an examination of events since 1963, an attempt was made to identify the forces which seemed to be dictating educational policy and developments in the post-primary sector. The preparation of post-primary school pupils to make possible the economic and technological development of the country, to an extent never before attempted, emerges as the main motivational force behind developments in post-primary education since 1963. To that extent, it might be considered to have become a rather major 'aim' of post-primary education. At no time, however, was it suggested that the more traditional view of second-level education as a preparation for life was unacceptable.

Chapter 3

General Education and a Preparation for Life

A basis for evaluation

Whatever else one might wish to say about the traditions of post-primary education in Ireland over the past century, based upon the considerations of the preceding chapter, it might reasonably be claimed at this point that these traditions had always seen as one of their main tasks the provision of a general education as a preparation for life. This was the idea, or at least the assumption, it would appear, which lay behind the old intermediate system and which has been central to the notion of secondary education from the beginning of the state. Vocational education also saw itself as aspiring to a general education and a preparation for life even if it adopted a quite different approach to the matter. In more recent times, with the emergence of a somewhat more unified concept of second-level education than had obtained in earlier times, the notion of post-primary education as a vehicle for the preparation of pupils to meet the economic and manpower needs of the country became more pronounced. What this implied for the traditional ideal of a general education was not always clear, I have argued. For while even intermediate or secondary education, with its strong literary and theoretical emphasis, was sometimes defended on the grounds that it provided a form of education which was suited to preparing pupils for entry to the professions, the civil service, and further studies, a feature of the changes of the 1960s was the intention to make post-primary schooling more directly preparatory to employment. It was also intended to make it preparatory to a considerably wider range of employment possibilities than before, notably in the technical and technological areas. As a consequence, today second-level education is no longer as dominated as it was in its concept by the academic or grammar school ideal of secondary schooling, even if it still does remain very much under the influence of this ideal in practice.

It is, of course, and always has been, a matter of some concern as to how well second-level education in Ireland, as elsewhere, has succeeded over the years in its task of general education, both as a preparation for life as well as for employment and university education. Already it has been seen that there are ample grounds for such concern, for example the lack of clarity on the question of aims and the dominating and narrowing influence of the public examinations. The approach to planning and policy-making, to co-ordination of the various levels of education, and to innovation to meet the changing social, economic, and educational circumstances of schooling in Ireland, moreover, has been at best sporadic. There are those, too, who believe that it is criteria for gaining entrance to the universities — aided and abetted by the public examination system — rather than considerations derived from a concern with broadly preparing pupils for life or for meeting the needs and interests of pupils, which largely dictates the content and the conduct of post-primary education in Ireland. If this is so, it might go some way at least to explain why the post-primary school curriculum is found unsuitable for large and growing numbers of post-primary school pupils.[1]

It is important to know how substantial the grounds for concern are and also to have some basis for deciding what constitutes substantial grounds. The provision of a general education as a broad preparation for life has been, and still appears to remain, probably the major goal of post-primary education in the Irish context. Accordingly, the extent to which the curriculum of post-primary education in Ireland is in a position to promote the attainment of this goal, along with the more recently espoused objective of meeting the manpower needs of the economy, would appear to be the most important and fundamental consideration in evaluating the curriculum of post-primary education in Ireland. Before this can serve as a useful basis for evaluation, however, greater attention to what is meant by a general education and what it implies by way of a preparation for life will be necessary.

This is an important question and one which is particularly apt at the present time. In a recent work in which he attempts to identify the causes of the present lack of confidence in schooling, Thorsten Husén, the noted Swedish educationist, observed that the present state of crisis is not only one of finance and confidence but also one of *raison d'être*.[2] Already in the discussion of the aims of post-primary education in Ireland in the preceding chapter I suggested that in Ireland this very issue has been dodged over the years. Abroad, some attempts have been made to come to grips with the issue. Witness the many commissions in the United States during the 1970s which probed the problems facing second-level education and made recommendations for reform.[3] Similarly, in England there has been considerable attention devoted to the discusssion of such matters since the inception of the so-called Great Debate by the Prime Minister in 1976. Witness also the reports and recommendations of the Schools' Council and the Inspectorate in the past two or three years. There particular attention has been devoted to the question of the curriculum of secondary education up to the age of sixteen and to proposals for a reform of the GCE examinations to facilitate curriculum reform at second level.[4] International organisations such as the OECD and the EEC have also begun to become involved, devoting particular attention to the role of the secondary school in preparing pupils for the world of work.[5] As will be seen, common to most reviews is a much broader view of the role of second-level education than has obtained in the past.

General education in the tradition of liberal education

Since its inception, the response of secondary education in Ireland to the problem of providing a preparation for life by means of a general education has been to adhere to a grammar school approach. This approach appears to arise directly out of a view of general education which is similar to the traditional idea of a liberal education, a view which is increasingly facing challenge. Accordingly, a consideration of this view can serve as a suitable starting point for our inquiry into the idea of a general education as a preparation for life.

The tradition which equates the idea of a grammar school or liberal education with the notion of a general education or a preparation for life is a long one and a proud one, and one which over the centuries has held the conviction of a great many educational theorists and institutions without sway. It dates its ancestry at least as far back as the Greek ideal of a liberal education, and ever since it has had an abundance of influential admirers and protagonists including such people as Cardinal Newman, Robert Hutchins and Jacques Maritain. More recently, prominent philosophers of education such as Harry S. Broudy and Philip H. Phenix in the

United States, and Paul Hirst and R.S. Peters in England, have sung its praises. It is, then, a tradition which cannot but be taken seriously; and even if there are elements in the tradition which may seem unsuited to the circumstances of today, it may still have much to offer.

In the traditional grammar school and intellectualist concept of secondary education, if we may so term it, there is little or no distinction made between the notion of a general education and that of a liberal education.[6] Central to each is the idea that education is concerned essentially with the development of mind, with the cultivation of the intellect. The idea of a liberal education had its origins in the Greek notion of an education considered proper for free men. Unlike the slave, the free man was not burdened with the need to earn a living or to engage in servile work and, accordingly, in his education he was free to pursue knowledge for its own sake and not for the sake of financial reward or vocational advancement. His education was shaped by the ideal of the development of what was thought highest and distinctively human in man, his reason. This is what is meant to develop man as man, and this became a feature of the ideal of a liberal education which has been maintained by advocates such as Jacques Maritain and Robert Hutchins in their insistence on intellectual education as the proper and direct purpose of the school.[7] Not surprisingly, then, in this scheme of things theoretical knowledge was to assume paramount importance in the curriculum.

If such a liberal education was considered proper for the free man in this sense, another dimension of the concept was to emphasise the liberating or 'freeing' effect of such an education on man. It made man free because it freed him from ignorance and the received ideas of his time and place — it enabled him to think for himself. As Maritain was to put it, 'education directed towards wisdom, centred on the humanities, aiming to develop in people the capacity to think correctly and to enjoy truth and beauty, is education for freedom, or liberal education.'[8]

Alongside the ideal of education for its own sake, for the development of man as man, there emerged also the notion that such development of the person entailed an education which was broad in scope. It is this element in the tradition which gave rise perhaps to the term 'general education' and its widespread use as a synonym for 'liberal education'. In time this idea would result in some quarters in programmes which tended to become unrealistically encyclopaedic in nature. More recently, however, this tendency has given way to an approach to general education, not by means of a broad general information but by means of an education which attempts to develop general powers of the mind by means of an introduction to the major divisions of knowledge which exist.[9]

The original Greek ideal of a liberal education has remained influential throughout the course of Western civilisation. It re-emerged prominently in higher Christian education from the time of St Augustine onwards, in the evolution of the medieval universities and in the Renaissance. It was the form which it took with the coming into prominence of the great nineteenth-century public schools in England, however, which has had the greatest influence on secondary education. Here the classics had come to dominate the curriculum and, as Matthew Arnold was to put it, the commitment was to passing on to pupils 'the best of what has been thought and said'. But another dimension was now also clearly in evidence. It was a dimension which had strong social-class overtones, and one which perhaps reflected the original Greek elitist origins of the ideal. Thus alongside strictly intellectual education, there was also an emphasis on the development of the social ideals and graces appropriate to the elite and the future leaders in society. And if the classics, and later on and more reluctantly other subjects such as mathematics, history and geography, modern languages and science, were to cater for intellectual education, social and moral education would be catered for no less surely in the organisation, sporting activities, customs and general moral atmosphere of the school.

While the grammar school or liberal education approach to secondary education evolved over time to form a rich and persuasive tradition, it did face objections on the grounds of being a luxury for the upper classes and one which was of little direct benefit or utility. Already it has been seen how the tradition of a liberal education had constructed a strong justification for its existence in terms of its value as a means of enabling the person to achieve his full and proper development as a human being. It did, however, feel pressed occasionally to defend itself against the charge of being useless. And along with its contribution to clarifying and promoting the liberal ideal, Cardinal Newman's celebrated work the *Idea of a University* was also to make a major contribution to this defence.

Essentially the defence stood on the argument that there was a strong degree of 'transfer' which could be effected from the studies pursued in a liberal education to all other areas of human endeavour. Thus, it was held, not only was a liberal education good and of value in itself; it was also of value as a preparation for life. Emphasising this latter point, R.M. Hutchins was to put it this way:

> An intellect properly disciplined, an intellect properly habituated, is an intellect able to operate well in all fields. An education that consists of the cultivation of the intellectual virtues, therefore, is the most useful education, whether the student is destined for a life of contemplation or a life of action.[10]

Whatever exaggerated claims may sometimes have been made for the values of a classical education in terms of transfer, this general view remains central to the position of those who argue for a liberal education as the core of a general education. Explanations offered by more recent writers such as B.O. Smith, Harry S. Broudy and others, however, make much more sense in the present-day climate of educational research.[11]

The argument for transfer frequently took the form that the exercise or training of the mental powers afforded in the study of the classics, for example, carried over into other areas of life. Likewise, advocates of the study of such disciplines as English, history, and mathematics have emphasised the unique contribution which they believe each of these studies can make to the refinement of intelligence and general development of mind. Intelligence developed through such studies, it is argued, could be put to good use in everyday living in the form of insights into and analysis of the predicaments of man, clarity of thought and correct reasoning.[12] But there is a further dimension to this general theory of transfer. Again, it is an aspect which has been well stated by Newman. One of the outcomes of a liberal education, as Newman saw it, was what he called the development of a 'philosophical habit of mind'.[13] And while this philosophical habit of mind was to find expression in the form of the calm and other social attributes of the gentleman, it also referred to something more fundamental. It referred to what is commonly called a philosophy of life, a world view in which the person, because of his broad knowledge and highly-developed powers of reasoning, had an understanding of the world in which he lived and a set of values to guide him in his daily living.

Just now I have been considering the defences which have been made by the advocates of a liberal education against the objections that it is not a very useful form of education. Strongly and consistently argued as these defences have been for the most part, however, they have not satisfied the objectors. Equally important, however, is the fact that many educators who hold the values of a liberal education in high regard have themselves begun to question the suitability of such an education for all pupils. Indeed one writer, G.H. Bantock, has gone so far as to recommend two quite distinct kinds of programmes of general education.[14] One, intended for the minority who are 'academic-minded', would be modelled on the traditional grammar school ideal. The other, to be followed by the majority of pupils who are not considered to be in a position to benefit from the more traditional fare, would have a curriculum based more upon folk culture. While Bantock has not attracted much of a following for this proposal, he is not entirely alone in the view that only a minority of pupils may be suited to the more traditional grammar school approach to general education.[15] If pupils are compelled to attend second-level education up to the age of fifteen or sixteen, it only makes sense that the programmes on offer should be such that all pupils may benefit from them. And this would appear to suggest strongly the need for a more open-minded approach to the problem of a general education than one associates with the advocates of a traditional liberal or grammar school view.

As was pointed out earlier on, second-level education has been undergoing a period of unprecedented attack. And insofar as secondary education in Western societies has been strongly influenced by the tradition of a liberal education, admittedly in watered-down fashion very often, the question simply has to be asked again: is the traditional secondary school type of curriculum — the dominant approach of post-primary education in Ireland today — suitable any longer for the purpose of second-level education which aims to provide all pupils with a preparation for life?

Here I propose to argue that while the grammar school tradition of a liberal education as I have described it may have an important contribution to make, it is not adequate as it stands as a concept of general education understood as the broad development of the pupil and as a preparation for life. It is not adequate, I shall argue, for two main reasons. In the first place, it does not, I believe, take a sufficiently broad view of the demands of a preparation for life in these closing decades of the twentieth century. In the second place, it tends to overlook, or at least it is unsympathetic towards, the many practical and pedagogical realities of second-level education today. I shall begin with a consideration of the first of these two issues.

General education and the demands of living

If the traditional concept of a general education does not take a sufficiently broad view of the demands of a preparation for life, how does one set about developing a more satisfactory view? It will be argued here that a more fruitful way of approaching the problem of a general education is to ground the enquiry on an analysis of what appear to constitute the major and likely demands of everyday living and what these appear to suggest by way of a preparation for living. This is similar in ways to the approach adopted in *Memo V. 40* which served as a guiding document in vocational education in Ireland for many years. There curricula and programmes were drawn up on the basis, in part, of an analysis of employment needs and other characteristics of the local areas in which the vocational schools were located.[16]

Considerations of the nature and structure of knowledge have always influenced thinking regarding the curriculum, but the approach to drawing up the curriculum of a general education on the basis of the perceived demands of life has had its advocates also. These have been few in number, however, and their influence has not been great. And while this approach, particularly as represented by some of its advocates, may have certain weaknesses, it does have an important contribution to make on the question of how one can begin to tackle the problem of the curriculum of a general education understood as a preparation for life. Herbert Spencer, the English social philosopher of the nineteenth century, adopted this approach in his main educational writings.[17] According to Spencer there are five 'leading kinds of activity which constitute human life'. These, he believed, may be arranged as follows: first, those activities which minister directly to self-preservation; second, those activities which, by securing the necessities of life, indirectly minister to self-preservation; third, those activities which have for their end the rearing and discipline of offspring; fourth, those activities which are involved in the maintenance of proper social and political relations; and fifth, those miscellaneous activities which make up the leisure part of life, devoted to the gratification of tastes and feelings.[18] Since the function which education has to discharge, according to Spencer, is to 'prepare us for complete living', a proper education was seen to consist in giving preparation in each of these areas. Greatest attention, it was thought, should be given in those areas where the value is greatest. If an education has to fall short of the ideal, attention would be given to the different areas in proportion to their value. Spencer does not say specifically that he has arranged these activities in order of their value, but he does say that the order in which they have been listed is 'something like the rational order of subordination'.[19]

Similar in many respects to the approach adopted by Spencer is that of Franklin Bobbitt in the United States. Writing in the 1920s, Bobbitt set about developing the curriculum for general education on the basis of an analysis of the activities which he considered make up, or which ought to make up, the lives of men and women. Bobbitt suggested the following list of ten general activities: (1) language activities; social intercommunication; (2) health activities; (3) citizenship activities; (4) general social activities – meeting and mingling with others; (5) spare-time activities, amusements, recreations; (6) keeping oneself mentally fit – analogous to the health activities of keeping oneself physically fit; (7) religious activities; (8) parental activities, the upbringing of children, the maintenance of a proper home life; (9) unspecialised or non-vocational practical activities; (10) the labours of one's calling.[20] Having identified these activities, the general curriculum task, as Bobbitt saw it, was to provide the pupil with the necessary experiences to enable him to engage in each of these life activities satisfactorily, thereby providing him with a general education as a preparation for life.

The general approach of Spencer and Bobbitt to drawing up a curriculum on the basis of what they considered to be the major life demands was never taken up and applied on a large scale. Yet there is a definite echoing of the approach in some recent developments in American education, developments such as the performance or competency-based approaches to teacher education, developments which have not escaped the kinds of criticism levelled earlier against the Bobbitt approach in particular.[21] The growing emphasis on the role of the school in preparing pupils for the world of work also bears some general resemblance to this approach. Undoubtedly, it was reflected too to an extent in the earlier tradition of elementary education in England.

It will be necessary to take cognisance of the criticisms levelled against the approach to curriculum development of Bobbitt and others of a similar view. It should be borne in mind, however, that the present study attaches greater importance to the general attempt of Bobbitt and others to ground the curriculum of a general education in the actual activities or demands of living rather than in the specific life activities which either Spencer or Bobbitt identified or, indeed, in the courses of study which were suggested. For, granted that the goal of the post-primary school is to prepare pupils for life, an approach to curriculum development and the selection of curriculum content which is based upon a view of the demands of living and of society would appear to stand a much better chance of success than one which is derived largely from a theory of the nature and structure of knowledge in which considerations of logical tidiness rather than relevance for living may be uppermost. And if the approach to curriculum development and the selection of content is best grounded in some view of the major demands of living, the same holds true for an assessment of a particular curriculum the objective of which is to prepare pupils for living. I do not propose to develop here a detailed list of life demands or life activities as a basis for evaluating the curriculum of post-primary education in Ireland. Nonetheless, some consideration of the kinds of criteria to be borne in mind in adjudicating the suitability of the curriculum from this viewpoint is necessary.

One way of viewing the demands of living is to see them as being social and personal in origin. Thus one can say that society demands of us that we abide by its customs and mores and that we play our parts in promoting and sustaining its well being. To meet these demands normally calls on one to engage in some socially productive activities and to adopt certain attitudes and skills in interpersonal behaviour. For, in important respects man is a social being, and the adoption of a socially acceptable life-style is necessary for his own survival and for the survival and continuity of society. The individual person also makes demands upon himself, demands necessary both for his mere survival and for his growth as a human being. Thus at the level of survival there are basic physical needs to be met, the need for food, shelter and companionship. There are also higher needs, such as the need for esteem and appreciation, the need for achievement and acceptance, the need for knowledge, the need for a spiritual or religious life, and the need for what is

good and beautiful.[22] Accordingly, to talk of education as a preparation for life is to talk of preparing people to meet demands of
living such as these and others, depending on how one conceives
of living.

But if the demands of living might be said to be social and
personal in origin, what form do they take? Here I shall treat of
them under four main forms as follows: the vocational demands
of living; the recreational or cultural demands of living; the philosophical demands of living; and other important though somewhat
miscellaneous practical demands of living. One of the merits of the
emphasis on liberal education in second-level education which I
have discussed already is, I believe, that it attempted to cater for
what I have here called the philosophical demands of living. By this
I mean the need for each of us to form a philosophy of life or a
world view, the need to work out and adopt a system of values for
the conduct of living.

What can be said of the vocational demands of living and the
extent to which such demands should be met, if at all, in a programme of general education understood as a preparation for life?
The tradition of a liberal education has rejected the place of
vocational education in its scheme of things, a rejection which I
have adverted to already in discussing the *Report of the Council
of Education*. Nonetheless, the need for technical or vocational
education has been recognised in almost all educational systems.
During the past five or six years, however, much greater attention
than was the case earlier has focused on this issue, with many
national governments and international organisations stressing the
importance and urgency they attach to this question today.
Inevitably such attention has led to a particular effort to introduce
a strong element of work-preparatory education into programmes
of general education at post-primary level. In the EEC publication
From Education to Working Life, in which the question was discussed largely in relation to second-level education, the authors
have this to say on the matter:

> Work is a large and important part of life. At the same time, a
> job is only one aspect of the individual's life. Education for
> living and education as a preparation for work are parallel and
> complementary aims for educational institutions, but there is
> evidently a growing concern and necessity to give greater
> emphasis to certain qualities which are of particular importance
> in preparing the individual for the world of work. These include,

inter alia, a capacity to communicate more effectively in oral, written, numerate and social terms; the ability to exercise initiative and take responsibility, to work in a team on a common task, to handle practical problems involving manual skills, and to observe and learn through doing; an understanding of the diversity of the world of work, including the uses and implications of science and technology in society; a comprehension of the human and physical environment in which the individual lives as well as knowledge of the world beyond the local community; and an understanding of the decision-making processes affecting the young person's working conditions and work environment.[23]

There can be little question that for most people today, work is an essential aspect of living. It follows that any form of education which purports to prepare pupils for life ought to recognise this. What is helpful about the extract which I have just quoted is that it suggests how intricate and complex a matter it is to prepare pupils for work. In the light of this and the continuing criticism of the failure of academic forms of post-primary schooling adequately to prepare pupils for the world of work, it appears that the celebrated 'transfer' argument put forward by the advocates of second-level education in the grammar school tradition does not quite hold up in this area. At the least, more specialised studies seem called for over and above the liberal studies. And if the post-primary school claims to provide a broad preparation for life, at least a beginning ought be made there in such vocational studies.

But while one can argue for a place in post-primary education for an element of work-preparatory education, this is not to suggest that it should have a monopoly or be unduly dominant. For there are other demands of living to be met. Hence the need to point out, as is done in the extract quoted, that 'a job is only one aspect of the individual's life'. Furthermore, cognisance must also be taken of the growing problem of youth unemployment and its implications for general education. Additionally, work ought to be seen in a broader context than simply that of a job as a means of earning a living. In addition to providing the means of a livelihood and of contributing one's share to the community, work may also have an enriching influence, becoming a source of personal achievement, identity and self-esteem.[24]

In turning to the question of what I have called the recreational or cultural demands of living, we are turning to an issue whose importance has been recognised in the grammar school tradition. By the recreational or cultural demands of living I mean the need for leisure, the need to enjoy and perhaps create objects of artistic beauty, and the need to appreciate the beauty of nature itself. Other pursuits in the form of games or hobbies or special interests may also serve to meet in an acceptable way the recreational demands of living.

While the importance of this aspect of general education has been recognised in the traditional ideal of a liberal education, its practice has not always been entirely satisfactory. Witness the way in which the study of the classics tended to be reduced to purely linguistic and grammar studies, with all sight lost of the content in which they found their original justification. In the Irish context the recent report of the Arts Council on the arts in Irish education also paints a generally gloomy picture.[25] Nonetheless, this is understandable. Educational practice has always had difficulty in asserting itself in those areas where what is to be taught is not at all easily defined and where it is difficult to express it in concrete terms. Furthermore, education in the arts has always been seen as a luxury and for this reason, unlike other subjects found in the traditional curriculum, it has suffered accordingly. At a time of a greatly increased cost-awareness and accountability in education, such forms of education may need to be specially protected.

If there may be a need for special protection, there is perhaps a need also for a somewhat more broad-minded and realistic assessment of the nature of the so-called cultural or recreational studies. In the past attention has focused largely on areas such as music, art and literature. There has been little provision for the visual arts and many of the fine and performing arts, for drama, film and television. Likewise there has been a notable lack of provision for education in the appreciation of objects of natural beauty, architecture and design.

One further observation may be made in connection with education of this kind. A great deal is spoken about the increase in leisure time which has accompanied and is expected to accompany the growing computerisation of industry and commerce; growing unemployment can have a similar effect. As a result we are likely to be moving into a period in which greater numbers of people may have more leisure time than has been possible in times past.

Accordingly, the need to prepare for the fruitful use of leisure time is, perhaps, greater than ever. And if this is so it behoves the school to take cognisance of it.

We come finally to what I have called the practical demands of living. And this, arguably, is the area in which the traditional concept of general education as liberal education has been most deficient. In view of the all-pervasiveness of the practical in life, it is difficult to understand how it has been de-emphasised. Life, it seems, is predominantly a practical affair. It is a matter of doing, of planning and of decision-making. Life entails all of these elements in the conduct of our daily affairs, be it in earning a living, shaping a career, rearing a family, getting on with others, or an endless range of such activities. For to live is to be pursuing goals, to be active in mind and body.

The failure to attend to the various practical demands is surely at the root of a good deal of the criticism levelled at second-level education today. It is a failure which has given rise to the call for greater attention to pastoral care programmes, provision for personal and social development, health education, moral education, preparation for parenthood and an adult role in family life, and the like. It is, arguably, a failure which arises also from the failure to appreciate more fully that a preparation for life for the second-level pupil ought to include helping him to live the life of a teenager, with all of the distinctive stresses of adolescence, in a satisfactory and fulfilling manner.

To say this is not to deny that programmes of study drawn up to meet the other demands of living may have something to contribute towards an education for meeting the practical demands of living. Thus, it may be that an educated intelligence in the liberal education mould can deal in a satisfactory way with practical problems and make very good practical decisions, a belief which, as we have seen already, is central to the liberal education position. For, arguably, the making of good practical judgments has something to do with apprehension, the ability to see relationships, and the ability to come to grips with new concepts quickly. But the practical demands of living would appear to warrant greater direct attention also than they have received in the liberal education tradition. For there is good reason to believe that acquaintance and practice in the practical domain is necessary to increase understanding and to develop the facility to make good practical judgments, and to effect them.

Richard Pring, the English philosopher of education, has dwelt on this issue, and a consideration of what he has to say will be helpful at this point.[26] Having drawn attention to the fact, long recognised by most people, that theoreticians competent in their areas of specialisation might lack the ability to apply theory to practice, he continues:

> Thus the expert in learning theory fails to apply his theoretical insights to his own teaching about learning theory; the student of ethics cannot recognise his own moral failings; an army of economic theorists can't make an economy work, and the theorist in administrative practice lives in a state of practical confusion. What one says of such people, proven and certificated though they are in their own theoretical field, is that they 'lack judgement', they have no commonsense. Hence commonsense has this further dimension: the man of commonsense is a 'man of judgement', the master of certain practical arts. And it is the job of the school, or of any educational agency, to increase such practical powers of the mind, for without it (without the capacity to relate theory to practice) there seems little point in the theory.[27]

While Pring recognises that learning how to do something involves an adequate conceptualisation of the problem, it also entails coming up to scratch in one's performances, he maintains. Yet the school, he believes, does not give due attention to this aspect of 'knowing how' to do things. Instead it concentrates on the theory or 'knowing that'. But, he points out, this is hardly the best way to teach in the practical domain. The theory of making friends or of social success will not necessarily teach one how to make friends or how to succeed in social relationships. One learns how to do these things by trying to do them and by practice, not by talking about them or learning the theory of them.

Pring is correct in this, I believe. More importantly, however, he is correct in the reasoning behind it, namely, that too easily we lose sight of the fact that theoretical knowledge, knowledge as we have it in books, often arises from systematic reflection upon the practical know-how which is theorised about. Yet, as Pring adds, we continue to teach a great deal of knowledge in total disconnection from the practical world which gives it point. For this reason, he concludes, 'the curriculum has become academic. It has lost its roots in the often practical world with its practical problems and perplexities which generated the more systematic, theoretical investigation in the first place. Theory is of little use without the judgement to recognize the concrete cases to which it is applicable.'[28]

These considerations suggest, I believe, that there is need for more direct provision in the matter of preparing pupils for the practical demands of living than is allowed in the traditional concept of a liberal education. Such considerations will be supported also by a consideration of the interests and aptitudes of pupils, especially, as I shall argue later on, as a result of large increases in school enrolments. But if this is so there are signs that not only has the traditional concept of general or liberal education been deficient in this regard but that in the practices which have grown up with it, and others besides, it may actually serve to hinder the preparation of pupils for meeting practical demands of living in a number of important respects. It is a deficiency, moreover, whose magnitude has also grown with the substantial increases in pupil enrolments in second-level education in recent years.

Chief among the aspects of contemporary second-level schooling which might be mentioned here as having a somewhat inhibiting influence on the development of competence in the practical domain are the following. First, there is the tendency in conventional second-level education to elevate conceptual and verbal skills into an end unto themselves with a consequent neglect of other important matters. As one writer has observed, 'schools do little to develop thought in relation to action, which tends to make workers sceptical of the value of theory. It is another of the many ironies in education that the more emphasis that is placed on academic activities, the more scholars press for rigorous intellectual exercises, the less functional the school becomes for the man who desires to live the life of a labourer or skilled tradesman.'[29] Second, there is the marked tendency, arising out of prolonged and institutionalised schooling, for pupils to postpone the undertaking of adult responsibilities. It is a postponement which is the outgrowth of the sense of dependency generated by schooling, where 'students have become used to having their work planned in detail by the teachers hour after hour, day after day, year after year'.[30] And third, there is the tendency of formal schooling to promote individualism and a spirit of competition at the expense of a sense of co-operation and community among pupils. Much of this is effected through the various systems of examinations which obtain. And with growing importance being attached to good examination results, there is the possibility that matters might dis-improve further.[31]

Finally, in regard to the question of the practical demands of living, it might be noted that there is some evidence to suggest that many qualities of mind which would appear to be closely associated with the practical demands of living, qualities such as willingness and confidence to persist at a difficult task, are not even being sought in schools. Yet many people believe that such objectives ought to be sought. Thus John Raven, in his recent study in which he inquired into the objectives of education, concluded:

> . . . there was also substantial agreement between pupils, parents and teachers that many of the most important objectives of education receive only scant attention in the classroom. Yet the qualities teachers neglect to develop are the qualities which most determine the vigour of a nation and the human resources which it can call upon. They are qualities of character. They include things like willingness to think for oneself, to be original; willingness to notice the need for innovations; confidence that one has the ability to initiate such developments; willingness to persist at a challenging task; desire to seek out such tasks; willingness to entertain new ideas; willingness to *use* such intelligence as one possesses; willingness to set about adapting the environment to one's needs rather than lower one's objectives to conform to what the environment easily provides; and willing-ness to do things oneself rather than leave things to others; to be master of one's destiny rather than a pawn of fate.[32]

It would, perhaps, be unfair to lay the blame for all of these various failings on the traditional concept of a liberal education. Many of them have to do with matters of practice and others may be as much a function of the institutionalisation of schooling as anything else. What is of importance here, however, is that such deficiencies should be adverted to in discussing the concept of a general education as a preparation for life so that greater care may be taken to ensure that what can be done to eliminate them will be done.

Life, I have been suggesting, is very much a practical affair. I have also suggested that the concept of a general education ought to include provision for preparing pupils to meet the practical demands of living. It is necessary, however, when one is emphasising the importance of the practical in educational matters,[33] to be mindful that the charge of utility may not be far away. Hence the possible criticism of the position which I have been outlining that it tends to forego important educational values, values such as personal development, cultural enrichment and the liberating influence of education, for the sake of merely practical or utilitarian values such as a preparation for employment and other practical tasks of living. Likewise, the activity analysis approach to the curriculum of a general education adopted by Spencer and Bobbitt has been criticised for being blind to important educational values not suggested in their activity analyses as well as for being bound by the cultural context of an age or a particular period of time. Additionally, it might be suggested that while the activities of an age may represent its life-style and achievements, it might not reflect at all its aspirations; it may even incorporate practices which it finds objectionable on moral or other grounds.

While it is true that criticisms of the activity analysis or similar approaches to curriculum development must be borne in mind, these need not entail its complete abandonment. Modifications which take account of the criticisms but which preserve the life-tasks orientation of this approach, while not necessarily accepting the specific activities identified by Bobbitt, for example, are possible. It is true, of course, that some specific activities will have to be chosen in order to prepare a pupil at any given time under the heading of any of the more general life activities and that these specific activities might become obsolete, or reflect specific cultural or moral values. And while this might necessitate a review of curriculum content periodically to take account of developments, surely this is inescapable anyway, and hence a feature which is common to all curricula if they are not to become obsolete. This has been the experience in even the most traditional of school systems. Likewise, the moral and value aspirations of a society can be applied to the selection of life activities to be satisfied by the curriculum. Dope-peddling or granny-bashing do not have to be included in the curriculum just because they are identifiable activities any more so than some other activities are to be excluded because they may not be as widely practised as one might wish. If one wishes the selection of life activities to be recognised by this approach to curriculum development to be bound by the moral and value aspirations of society, this requirement can be met.

The possible criticism that the approach to the curriculum of a general education being considered here is too 'utilitarian' in character, is a very odd criticism. It is odd because of the fact that historically general education in Ireland has been conceived largely as a preparation for life. If the approach to the curriculum of a general education being suggested here can be said to be utilitarian it is simply because it attempts to orient the curriculum to its expressed objective of preparing pupils for life. If this should necessitate a curriculum with a utilitarian character, then so be it. What might be at fault in that case is not the type of curriculum which this view entails but the type of curriculum that has had currency in the past. For if the type of schooling which a preparation for life calls forth is utilitarian, then the highly literary and academic curriculum of times gone by might not have been quite as broadly relevant as was thought. Thus it can be said that in so far as the aim of a general education is to prepare pupils for life, and in so far as a preparation for life entails a practical or utilitarian emphasis in the curriculum, the curriculum of a general education should include such an emphasis — irrespective of whether this makes it utilitarian or not.

Practical and pedagogical issues affecting general education

It is time now to turn to a consideration of the second of the two broad reasons why the predominantly academic tradition of second-level education is inadequate for the purpose of general education as a preparation for life. This is its tendency to underestimate the practical and pedagogical aspects of the problem of general education, aspects which have assumed much greater prominence owing to the large increase in the second-level school-going population since the 1960s.

R.M. Hutchins, the American educationist and strong proponent of the liberal education ideal, once wrote: 'you cannot say that my content is wrong because you do not know the method of transmitting it. Let us agree upon content if we can and have faith that the technological genius of America will solve the problem of communication.'[34] Leaving aside the suggestion implicit in this statement that teaching is a matter of 'transmitting' or 'communicating' alone, it illustrates an attitude long prevalent in educational thinking. It is an attitude wherein the problem of curriculum is seen in terms of content alone, with pedagogical considerations receiving little or no attention. To focus upon content alone, however, and to ignore the question of the teaching of that content, and the implications of the one for the other, is to ignore a pedagogical problem which lies at the very heart of schooling. As John Dewey has pointed out, content in itself is of no educational value. It is of value only in so far as it can be psychologised to the point where the pupil, from his particular stage of development or experience, can benefit from interaction with it.[35] Thus, to psychologise or adapt curriculum content is a major problem of schooling and a fundamental issue in the implementation of every school programme. It is a problem which necessitates that, in addition to questions of curriculum content, a number of related issues such as curriculum organisation, teaching and examining must be taken into account in the development of curricula and programmes. Above all, perhaps, it calls for a careful attention to the nature and needs of the pupils to be educated.

In view of the extent to which the problem of curriculum is seen largely as one of content, it is inevitable that when something begins to go wrong we have focused primarily on the formal content of school programmes. This is certainly true of the approach in the *Report of the Council of Education*; it also characterised very much the response of the 1960s to the challenge of post-primary education in Ireland. On an international level, and particularly in the United States, it is also true that in the earlier stages of the curriculum reform movement which began in the late 1950s the focus of attention was upon theories of the nature and structure of knowledge as a basis for curriculum reform. It may be that this is explained in part by the relative poverty of the contribution of the psychological work in education there at the time. But it is surely a reflection also of the traditional hesitancy, particularly within the tradition of a liberal education, to give much weight to considerations of the interests and needs of the individual pupil in his own education. It is noteworthy, then, that it is very much on the basis of considerations having to do with the interests and needs of pupils that the growing concern regarding the limitations of second-level education today is rooted. And irrespective of what the theory of any particular approach to second-level education might maintain regarding its efficacy, it is only at our peril that we ignore the actual realities of schooling and pupils' responses to them.

Among the background realities of post-primary education in

Ireland today, as elsewhere, is the fact that we are now engaged in mass education at this level. This is a big remove from the situation which existed 100 years ago at the time of the setting up of the intermediate system. Accompanying this development there has also been a major change in the socio-economic composition of the pupil body and in the variety of family and home backgrounds from which pupils are drawn. And with this, in turn, has come a widening of the range of interests, aptitudes, educational achievements and needs of pupils.

Important changes in society which affect schooling and popular attitudes towards it have also taken place. Despite the criticisms levelled at schooling, formal schooling is still held in high esteem in most places. Indeed, generally, higher expectations of education were generated during the expansionist and optimistic mood of the 1960s. And while there is a growing awareness of the need for technical education and skills, academic education and qualifications are still a major attraction for parents and employers. With growing youth unemployment, this puts a premium on academic and examination success by pupils. Other developments of note include the raising of the minimum school-leaving age in most countries, a move about which some doubts are now being expressed. More recently, there are signs too that the political significance of education is diminishing in the eyes of governments, a development which has also been accompanied by a general tendency towards cut-backs in educational expenditure. Finally, schools have now to compete to an extent not true in the past with other educational or quasi-educational institutions, notably radio, television and popular literature.

It is the actual impact on schooling of these changes in schools and society over the past twenty years or so, however, which is of central concern from the point of view of the curriculum. And chief and most disconcerting in this connection is the general air of disenchantment with and negative attitudes towards schooling which is found among young people. This is a development which has been documented by John Raven in Ireland independently of evidence available in other countries.[36] It is a development which is seen as leading to serious problems of motivation and discipline. Many pupils feel caught in a bind: on the one hand they often find their studies to be too academic and irrelevant; on the other hand they find themselves in a situation where a good performance in those very studies may be necessary to meet with success in an increasingly competitive job market or to gain entry to third-level education.[37]

I have suggested already that it is at our peril that we ignore the views of pupils concerning the education which they receive. It is important also to take cognisance of the other realities of the post-primary school which have come in for attention in the past five or six years. What, then, we must ask are the implications of the above matters for the question of general education as a preparation for life? There are two main implications. The first is one which I have largely dealt with already in discussing the implications of the vocational and practical demands of living for the content of a general education. The second main implication has to do with what might be termed the pedagogy of the curriculum.

It is important to build into the theory of a general education a definite recognition of the pedagogical aspects of schooling. For there is a serious need to take cognisance of the implications for general education at second level of such factors as substantially increased enrolments, the inevitable variety in pupil intake arising from this, the particular needs of adolescent pupils, and the impact of developments such as radio and television. Cognisance will also need to be taken of the implications of prolonged and institutionalised schooling for the socialisation of pupils, particularly in respect of undertaking the responsibilities of adult life, and the tendency for schooling to promote merely conceptual and verbal skills at the expense of personal initiative and a more action-oriented life-style.

To take cognisance of these matters will undoubtedly mean that attention must be given to individual differences among pupils and to the need to make curriculum provision which allows for choice and flexibility. It will call for attention to the manner in which curriculum content is organised for pupils and how various aspects of the educational system relate to one another and influence one another. In particular, attention will need to focus upon the impact of examinations both on schooling itself and on pupil learning and attitudes.

What is noteworthy about observations of this kind is that they go significantly beyond what has traditionally been conceived as the major concern of a liberal education, namely the content of the formal curriculum. Already I have quoted from R.M. Hutchins on this point. The implication of the points I have just raised, however, is that no longer can the question of a general education be seen as simply one of 'agreeing upon content if we can' and leaving it to technological genius to 'solve the problem of communication'. For the content itself is part of the problem of communication, and all the more so when it is bound up with a whole set of traditional school practices such as the emphasis on book learning, classroom-based instruction and the like. Education, like politics, is the art of the possible, one in which the factors of motivation and relevance must be given due recognition. Accordingly, central to the question of the content of the curriculum of a general education is the question of what can be done when all the considerations – practical, psychological, sociological and philosophical – are pooled together. It is, as I have called it, a question of pedagogy. And acknowledgement of this question can no longer be omitted from the theory of a general education.

Conclusion

It is time now to bring together the foregoing considerations with a view to setting forth what is understood here by a general education and what it entails by way of education as a preparation for life in Ireland today. General education, as it is understood here, is broader in scope than the traditional concept of a liberal or grammar school education such as that set forth in the *Report of the Council of Education*. This broader concept is necessary because a general education, understood as a preparation for life and the all-round development of the pupil, must take account of the various demands of living and provide curricula which respond to the need to prepare pupils to meet these demands. Accordingly, it has been argued that a general education ought to include specific recognition of the fact that in today's world adults are generally required to engage in productive work and to earn a living. Any education which fails to recognise this, and to make curriculum provision accordingly, cannot claim to face up realistically to what is entailed in a preparation for life. There has always been serious doubt regarding the transferability of the general knowledge and skills acquired in the grammar school tradition of second-level education. In light of the enormous complexity of social and technical knowledge, attitudes and skills required for many forms of work in the world of today, the burden of proof can only lie with those who fail to recognise the need for adequate vocational preparation as part of a general education.

According to the position adopted here the idea and the curriculum of a general education will be of sufficiently broad vision to cater for many of the other practical demands of living. As was mentioned earlier on, traditional grammar school practice did build into its overall approach what might be termed a 'hidden curriculum' of moral and social education. At the same time it was hesitant to make any explicit provision for it in terms of the more formal curriculum. Whether one had best cater for this demand by means of the overt or formal curriculum or by paying greater attention to aspects of school organisation and special programmes of pastoral care and guidance, or a combination of both, might be left an open question at this point. What must be insisted upon, however, is that adequate recognition of the place and provision for a quite broad range of the practical demands of living ought to be included in any general preparation for life. In some cases these take the form of general 'intellectual' skills and attitudes such as critical thinking and independence of thought; at other times they will range from the need for family-life education and inter-personal skills to moral and religious development and preparation for the acceptance of adult responsibilities.

Turning to the question of what I have termed the philosophical demands of living, the idea of a liberal education recognises in principle the importance of education of this general kind. Indeed, with its emphasis on intellectual education and the development of man as man, along with its emphasis on a blend of humanistic and, more recently, scientific studies, one must recognise that the tradition of a liberal education has an invaluable and essential contribution to make to the ideal and the practice of a general education in the broader sense in which I conceive of it here. It may be necessary in practice, however, to adopt a more flexible approach than one associates with the grammar school tradition in this area. And much the same can be said here regarding the place of education to meet the recreational or cultural demands of living.

Finally, a word about the pedagogy of a general education. According to the general approach adopted here, general education intended as a preparation for life must address the needs of all pupils, and all the more so when they are compelled to attend. Traditional appeals to a highly intellectual form of education must be tempered by the actuality of pupil interest, motivation, aptitude and educational achievement. Accordingly, programmes may need to be varied and shaped differently for different kinds of pupils. And sight must not be lost of the possible negative effects of the prolongation and institutionalisation of formal general education.

To summarise regarding the idea of general education, then, I would argue for a broader concept of general education than one associates with the traditional liberal or grammar school approach. The emphasis would be on broadening the concept to take account of the actual demands of living and the practical realities of mass education. The idea would not be to exclude the liberal education component. It would be rather to recognise its limitations in scope and approach. Particular attention would be directed to accommodating all pupils by the recognition and introduction of alternatives in curriculum and general approach. It remains to be seen now how well curriculum provision in Irish post-primary education today stands up to these requirements.

Chapter 4

The Public Curriculum

Preliminary considerations

The broad basis for the evaluation of the curriculum of post-primary education in Ireland today has now been set forth. The knowledge, skills and attitudes needed to meet the practical, vocational, recreational and philosophical demands of living are seen as the main values to be promoted through the curriculum. The curriculum, in turn, must be designed and implemented with due recognition of the practical and pedagogical realities of schooling. In this chapter attention will be devoted to a consideration of the adequacy of the formal or public curriculum, that is the various programmes and subjects of the post-primary school. In the next chapter the analysis will centre on a consideration of a number of pedagogical aspects of the curriculum. Before proceeding, however, a number of secondary considerations are in need of attention.

The analysis in this chapter and the following chapter is, of necessity, rather general in nature. It is not my intention to analyse in detail and assess the various contributions which may be made by each subject on the curriculum. For while such an approach may have merit, it is not the only way to proceed. Benefit may also derive from a characterisation and evaluation of the general nature, scope and structure of the curriculum. It is from such a perspective, for example, that one is enabled to assess the merits of the overall curriculum as distinct from any of its parts. A general analysis of this kind allows one to look at the full extent of the curriculum in assessing the suitability of curriculum provision to meet the various goals and objectives being sought. Thus, for example, in assessing the adequacy of the curriculum for the purpose of preparing pupils to meet the various demands of living, it must be borne in mind that a variety of subjects might be suited to attaining any one broad objective. Similarly, different objectives might well be promoted by the one subject. Thus, the study of literature may well have a contribution to make towards meeting the philosophical demands of living as well as the recreational demands; or, depending on the pupils in question, the vocational demands of living might be equally served by any number of business or technical subjects on the curriculum.

From the point of view of the curriculum of a general education as a preparation for life, it is probably true to say that all subjects which are now recognised officially as subjects of the curriculum of post-primary education in Ireland have some value; yet it is possible that many subjects not on the curriculum may be equally valuable or even more valuable than some which are. Accordingly, an important consideration to bear in mind in evaluating the adequacy of the curriculum, and its various programmes and subjects, is not merely whether it is valuable but whether it is as valuable as it might be. The matter, however, is not quite as cut and dried as that; there is some question as to how sure one can be as to what is of greater or lesser value as a preparation for life. This is so because one can speak in only a rather tentative and general way as to what constitutes a preparation for life in advance of living it. For no one can say what demands, what unforeseen circumstances and events, the future holds.

This situation is compounded by the fact that if one grants that considerable differences may exist among pupils, then one must also expect that the type of schooling or curriculum suitable for one pupil might differ from that required for another. Thus a pupil with a career interest in languages or music, for example, may benefit more from an education which differs in some important respects from a pupil with a career interest in business or industry. Likewise, pupils may differ from one another in their leisure, recreational, or artistic interests and aptitudes. One may have a decided flair or preference for outdoor and physical recreation activities while another may be more inclined to the literary or the musical. Furthermore, differences in general and other abilities may also suggest different rates of progress and different kinds of study for one pupil from another. Thus, while the goal of a general preparation for life remains central to the notion of a general education for all pupils, it may well be that the specific content of a general education or preparation for life for one pupil will not be common to all pupils. A general education for all, that is, might not imply a common education for all. For content which might be of great value for one pupil might not be quite so valuable at all for another.

Having said this, however, and in line with what has been said already regarding the social demands of living, there is more to life than the perfecting of one's own talents or the uninterrupted pursuit of one's interests. The world in which we live out our lives presents its own demands, demands which do not always respect the peculiar interests, circumstances, or aptitudes of the individual. And if a consideration of the individual pupil to be educated, and his or her unique personal make-up, draws attention to the desirability of shaping schooling to meet the particular requirements of each pupil, likewise the demands of living, and of the society in which we live, emphasise the necessity to include elements in the curriculum which may be common to all pupils. Not surprisingly, then, the notion of a common curriculum for all which has been attracting so much attention in the current educational debate in England has been with us for a long time.[1] It is a notion which is grounded in the fact that all societies, even multi-cultural societies, possess some basic common culture which makes common demands on everyone. Thus, the need to communicate with one's fellows and the importance of basic literacy and numeracy today, makes it virtually imperative to ensure that a certain minimum education is given in these areas within most societies or cultures if pupils are to be considered in any way prepared for life. Likewise, an initiation into the fundamental values, institutions, and customs of the society in which one lives would appear to be essential both for personal growth and for the welfare of the society in question. And this too holds true even in a multi-cultural society. For without the cohesion provided by certain shared values and customs there can be no society.

The practical demands of living

If, as has been suggested, life is predominantly a practical affair, the question then becomes whether the curriculum of post-primary education in Ireland is such as to prepare pupils adequately to meet the various practical demands of living. Is it such as to provide pupils with the range of knowledge, attitudes, and skills necessary for making good and informed practical judgments and taking practical action across the broad range of areas encountered in living?

From the outset it can be said that in some major respects post-primary education in Ireland is not designed to cater adequately for meeting the practical demands of living. This is not to say that there is not quite a number of what might be termed practical subjects on the curriculum, nor that the contribution of transition-year and pre-employment programmes, for example, are to be dismissed. Neither is it simply to advert to the fact that, although there are a number of practical subjects available, the actual subject choices made weigh heavily in favour of the less practical or non-practical subjects. It is to advert, rather, to the nature of the practical subjects in question as well as to the overall character of the curriculum.

If one takes the practical subjects on the curriculum, subjects such as accounting, building construction, business organisation, metalwork and woodwork, it can be said that they are rather specialised in character. By this I mean that their main uses in life come in the form of a career or vocational speciality. Aside from subjects which have this vocational or specialised orientation, however, there are very few subjects of a practical nature where the explicit concern is some area or areas of everyday living which are the immediate and continuing concern of everyone. Civics is one such subject; several elements in the home economics (general) course in the Leaving Certificate programme are also of this kind; elements of other subjects, notably the 3 Rs and religious education, also fall into this category. Yet these are, arguably, among the most neglected areas in the curriculum of the post-primary school.

The neglect of practical education of this basic and general kind is a feature of post-primary education in Ireland which has begun to attract the attention of educators of late. Adverting to this point recently, Seán O'Connor had this to say:

> Except for the help he receives from religious instruction, the student's progress is based on trial and error. He receives little assistance from his formal schooling towards his understanding of the problems of living with people and playing his part in the life of the community; yet, surely, education should put as much effort into preparing the student for adult living as it puts into preparing him for a job.[2]

The point is made at greater length in a recent publication of the County Tipperary (NR) Vocational Education Committee entitled *Post-Primary Education 1985-2000 and its Relevance to the*

Economy: A Policy Document. This same topic was also the theme of the AIM Group seminar on education to mark the Year of the Child.[3] In *Post-Primary Education 1985-2000* the broad outlines of a programme which runs throughout the entire course of the post-primary school programme, and which is entitled 'Education for living: Pastoral Care Programme', is sketched.[4] It suggests a number of areas of study where the concern is with practical education of a general kind, and it may serve as a useful starting point in any consideration of how the schools might set about filling the vacuum that exists in this area at the present time. It is more in order at this point, however, to take a closer look at the way in which practical education of a general as opposed to a vocational or specialised kind is neglected in Irish post-primary education. This can be done here by reference to the subject of home economics in the Leaving Certificate course.

At the present time pupils may study only one of the two home economics syllabuses which are offered. These are the home economics (general) syllabus and the home economics (scientific and social) syllabus. Originally, and up until 1970, there was just one home economics course for the Leaving Certificate programme. This was expanded into two syllabuses, however, with a view to being accepted for university matriculation purposes. One of these syllabuses, the home economics (scientific and social) syllabus, has been accepted since 1977 for matriculation purposes by the National University of Ireland. Both this syllabus and the home economics (general) syllabus are acceptable for matriculation purposes by the University of Dublin.

The home economics (general) syllabus, at least in some important respects, may reasonably be characterised, both in intent and in content, as a practical subject in the sense that I am using it here. It is practical in that it prepares pupils to deal satisfactorily with a range of issues commonly encountered in everyday living, issues such as diet, consumer matters, dress, hygiene, household management and budgetting.[5] It is this orientation that provides the course with its justification and which makes it an example, at least in some important respects, of a practical subject of a general kind. Thus it treats of the topics which it does, not because they are central to some particular discipline or body of knowledge – in the way that one might treat of the concept of mass or energy in the study of physics or of climate in the study of geography – but because they are central or fundamental to living well, that is to meeting a range of practical demands of everyday living. The treatment of topics in the course is not merely descriptive or explanatory; it is also prescriptive as the course suggests principles or guidelines for the conduct of everyday affairs. This orientation is manifest throughout the syllabus. In Section C of the course dealing with 'Management of the Home' we read, for example:

> The aim in this section of the course should be to give students a good general knowledge of the importance of good work methods, initiative, good planning; correct use of time and leisure; and the practical application of good homemaking practices. A basic study of the principles underlying good home management practices and efficient work-methods (including use of modern labour-saving equipment) should be covered.[6]

It continues by way of outlining the syllabus for a topic on 'The Home: A study of the house and its environments' as follows:

> Guidelines to choosing a house; aids to buying and renting houses, maisonettes and flats (furnished, unfurnished). Modern methods of ventilation, heating, lighting and sanitation; central heating.[7]

To say that the course is a practical one, that it is concerned to treat of issues because of their importance to meeting a range of practical demands of living rather than their importance to a body of knowledge, is not, however, to say everything about the course. Thus while the orientation is practical, a scientific or theoretical element is also included; that is to say, the course aims not simply at giving guidelines and skills but also at providing an understanding of the issues being treated. Thus, in a unit on foods in the nutrition and cookery section of the course, there is provision for the study of essential food constituents such as proteins, carbohydrates, vitamins, and so on. The same is true of the other topics treated.

Turning to the scientific and social syllabus, one is perhaps more impressed by the seeming similarity between this and the general syllabus rather than the differences. The actual format of the two syllabuses, however, is quite different. The general course has a more practical orientation as opposed to the somewhat more scientific and theoretical orientation of the scientific and social course. Thus, the scientific and social syllabus would appear to be primarily concerned with promoting an understanding of the issues which are treated; there might even be the suggestion that it is a form of understanding which is not greatly concerned with the application of what is known for purposes of everyday living. Thus a unit on the family in the scientific and social syllabus which appears to be primarily academic, and the sections in the scientific part of the course which are narrowly scientific in orientation, might well be dealt with in isolation from the context of their everyday applications.[8] As I have intimated, however, there appears to be a greater overall similarity rather than dissimilarity between the two courses, and it may well be that this is even more true in practice than on paper.

However great or slight are the actual differences in practice between the two courses in home economics, they bear further consideration for a number of reasons. Firstly, they shed important light on the forces which bear on the curriculum of post-primary education in Ireland. Whatever the differences between the two courses, it is important to note that one of them is acceptable for university matriculation purposes in the National University of Ireland and the other is not. Granted the Irish university tradition, and the circumstances surrounding the introduction of two syllabuses in home economics, it is reasonable to conclude that the scientific and social syllabus is considered to be acceptable over and above the general syllabus because it is perceived to possess a body of theoretical knowledge of some significance not contained in the general syllabus. But the difference between the attitudes towards these two syllabuses is of greater significance than this distinction alone might suggest. It is a difference between a commitment to what is apparently considered to be a more theoretical form of knowledge as opposed to a more practical form of knowledge, a practical form considered important enough by the state Department of Education to maintain it on the Leaving Certificate programme even though it is not recognised by the National University of Ireland for university matriculation purposes. If the difference of emphasis in these two courses, one theoretical and the other practical, is the essential difference between them, and if this is also the reason why one is acceptable for matriculation purposes and the other is not, then it is worthy of reflection; it says much about the influences which bear on the post-primary curriculum and the not inconsiderable difficulty encountered by those who wish to promote forms of education which may be considered to contribute to the practical education of pupils at post-primary level. And while the university may have very good reasons for thinking that the general syllabus is not suitable for matriculation purposes, it still raises serious questions regarding the interrelations between second-level and third-level education. This is a point to which I shall return in the next chapter.

To draw out the contrast between the home economics (general) and home economics (scientific and social) syllabuses is important, secondly, because the contrast exists not just between these two courses alone but between the type of course that the home economics (general) course is and the majority of the other non-vocational subjects on the curriculum. That is to say that while living may be a thoroughly practical affair, calling for practical judgment and action, much of the curriculum of the post-primary school appears to be predominantly non-practical or academic in character. Thus, there is little that one finds or, in some cases, that one would expect to find in a number of subjects on the school programme which is of a directly practical nature, one wherein there is an explicit concern to assist pupils in meeting and in dealing in a successful way with practical issues as they arise in life. This is true of such subjects as Latin and Greek, history, geography, mathematics, applied mathematics, physics, chemistry, biology, economics, economic history and other non-vocational subjects. Similarly, a number of subjects which do have the potential to address themselves to practical issues, subjects such as religious education, civics, physical education, and some language and so-called 'cultural' subjects, are either ill-conceived in their present form or are in some way inhibited from exploiting their potential in this regard. Still other possible subjects with such potential, such as health education, family-life education, consumer education, education in interpersonal relations and community living, and media education, are almost entirely ignored.

It is not my intention here to dwell upon the way in which the subjects mentioned do not exploit their full potential in regard to the practical. Yet some further elaboration is in order, and this can be done with reference to the area of language studies in English. While Irish and modern European languages have an important place in the curriculum of post-primary education in Ireland, both for reasons of culture and communications, English remains the major language. Accordingly, its place in the preparation of pupils for living is of the greatest importance. But how well does the teaching of English at post-primary level meet this challenge, and how adequately does it cater for the practical demands of living? It has long been a criticism of language studies in Irish post-primary education that they have neglected the spoken word,[9] a criticism which can be applied to the teaching of Irish and modern languages as well as to English. Arguably, other aspects of the communications element in language, aspects such as the critical reading of the daily newspaper, which are so central to the use of language for everyday purposes, have been neglected just as much.

In everyday living the oral use of language for communication purposes takes the active forms of conversation, discussion and debate. Radio and television constitute its main passive forms for most people. The everyday use of language in the form of reading and writing finds expression mostly in the shape of newspapers and magazines, books, notices, advertisements, official letters and forms, and personal correspondence. Yet, it must be asked, what attention do these matters receive in the language studies of the post-primary school. True, it might be argued that the basics of reading and writing belong to the primary school, and that in fact some attention is given to some of these matters in the post-primary school. But this can hardly be said of the development of skills such as critical reading, interpretation and evaluation, discussion and debate of current and political affairs, for example. And while there has been some widening out of the scope of language studies in recent years, it has not addressed itself satisfactorily to these sorts of matters. The emphasis in language subjects still seems to be that of the classical studies and literary traditions in which the formal study of works of established literary repute receive the main attention and in which the oral and communications aspects in their various forms — and especially as employed for purposes of everyday living — continue to be neglected.

These various points can be borne out by reference to the programmes and syllabuses in English at the Group Certificate, the Intermediate Certificate and the Leaving Certificate examination levels. The most striking aspect of the syllabuses in question is their all but complete avoidance of the oral element. In no case is there direct provision for attention to the oral element in the syllabuses, though the desirability of some such attention is adverted to in the discussion of aims of both the Intermediate and Leaving Certificate courses in the subject. There is also provision for an optional oral assessment in English at the Intermediate Certificate examination. It is a feature of all three syllabuses, moreover, that they are set forth very much within the context of the certificate examinations, a context which provides the opportunity to warn that 'incorrect spelling and punctuation will be penalised in all sections of the examination papers'.[10] In no case is any specific attention given to the study of language in the context of the realities of present-day communications and mass media.

In an age of mass communications when, perhaps, language is used in a greater variety of forms for communication purposes than ever before, forms such as advertising, propaganda, election-eering, official and unofficial information purposes, radio and television newscasts, political commentary and debate, is it not remarkable that so little attention is given to education in language as communication, either in oral or written form? Thus there is little or no direct provision for the preparation of pupils in group or public debate, in the discussion of current affairs, or in develop-ing critical skills of interpretation towards the content and, indeed, the various forms of communications used, often for conflicting purposes. I am not suggesting that the formal study of com-munications or the like should be introduced into the school programmes; rather what is lacking is attention to the practical aspect of language studies demanded in the present day and age.

The above criticism is not to say, however, that the schools are teaching nothing that is valuable from a language point of view. To hold this would be patently silly. Through the study of English as it is constituted at present, most pupils' language proficiency will undoubtedly be improved. That this is intended, moreover, is actually stated in the introduction to the syllabuses for the Inter-mediate and Leaving Certificate courses. The reading, writing, listening, and speaking which a pupil does in school may also be of all-round benefit from a language point of view and for purposes of communication.

In talking of the place of the practical in education it becomes evident that practical knowledge is of many different kinds or has many different facets and applications. Thus the practical as I have been discussing it with reference to home economics is somewhat different from what is in question in the discussion of English. In the one, the focus of attention is on questions having to do with the development of guidelines and principles for the conduct of personal and family affairs; in the other, the emphasis is more on the analysis and interpretation of ordinary language as used for various everyday purposes of communication and persuasion. The basic orientation in practical education remains common, nonetheless, namely, a concern with the application of knowledge required for the purposes of everyday living.

Before leaving this discussion of the practical in education, some attention must be given to practical education in which physical skill plays a significant part. Physical education and manual instruction have had a long association with formal schooling. And while various and even conflicting justifications have been offered in their support, their place in the curriculum of the school has a certain common-sense appeal. It is an appeal at the basis of which lies, perhaps, a recognition of the importance of physical skill and dexterity in the conduct of many important affairs of everyday living from bodily exercise and comportment to driving a motor car, decorating a house and, at its highest levels, to professional expertise in a range of vocational specialisations calling for a high and very responsible level of physical skill and its associated understandings (think of the electrician, the motor mechanic, the dentist, the surgeon).

There has not been a strong tradition in Irish post-primary education, particularly in secondary education, in practical education of these kinds. Recent years have seen some improvement with the introduction and encouragement of a number of practical subjects. The introduction of improved facilities and a degree programme for the education of specialist teachers of physical education also marks an advance. Nonetheless, the combination of relatively low levels of pupil participation in practical subjects of this kind especially at senior cycle, the relatively disadvantaged position of these subjects from a university matriculation point of view, and, in the case of physical education, the competition it receives from examination subjects, still militates against them. Their historical non-secondary status does not help matters either. Despite this, however, the increased importance which might be expected to be devoted to many of these subjects for economic reasons in the future will undoubtedly influence their fortunes. This, of course, is not to say that such practical subjects can be justified only in relation to work or economic benefit. Indeed, the case has been argued that such studies merit attention in education purely in their own right.[11] Nonetheless, it is as vocational subjects that these practical subjects have grown in importance in recent years, and as such further attention must be given to them.

Before leaving the discussion of the extent to which present-day curriculum provision in Irish post-primary education supports education of the general practical kind of which I have been talking, one further point bears comment. If one considers the place of the established subjects on the curriculum of the post-primary schools in Ireland it will be found that the tradition of a liberal education and the position of influence of the universities has done much to press for and support the position of many of these subjects. In the case of other subjects, the newer and the more vocationally-oriented subjects very often, there is again a substantial interest group in society which can exert influence to boost and support the place and interest of these subjects in the curriculum. But in respect of the kinds of studies of a general practical nature, civics for example, from where do these get their support? No source of support for education of this general practical kind which can compare in influence with the universities and vocational interest groups exists. Accordingly, their cause tends to be a neglected one but surely it is none the less important for this.

The vocational demands of living

One of the more obvious demands of living is the vocational demand, the need to engage in gainful employment. The traditions of technical, vocational, and apprentice education have always given attention to the preparation of pupils in specialised knowledge and skills. The concept of the work-preparatory in recent years, however, has broadened out to include the notion of emotional and attitudinal orientation and other aspects of education for employment as well. Through the vocational education system, the post-primary sector in Irish education did much over the years to cater for the vocational needs of a range of pupils and of society. The changes brought about in Irish post-primary education over the past ten to fifteen years, however, have had important implications for the vocational school tradition. To a lesser extent they have had implications also for the secondary tradition which, historically, did not see itself as being primarily vocational or work-preparatory in orientation. Accordingly, the focus of attention here will be in assessing the present-day provision made for the vocational or career demands of living in Irish post-primary education. Two aspects of this question, in particular, will be examined. Firstly, there is the question of the place of vocational subjects *vis-à-vis* general education in the post-primary school; and secondly, there is the broader question of general orientation towards the world of work.

There is now quite a number of subjects of a vocational kind which are to be found at all levels of the post-primary school, be it secondary or vocational school. The Group Certificate programme, however, still remains the most vocationally oriented of the three main programmes in the Irish post-primary education system, even though its vocational orientation has been diluted by recent reform measures.

The stance which has been taken in the matter of the curriculum of vocationally-oriented subjects, that of a midway position between the pure or theoretical studies on the one hand and specifically trade subjects on the other, has much to support it. This is an important stance and one which warrants some consideration here. In speaking of the place of subjects such as commerce and woodwork in the curriculum of the secondary school, the Council of Education went out of its way to say that the proper concern of the secondary school with subjects such as these was not one wherein the intent would be to prepare pupils for employment. Such subjects were to be included in the curriculum only because of their inherent educational value. This same view, moreover, is reflected in the current *Rules*, for example in the preamble to the Intermediate Certificate syllabuses for woodwork and metalwork.[12]

While the purity of intention sought by the Council of Education in advocating the study of practical or technical subjects might not have been fully realised, neither has the study of these subjects in the Group, Intermediate, or Leaving Certificate programmes been treated as constituting merely a direct preparation for a specific trade. Moreover, it was never the intention that continuation education as provided for in the vocational education system should cater for any such specific training. This is a position which has been emphasised in recent years with the emergence of AnCO as the national agency for apprentice education in the various trades. Likewise, with the introduction in some schools of pre-employment programmes in recent years, the emphasis is on general preparation and orientation rather than training for a specific job. Accordingly, in even the most applied or vocationally-oriented subjects in any of the post-primary school programmes the emphasis is on the development of general understanding of principles and skills rather than on principles and skills specific to any particular trade or occupation. And even in the few cases where a particular subject may be closely related to a specific trade, for example woodwork *vis-à-vis* carpentry, there is much more demanded in the post-primary school programmes than the study of just one such subject. In fact, the point made in the prefatory note to the Leaving Certificate syllabus in technical drawing, where the course is clearly not seen as a training for immediate trade employment, may be taken to be representative of how far any of the vocational subjects are prepared to go in this regard. It reads:

The course will be of two years duration and the syllabus is so designed that it continues and extends the studies outlined for this subject at the Intermediate Certificate level.

A course in plane and solid geometry with associated technical applications is an excellent training ground for students in spatial comprehension. The course is on this account eminently suited to those interested in pre-University, pre-Technological College, or pre-Technician training leading to careers in Architecture, Building Industry, Engineering and various other occupations of a technical nature.[13]

From the standpoint of a general education this approach would appear to have much to commend it, both from the point of view of the personal and vocational preparation of the pupil and from the point of view of manpower development in the interests of the community. Thus a pupil is not limited to knowledge or skills which would be too specialised to provide a more general competency in a range of employment areas such as might emerge and might be consistent with the interests of the particular pupil in question. While a pupil is brought to a point where specialisation might commence he is also equipped with a breadth of knowledge and skills which may serve as a safeguard against all but severe obsolescence of knowledge and skills. At the same time a basis is laid for immediate specialised training in a range of areas, rather than just one, and for whatever subsequent forms of retraining which the increasingly rapid rate of changing working conditions might necessitate. In this way also the wider manpower interests of the community might best be served – a point to be borne in mind when pressure to make the school merely serve the labour force may be such as to pressurise schools into mere training of possibly short-term value.[14]

A number of points arise following the adoption of this middle position concerning the place of vocational studies in the post-primary school, that is the inclusion in the curriculum of a number of vocationally-oriented subjects, and the study of these at a general level rather than at the level of preparing pupils for specific trades. The first point I have already adverted to, namely the low level of participation in vocational subjects. However sensible may be the curriculum position which has been adopted in relation to vocational studies, it is of little value unless these subjects are actually studied. The second point is related to this. Insofar as the aims of the post-primary school entail a commitment to providing a preparation for life as well as meeting the manpower and economic needs of the community, then the schools must include subjects which prepare pupils for employment. Insofar as the state has made some provision for vocational subjects in the curriculum, it has done something towards meeting the vocational and employ-ment needs of pupils and of the community. But has it gone far enough? I am inclined to think not. If these objectives are to be sought in a determined way, then participation rates in various vocational subjects must be brought to a level which is in some way related to the need for them. Additionally, however, the subjects made available for study must also be related in some way to the nature of the employment or work demands of the community.

A number of studies in recent years including *Investment in Education* have turned their attention to this particular point. Bearing in mind some of these studies, the policy document of the North County Tipperary VEC has drawn out some of the impli-cations for post-primary education and it appears that the actual vocational subjects on offer in the schools do not tally fully with the areas of economic demand. This is not to say that the vocational subjects which are on offer have no relevance. They have. Indeed it is arguable that not only should they be retained but they should be even better attended. But there are also areas of economic and social need for which a number of suitable subjects are not available at all in the schools. Thus, while recent measures have been taken to develop on a pilot basis some of the areas listed below, there would appear to be insufficient provision in post-primary education in general for many areas of vocational potential. Areas which have been mentioned include the following: various forms of engineering; building crafts; secretarial; communications and the media; local and public administration; business management; farming and farm management; computers; and the oral aspects of modern languages.[15] One might also investigate the possibilities in areas such as public health, social services, public relations and so on.

Until recently there has been a lack of a clear identification of the likely areas of vocational needs on a national scale as a basis for drawing up new vocational subjects, content and programmes to be included in the curriculum of the post-primary school. With the introduction recently of *Manpower Information Quarterly*, a publication of the Vocational Manpower Service of the Department of Labour, some information of this kind has been made more readily available. Yet before any work on the drawing up of courses and programmes can be seriously undertaken, further studies in the form of the identification of the work needs of the community may need to be undertaken on a basis designed to provide the kind of information that educationists and curriculum developers will need.

It is true, of course, that one cannot simply sit back and wait for the completion of studies of this sort, important though they may be; one must make the best of the situation in which one finds oneself. And to an extent this is what the Department of Education and the schools are doing by providing courses leading to examinations in the vocational subjects recognised by the Minister for Education. In addition to this, however, a number of schools have, at the prompting and encouragement of the Department of Education and the EEC, introduced year-long programmes, programmes which have gone by names such as transition-year programmes, pre-employment programmes, and the like.[16] Vocational education authorities have gone further and have called for provision to be made for the introduction of a two-year work-preparatory programme which would run as an alternative to the current Leaving Certificate programme.[17] In most of these programmes there would be a substantial emphasis on establishing a link for pupils between the world of school and the world of work.

A recent survey carried out on the transition-year programmes shows that aspects of these programmes vary from one to the other.[18] Some have a work-preparatory element and all have a rather strong cultural and personal development dimension. There is recognition in the *Rules* for these transition-year programmes.

As originally envisaged, however, these programmes were designed to serve as an aid either for the purpose of transition from the junior cycle to the senior cycle of the post-primary school or for transition from school to work.[19]

Along with the introduction of transition-year programmes, the Department of Education, in line with the resolution of the Council and of the Ministers of Education of the EEC of 13 December 1976,[20] has also been engaged in a larger-scale project. The purpose of this project is to promote pre-employment programmes. These are based in vocational, comprehensive and community schools. In these programmes the pre-employment orientation is very marked. In 1977/8, eighty schools participated and in 1978/9, over 100 schools were involved.

While schools have a fair share of freedom in developing pre-employment programmes, in general there are three broad sections in each programme. In the first section, the 'technical modules' section, the emphasis is on general technical skills and over-specialisation is avoided. The second section is a general studies section consisting of studies in communications, mathematics and social and industrial studies and there is also provision for personal and social development; overall, there is a concern to provide the pupil with 'the knowledge and skills to move from the dependency of school life to the relative autonomy of adulthood'.[21] The third section consists of a variety of work experiences.

Perhaps the most welcome feature of the various work-preparatory programmes which have been put into operation in recent years is the inclusion of actual work-floor experience in the programmes. Another important feature of these programmes is the extent to which they have addressed themselves to the attitudinal aspects of preparation for employment. This is a feature which can be overlooked when the emphasis is on the impartation of specific knowledge and skills in a subject, be it business organisation or building construction. And while it is far too early to say how successful these work-preparatory programmes will be in educational terms, in general terms they are to be welcomed as a new initiative in orienting the post-primary school to the demands of employment and the world of work.

Despite a number of encouraging aspects of the situation in regard to preparing pupils for the vocational demands of living, a major stumbling block still remains. It is the absence of a well-developed concept or philosophy of post-primary education, and the subsequent development of programmes based on this philosophy. In such a philosophy the notion of post-primary education as a preparation for life in the present day and age would be worked out and the demands of vocational preparation would receive explicit recognition and provision in accordance with this. That thinking of this sort existed during the reform attempts of the 1960s cannot seriously be doubted, but what can be said is that it was never fully harnessed, focused or developed into a coherent philosophy leading to explicit programmes. As a result, in the absence of such a guiding philosophy, the traditional philosophy, as determined by traditional practice, expectations, institutions and structures, remained dominant. It was the philosophy of intermediate or secondary education, in which there was little or no recognition of the place of vocational education. It was a philosophy which was at odds with the innovative spirit of the times and against which this spirit has only been able to inch its way.

The recreational demands of living
In addition to the practical and vocational demands there are also what I have called the recreational or cultural demands of living. While these recreational needs may be met in a wide variety of ways, throughout the course of history the arts have achieved a special place in this regard.

There is a long tradition of dissatisfaction with the attention given to cultural education of this kind in Irish secondary and post-primary education but some provision is made. Thus music and musicianship and art (including crafts) are recognised subjects at post-primary level. There are, furthermore, substantial literary components in the various language subjects, especially in English and Irish. The introduction of physical education into the schools on a somewhat wider scale in recent years has also added to this element in the school curriculum.

It is one thing, as has been seen already, to have a subject included among the approved subjects. There are also the questions, however, of participation rates, the adequacy of the programmes and teaching provisions, and the overall image of the cultural which is transmitted, and those subjects and areas which are not included in the curriculum. The participation rates in the two exclusively art or cultural subjects, as they are called, namely music and art, are extremely low. The numbers of boys and girls taking art and music in the Intermediate and Leaving Certificate examination in 1979 are given in Table 6.[22] With fairly minor variations, these figures are representative of the participation rates in each year over the past five or six years. As is true of home economics, these subjects would appear to be considered more appropriate for girls than for boys.

Table 6: **Numbers of candidates taking art and music at Intermediate and Leaving Certificate examination, 1979**

Examination	Total Number of Candidates	Art	Music
Intermediate Certificate	Girls (26,224)	12,525	5,546
	Boys (23,756)	6,679	1,464
Leaving Certificate	Girls (19,726)	4,088	527
	Boys (15,784)	1,957	102

The participation rates in literary studies, which form a part of each of the language subjects are, of course, much higher than those for music and art. The same is true of physical education at both junior and senior cycles; in this case, however, since physical education is not an examination subject, there is probably a great deal of variation from school to school as to how much time is allotted to the subject and what aspects of it are taught. Dance, gymnastics and athletics, as well as various games and other pursuits, form part of the official programme.[23]

Turning to the area of literature, the art area to which greatest attention is devoted in terms of programmes, resources and pupil numbers, it is to be welcomed that the major areas of poetry, prose and drama are given attention. Changes in the syllabuses which have taken place over the past decade or more and which have led to a broadening of the range of materials included, the introduction of more modern and contemporary material, as well as Anglo-Irish literature in the case of English, are all to be welcomed. Nonetheless, one cannot but agree with the report of the Arts Council *The Place of the Arts in Irish Education* when it calls for constant diligence in the selection of materials. And in this connection one is simply forced to ask if the present selection of materials is the most suitable, given the times in which we live and the ages and composition of the pupil body.[24]

There are, of course, other areas of concern regarding the provision for the cultural subjects in the curriculum and, although these may be expressed in relation to some other subjects in the curriculum, it would not be out of place in the case of the art subjects, to draw special attention to the questions of the adequacy of the teaching facilities, the formal qualifications of many teachers of the art subjects, the pressures of the examinations system and university matriculation requirements. These are points on which the report of the Arts Council has expressed its own concerns.[25] Finally, at a time when the rate of youth unemployment is expected to be high, one would wish the recreational studies to play an important part in preparing pupils for this eventuality.

Education and a philosophy of life
Hitherto I have been examining curriculum provision for the practical demands of living, the vocational demands of living and the recreational demands of living. I have argued that any school programme which purports to provide a general education ought to prepare pupils to meet these demands, and that the tradition of post-primary education in Ireland has been somewhat delinquent in doing so. Yet, over and above the practical, vocational and recreational demands there is a fourth demand. It is a sort of 'quintessential' demand, a demand that pervades all of the above demands and all of living. It is that demand, arguably, to which the classical notion of a liberal education addressed itself: the need to understand, to make sense out of events and phenomena, and to shape our lives and destinies eventually. It is the demand for a philosophy of life, a world view, and a set of values by which to guide our thoughts and actions.

The literary embodiment of the educational ideal to meet this demand has been created over and again in such characters as Plato's philosopher king, More's Hythloday, Rousseau's Emile, Newman's gentleman and more recently the educated person of Hirst and Peters. Curriculum proposals for the attainment of the ideal have been no less numerous. There are some differences of viewpoint both in conceptions of what constitutes the ideal and the curriculum measures proposed by which to achieve it, but happily, there are areas of agreement also.

A general education as I have conceived of it consists of preparing pupils to meet the various demands of living. This notion

I have distinguished from that of the traditional idea of a liberal education which, as it developed, did not contain the practical or utilitarian emphasis found in the concept which I have set forth. Understood in the traditional way, a liberal education was intended, as we saw earlier on, as a form of education in which the central idea was a concern with the development of intellect as a good or end in itself without any concern for what its uses in life might be. And although such a form of education may have been widely hailed as being the most useful type as well, it is important to note that the criterion of utility or practicality played no part in drawing up the ideal itself or the curriculum by which it was to be achieved. Hence, the highly literary, academic and non-vocationally-oriented curriculum with which it became identified. And although it is true that in recent times many have come to speak of a general education meaning a liberal education in the sense described here, and the curricular programmes for general education which they propose are equally 'liberal' or non-practical in character, such is not the view of a general education which I have in mind. It is too narrow a view.

Liberal education understood as the development of a 'philosophical habit of mind', to use Newman's phrase, is not co-extensive with the idea of a general education as I have expressed it here. Yet insofar as it aims at the development of intellect and a philosophy of life it constitutes an important element in general education and one for which provision must be made. But what, it must be asked, constitutes an adequate curriculum for purposes of liberal education, for education as the development of intellect and a philosophy of life? And how well does post-primary education in Ireland fare in the light of it?

There has emerged a strong tradition in recent educational thought in which the curriculum of a liberal or general education has been shaped by the view that there are different kinds of scientific or systematic knowledge, knowledge which has been developed by man in his attempts to interpret, understand and eventually shape and control the world in which he lives. The curriculum of a liberal or general education, it has been thought, ought to include in one way or another each of the major forms or kinds of knowledge (as being necessary for initiation into the culture, as a means of intellectual and personal growth, and as a basis for understanding the world in which we live). This is a view, and a general approach to the question of the curriculum of a liberal or general education, which has been adopted by many contemporary philosophers of curriculum, including Harry S. Broudy and Philip H. Phenix in the United States, R.S. Peters and Paul H. Hirst in England, and many others. In considering the question of what constitutes adequate curriculum content for purposes of liberal education, it will be helpful to refer to the views of authors such as these.

Hirst and Peters have set forth a tentative classification of knowledge into seven forms including mathematics, science, inter-personal knowledge, moral knowledge, aesthetic knowledge, religious knowledge and philosophical knowledge.[26] Each form, it is claimed, corresponds to a distinctive mode of experience and knowledge which is the product of man's attempts to understand the world around him. The full development of intellect, more-over, will necessitate study of each of the seven forms. A 'general education', it is pointed out, aims at no exhaustive mastery: 'its concern is that the pupil will be sufficiently immersed in each form of understanding to appreciate its character, to employ its major elements that have application within the context of everyday life, and to be aware of the further possibilities in each area, given the time and inclination to pursue these'.[27] This latter point is in line with Hirst's insistence that what is important in liberal education is the development of the mind and not the study of different forms in themselves. One studies the forms simply because these are the means available to us to develop the mind. And any course of studies that does not expose a pupil to all of the forms cannot, in Hirst's view, claim to provide an adequate liberal or general education. Accordingly, when Hirst comes to a consideration of different subjects on the curriculum, his concern is less with the actual subjects studied or the curriculum organisation which is employed than with the fact of whether all of the forms are represented.

Hirst has leant heavily on the notion of the development of mind as the object of a liberal education and in doing so he believes that he has relieved the justification of liberal education of its dependence on the classical realism theory of truth.[28] This he con-sidered to be a weakness of the original Greek theory. This latter position is still maintained in the classical realist position of Harry S. Broudy. Approaching the question of what ought to make up the curriculum of general education from a consideration of 'the ways that schooling or school learnings are used in modern life',[29] Broudy identified four major uses of knowledge. These are what he terms the associative, the replicative, the applicative and the interpretive.

Arguing that the applicative use of knowledge is found usually only in the specialist, the associative, replicative and interpretive uses remain for the non-specialist. And although Broudy puts important store by the associative and replicative uses of schooling,[30] a special place seems to be reserved for the interpretive. Thus, we read:

> Whether a boy is heading for the practice of law or the manipulation of buttons on the instrument panel of an automated refinery, as a citizen he needs highly general cognitive and evaluative maps. On these maps he will maneuver [sic] all of his problems for understanding, appraisal, and, hopefully, for solution. This interpretive use of schooling determines the way he perceives his world, the way he thinks and feels about it, and the way he makes choices concerning it. It is also the base on which his specialist training can be built.[31]

Attempting then to provide the outline of a programme which will include the 'key ideas and criteria' and the 'indispensable symbolic and logical operations without which interpretation cannot be adequate',[32] Broudy comes up with five main areas of study. These are what he calls the symbolics of information and include languages and mathematics; basic sciences, including general science, chemistry, physics, and biology; developmental studies including history, geography, politics, economics, and technology; exemplars including art appreciation and value education; and molar problems, the study of which will aim at instruction in the art of collective deliberation.[33]

Despite the differences of viewpoint between philosophers of curriculum, both in the grounds upon which they base their selection of curriculum content for purposes of liberal or general education, and the differences which exist among their guidelines for the selection of content, common to almost all is a unifying curriculum principle by which it is determined that certain curriculum elements are essential for purposes of liberal or general education. These elements cover a wide range of subjects including the natural sciences and mathematics, the arts, the humanities and the social sciences. It is noteworthy also that it is this kind of thinking which lies behind many of the recent efforts in England to broaden the curriculum of secondary education there and which has also led to attempts to re-organise the pattern of the GCE 'O' and 'A' level examinations accordingly.[34]

With this we come to an assessment of the present-day position in Ireland. The question is how adequate is curriculum provision in Irish post-primary education for preparing pupils to meet what I have called the philosophical demands of living. Turning first of all to the question of an underlying philosophy of post-primary education in Ireland as a source of curriculum unity, I have argued already that no explicit philosophy of post-primary education exists; not even since the attempted reforms of post-primary education in the mid-1960s has there been an explicit attempt to define what is understood by post-primary education in Ireland, what it aims to achieve, and what general measures and procedures it ought to take to achieve its ends. This is not to deny that there has been a growth in comprehensive schools and curriculum at post-primary level, or that efforts have been made to promote technical and applied subjects. It is simply to say that such changes have taken place for the most part on a piecemeal basis and within the context of the existing traditions of secondary and vocational education rather than within the context of a newly developed and explicit philosophy of post-primary curriculum.

This being the case, it is not surprising that with the abandonment of elements in both the vocational and secondary school traditions the unity and sense of purpose of the original Group Certificate programme, and to a lesser extent the Intermediate Certificate programme, began to be diluted. The Leaving Certificate programme never had any worthwhile principle of unity or selection, save that Irish has been a compulsory subject of study since the 1930s. Accordingly, when it comes to the question of identifying a basic underlying philosophy of curriculum, one which might reasonably be expected to have faced up to the question of the place of general education in Irish post-primary education today, there is none to be found. In the absence of any such principle of curriculum unity one's hopes for an education fitted to meeting the philosophical demands of living are immediately dampened. Furthermore, as was the case in discussing the aims of post-primary education in an earlier chapter, if one is to identify elements of a guiding philosophy one has to fall back on a consideration of the rules and regulations governing programmes, choice of subjects and examinations. Nor is this situation likely to change since few indicators are contained in the *White Paper on Educational Development*.

All pupils studying for the Intermediate Certificate course must take Irish, English, civics and mathematics. In addition, pupils in secondary schools must normally take history and geography. Pupils in vocational schools may not, seemingly, fulfil the requirements completely by taking history and geography, though they are permitted to study these subjects; instead, such pupils must take either mechanical drawing or art or home economics or commerce. All pupils are required to take two other approved subjects in addition to the above. As an apparent exception in principle, if not in practice, pupils in comprehensive and community schools wishing to take the Intermediate Certificate examination are required merely to follow 'an approved Intermediate Course' as a pupil of such a school. And it is added that the 'approved course for a pupil in a comprehensive school shall include the subjects which from time to time comprise the compulsory common core of subjects in the curriculum of comprehensive schools'.[35]

The situation in relation to the Group Certificate course is somewhat similar. All pupils are required to take Irish, English and civics. In addition to this basic core, Group Certificate pupils must also take the compulsory subjects of at least one group of the Group Certificate groups of subjects. Thus, a pupil following the commerce (general) course would be required to take book-keeping, commerce and either commercial arithmetic or arithmetic in addition to the basic core. The requirements at Leaving Certificate level are quite different from those for both the Intermediate and Group Certificate courses. At this level pupils are required to study just five approved subjects, one of which must be Irish.

From a consideration of these regulations it would appear, at least on the face of it, that an attempt is made to cater for the demands of breadth of knowledge, one of the criteria employed by Hirst and Broudy. Thus, any pupil who completes the junior cycle of the post-primary school will have been exposed to second-level education in mathematics, languages and literature (including Irish language and literature) and social studies. If one counts language and literature as including art and humanistic studies, however limited they may be in this regard, all but one of the major areas of study widely agreed by curriculum theorists as essential would have been included. The requirement for pupils to follow a fairly common core of studies up to Intermediate Certificate level, and the requirement to study five subjects at Leaving Certificate level, would also appear to meet to some extent the kind of breadth of studies being sought after in England at the present time. An area of study which is omitted, however, is the natural sciences.

While it is important to recognise the actual range of studies which exists in the Irish post-primary school, I have been putting the most favourable construction on it. For while it is undoubtedly the case that many pupils enjoy courses of study which might be regarded by some as fulfilling a satisfactory range of subjects for purposes of liberal education, much is also left to chance.

In the first place one cannot be satisfied with any programme of general studies from which the study of the natural sciences is omitted. It is not necessary here to rehearse the values of scientific study in an age which has become so dependent upon science. Secondly, it is questionable that adequate exposure can be given to the development of the skills of expression and appreciation in the arts through the study of literature alone; likewise the value of social studies which rest on the study of civics alone must be open to question. Yet, under the existing regulations, pupils may complete junior cycle education, be it in the Group Certificate or the Intermediate Certificate courses, without any more exposure in these areas. The complete or almost complete absence of regulation at senior cycle, especially when one considers what may be the case at junior-cycle level, is also a cause for some concern. Formal provision for values or moral education seems particularly suspect. Religion, it might also be noted, is not a recognised subject of secondary education in Ireland.

Considerations other than breadth of knowledge are necessary, however, when one is evaluating the suitability of school programmes for developing in the pupil a broadness of mind and the wherewithal to develop a philosophy of life. One of these considerations is the grounds or criteria for the selection of content within the subjects of the curriculum. It is one thing to decide what range of subjects is required; it is another to select content from within each of the required subjects. Thus, it is not enough simply to say that a pupil should study mathematics or history — one must also say something about the kind of mathematics and the kind of history. In their discussion of the depth of study in each of the forms of knowledge which should be required of pupils,

Hirst and Peters argued that this, to a certain extent, ought to be determined by the interests of the pupils in question.[36] I agree that individual differences ought to be borne in mind in the matter of curriculum provision but the purpose of a general education under consideration here — to help pupils to develop an understanding of the world, to develop the beginnings of a philosophy of life — must also be borne in mind when it comes to the selection of content within the subjects of the curriculum; that is there is the question of relevance to the world in which the pupil is to live and the issues which he must face. There are also issues which are imposed upon him — and not in any contrived 'educational' way — by the age and circumstances in which he lives. Already considerations of this sort have led to the suggestion of a common core of studies for all pupils; they have also led to the suggestion that the principle of selection within such a core ought to be determined by the general explanatory power and relevance of the content for the purpose of a general understanding of the world rather than with a view, for example, to making pupils into subject specialists. For while it is not an infrequent criticism of the curriculum of post-primary education that it bears little relevance to the interests and needs of the pupils, there would appear to be a degree to which it is not as relevant as it might be either to the issues of the day and age in which they live. The emphasis, it would appear, is academic and specialist; it is in many respects on the static rather than on the living and vital. Moreover, as will be argued in the next chapter, the dominant working ethic of the schools appears to be one of examination success as opposed to general education as a preparation for life.

What do I mean when I say that the content of the curriculum is heavily academic, specialist, and static as opposed to being living and vital? I mean that it does not take sufficient cognisance of the realities of the present day, that it has been drawn up on the basis of traditional selection patterns, that it is inward-looking and concerned with matters more of a scholarly or academic interest than of interest to the world of living as it takes place and changes from day to day. This preoccupation is noticeable in various elements in the curriculum. Thus, in the so-called cultural studies area one finds a preoccupation with traditional art forms, good in themselves but hardly such as to warrant exclusion of other forms such as television and film, to pick the more obvious ones. Banished altogether from this domain is even the most modest attempt to devote attention to popular adolescent culture in the forms of popular music and dance. Furthermore, nowhere does one find an attempt to relate the aesthetic to the matter of every-day living. Art and culture are conceived in terms of the museum and the art gallery. Little is made of the aesthetic in personal cleanliness, appearance and deportment. The beauty of nature as manifest in living things and physical phenomena receives no attention. Also overlooked or forgotten is the aesthetic in our public places: filthy streets, dirty and unsightly buildings and so-called development plans are never considered in the context of aesthetic education. Yet, can there not be an undefinable beauty in the running water, the gathering cloud, the bird in flight? Or consider the constructs of man: the shapely, airy-light bridge, the majesty and power of a jet-liner. Consider too the beauty manifest in athletic endeavour: the flight of a ball, the skill and composure of the master of his craft. But where in our schools do we attend to these? Can it not be said that as conceived in the curriculum of post-primary education in Ireland there is a radical separation of the artistic and the aesthetic from the fabric of everyday life? It is conceived and portrayed in terms of the static, the bookish, the non-vital. The aesthetic in our schools, it seems, is confined to the recognised, the classical. It is portrayed, like many of the academic subjects, as having little to do with everyday living.

In the matter of social studies, content is again conceived and pre-sented in conventional and academic terms. While one appreciates that the study of history and geography, as well as other social science subjects such as economics, politics, anthropology and sociology, may be fundamental to the analysis and the discussion of social questions, this can hardly be taken to mean that such questions cannot be discussed or examined without a prior sub-mersion in a number of the social sciences. If this were so it is difficult to see how such questions could ever be faced up to. Rather, one might argue that it is one of the tasks of the skilful social studies teacher to lead his pupils in the discussion of relevant social, economic, and political issues, to appreciate the complex issues involved and the necessity of taking a disciplined, analytic, and scientific approach to the discussion of such questions. Indeed, it is the absence of such an approach in the social studies that leads one to the view that in this realm also there is a lack of concern for the actual social and political issues around which the conduct of our day-to-day lives revolves. In their place we have the academic study of academic issues and questions in history, geography and so on. The focus, one is led to conclude, is on these subjects as bodies of knowledge unto themselves rather than as ways of seeing and understanding and coming to grips with the social reality in which we live. And while a radical separation of both of these approaches to a subject may not be possible, one may well ask if the prime value for social studies as part of a general education lies not more in an issues-centred rather than a subject-centred approach. Social studies for purposes of general education appear to have become confused with the pre-professional study of self-contained academic subjects.[37]

In the case of science, likewise, the study has become somewhat isolated from the context of general understanding and knowledge. In the science syllabuses there is little if any attention devoted to a consideration of the social and moral implications of science. And although one of the science syllabuses in the Intermediate Certificate course attempts to place science within the context of the more everyday experience of the pupils, the emphasis in most syllabuses is narrowly academic and specialist.

And so it is that these aspects of the curriculum of the post-primary school which form the bulk of the core or compulsory studies have been developed at a remove from the concerns of everyday life. They have been developed in the interests of subject specialisation, where the concern appears to be with the initiation of pupils as 'mini-specialists' into subjects rather than with promoting a view of the world for purposes of general understanding. That specialist subject preparation may have a role in developing such understanding, I do not wish to deny. What I do wish to object to is transforming what claims to be education of a general kind at post-primary level into education of a specialist kind. Whitehead put it well when he wrote that 'the problem of education is to make the pupil see the wood by means of the trees'. He continued:

> The solution which I am urging, is to eradicate the fatal disconnection of subjects which kills the vitality of our modern curriculum. There is only one subject-matter for education, and that is Life in all its manifestations. Instead of this single unity, we offer children — Algebra, from which nothing follows; Geometry, from which nothing follows; Science, from which nothing follows; History, from which nothing follows; a Couple of Languages, never mastered; and lastly, most dreary of all,

Literature, represented by plays of Shakespeare, with philological notes and short analyses of plot and character to be in substance committed to memory. Can such a list be said to represent Life, as it is known in the midst of living it?[38]

To summarise, at no point in the consideration of the curriculum of post-primary education in Ireland am I satisfied that it is to any substantial degree a coherent, philosophically inspired, or unified affair with a clear goal of enabling pupils to develop a philosophy of life, a world view, or a well-grounded set of values. And while some attempt is made to develop programmes at the junior cycle, individual subjects are still seen as self-contained units, having few if any relations with other subjects or with issues of substance which have a bearing on our daily living. The various subject syllabuses are set forth by authorities, to be followed by pupils and teachers alike. Thus, in place of a unified course of studies, pupils are left adrift with a handful of subjects, '. . . from which nothing follows'.

Concluding remarks

It is necessary now to draw together the various threads which I have been weaving in this chapter, the purpose of which is to evaluate the adequacy of the existing curriculum provisions at post-primary level for the purpose of general education. Specifically, the concern has been with the public curriculum, that is the stated programme and subjects, and with its adequacy in providing for a preparation for living. In an earlier chapter it was argued that a general education has been understood, in the context of post-primary education in Ireland, to mean a preparation for life. And a preparation for life, it was argued in the last chapter, was an education which aimed at preparing pupils to meet successfully the various major demands of living as experienced by all of us.

Measured against requirements such as these, the public curriculum, I have argued, falls short on a number of counts and does somewhat better on others. Firstly, regarding many of the practical demands of living, it falls short in a number of respects and one is reminded of the words of Spencer which, if they overstate the case in an amusing way, nonetheless draw attention to the point. He writes:

If by some strange chance not a vestige of us descended to the remote future save a pile of our school-books or some college examination papers, we may imagine how puzzled an antiquary of the period would be on finding in them no indication that the learners were ever likely to be parents. 'This must have been the *curriculum* for their celibates,' we may fancy him concluding. 'I perceive here an elaborate preparation for many things: especially for reading the books of extinct nations and of co-existing nations (from which indeed it seems clear that these people had very little worth reading in their own tongue); but I find no reference whatever to the bringing up of children. They could not have been so absurd as to omit all training for this gravest of responsibilities. Evidently then, this was the school course of one of their monastic orders.'[39]

That is to say that although one's personal or private life, and indeed a great deal of one's public or social life, entails grappling with an unending host of practical matters, the school curriculum is largely dominated by a concern for the academic and the theoretical. There is a neglect to prepare pupils directly for the wide range of practical demands of living; it is arguable, indeed, if one omits the practical subjects of a vocational kind, that it is in respect of the practical demands of living that the greatest neglect is found in post-primary education in Ireland. It is an area also in which, as I have remarked already, no strong pressure group in society exists to support its requirements.

Turning to the area of the vocational demands of living, there can be little doubt as to the greatly increased awareness expressed both in word and in action especially since the introduction of the reform measures in Irish post-primary education since the early 1960s. And, as has been stated already, substantial measures have been taken to promote education in this area at post-primary level, although they have not yet borne full fruit in terms of pupil participation in vocational-type subjects but nonetheless offer promise. Further developments are also underway, notably the developing of new programmes and pilot programmes in the area of the relationship between the world of school and the world of work.

But while welcome developments of the kind noted have taken place or are still underway, the impetus sought in this area has suffered from the lack of the necessary philosophical support for, and more comprehensive identification of, areas of need. As a result the movement has experienced substantial misunderstanding (by universities and parents, for example) and delay in implementation. Secondly, and related to this failure to develop a broad philosophy of post-primary education in which explicit consideration would be given to education of a vocational kind, there has been a failure to identify and set forth a comprehensive range of the areas of employment needs in the country. Unless something like this is done, preparation for employment will never attain its due place in general education, let alone its full realisation in school programmes; neither will vocational education make its full contribution to the economic needs of society.

But if there has been a neglect in the preparation of pupils to meet the varied practical, recreational and, to a lesser extent perhaps, the vocational demands of living, there may well be those who will argue that this is so for very good reasons. Thus, it may well be argued that the purpose of the school is specifically intellectual and academic rather than practical or vocational in character. This view has long held sway both in the conduct and in the justification of secondary education in Ireland. This being so, the question then is has this opting for the academic, the theoretical, the liberal, been satisfactorily served in the curriculum? The answer, it seems, must be at least partly in the negative.

This is so, as I have argued, for a number of reasons. To begin with, there is inadequate provision for the kind of breadth and representativeness of studies with which the notion of a liberal education is now associated; likewise the curriculum fails to provide an adequate basis for understanding the world in which we live through a treatment of major issues of contemporary importance. Such issues include religious and cultural toleration, environmental protection, terrorism and political action, poverty, industrial relations and sexual morality, to mention but a few. As a result the existing pattern of curriculum provision does not cater adequately for the ideal of developing in the pupil a philosophy of life, a world view, a set of values and principles by which to enable him to understand, to interpret and to make judgments in such matters in an informed and educated manner.

Where, then, one must ask, is the curriculum provision for purposes of liberal education for which it has been deemed necessary to forfeit the more directly practical studies? It does not exist. And it never will without a substantial re-drawing of the curriculum. In doing so a number of factors will need to be borne in mind. The liberal education element of a general education may well be impossible to attain unless it is linked in some way to a concern for the various practical demands of living. It is to these that it may have to turn for the source of its relevance, its vitality, its seriousness and ultimately its justification. For it is the various practical demands of living which determine, in the final analysis, the bounds of probability and of possibility within which each of us has to live out his life.[40]

Secondly, if pupils are ever to hope to develop the critical and philosophical habit of mind, a determined break with present-day curriculum thought and practice in Ireland will be necessary. For underlying the present curriculum provisions of post-primary education is a fundamental mistrust of pupil and teacher alike. As long as curriculum content is conceived and sanctioned in terms of pre-decided and pre-packaged content to be consumed by unwitting pupils and transmitted by unwitting teachers, the philosophical and critical habit of mind will not develop. For this to be possible the pupil must be encouraged to contribute, to create, to be critical and to work things out for himself.[41]

I have already drawn attention to the view that a liberal education ought to be based on a curriculum demonstrating a certain breadth and representativeness of knowledge. If this ideal is to be attained and if, at the same time, the demands of social and individual relevance are to be maintained, it will be necessary to devise programmes geared to these ends. The criteria upon which such programmes will be devised and regulated will call for the development and setting forth of an explicit philosophy of curriculum for post-primary education. It is a philosophy which will have to take into account the practical, vocational, recreational and philosophical demands of living and which will have to match them with the kinds of pupils found in post-primary schools, pupils who differ from one another on grounds of interest, aptitude, background and aspiration. Out of such considerations there ought to be shaped programmes which attempt to cater for both the various demands of living and the individual demands of pupils of very different kinds. Not until measures of this sort are taken can post-primary education in Ireland be said seriously to aim at providing a general education as a preparation for life for all of its pupils. These are matters, however, which must await a fuller discussion in the final chapter.

Chapter 5

The Pedagogy of the Curriculum

The pedagogical problem

Earlier on I suggested that in dealing with the problem of a general education the practical and pedagogical aspects of the problem have very often been overlooked or neglected. This tendency to focus on questions of content to the virtual exclusion of pedagogical and other relevant considerations, such as the interests and abilities of pupils or the impact of institutionalisation on schooling and learning, is an important feature of the major reform attempt in Irish post-primary education during the 1960s. This reform effort, as has been seen already, consisted largely of the opening up of existing subjects in the vocational and secondary sectors to all post-primary school pupils and the introduction of a number of subjects of a technical and business studies kind. Innovation in the form of curriculum organisation, teaching methods and examining was slight. More recently, a number of projects have attempted to institute reforms in the areas of curriculum and examinations which would involve pedagogical innovation. These have not been carried out on a large scale, however, and it still remains to be seen what the impact of these undertakings will be on the day-to-day work in the schools. The focus of attention in the *Report of the Council of Education* on the curriculum of the secondary school, published in the year before Dr Hillery announced his plans in respect of post-primary education in 1963, was also very largely on questions of content to the exclusion of pedagogical issues.

Bearing these points in mind, as well as what has been said already on the question of the importance of practical and pedagogical considerations in providing general education for all pupils, attention in this chapter will focus on how well the content of post-primary education in Ireland is handled from the point of view of facilitating successful teaching and learning. The importance of the pedagogy of the curriculum can easily be overlooked in the search for new and improved curricula and with it the prospect of substantial reform jeopardised; it is difficult, however, to analyse and discuss the pedagogical issues affecting curriculum, not least because of the rather intangible nature of the issues involved. Here I propose to concentrate on four aspects of post-primary education in Ireland with a view to identifying their actual or potential impact on learning. These include, firstly, the broad pattern of formal education in the country, of which post-primary education constitutes one element. In particular, attention will be directed to the relationships between post-primary education and primary education on the one hand, and between post-primary education and third-level education on the other hand. Secondly, consideration will be given to the general pedagogical character and structure of the post-primary curriculum, with particular reference to the influence of the structure of the curriculum on the actual curriculum content of everyday schooling. Thirdly, attention will be given to the question of individualised instruction; that is to say, if the problem of curriculum is not just one of selecting content which may be of educational value, but also one of ensuring that it can be taught and learned, consideration must be given to the suitability of both the content and how it is organised for purposes of teaching and of learning by an increasingly wide range of pupils of varying interests, aptitudes and abilities. And fourthly, attention will focus on one of the perennial problems of post-primary education in Ireland ever since the establishment of the intermediate system in 1878, namely the problem of the public examinations. For while there has been widespread recognition of the impact of external examinations on schooling, over the years there has been a distinct failure to come to grips with many of the criticisms and alleged difficulties associated with the public examinations at post-primary school level in Ireland.

Coordination of sectors
While the 1960s and 1970s were to be a time of rapid growth and change affecting many aspects of post-primary education in Ireland to an extent unknown since the early years of the new state, considerable change and, in some cases, substantial growth were also the experience in primary and third-level education. In their workings and their inter-relations with one another during the preceding thirty or forty years, a period more noted for stability

than change in educational matters in Ireland as elsewhere, the three sectors of the educational system had grown to understand and accommodate each other. During the 1960s and 1970s, however, they were each to experience the two-fold shock of internal change and change in the other sectors which affected themselves. And during this period of shifting relativities, and the insecurity which went with it, the post-primary sector was to be more exposed than any other sector since it alone had direct boundaries with each of the other two.[1] Lulled, perhaps, by the relative inactivity of earlier times into taking for granted the educational framework within which it operated, post-primary education seemed ill-prepared to cope with the sudden changes which were to take place. It was a difficult situation compounded no doubt by the fact, as was argued earlier on, that post-primary education did not have any very well developed guiding philosophy of its own. Under such circumstances, and with so much demanded of it so suddenly, problems of adjustment and orientation were to be expected in the years that followed.

Turning first to boundaries between the primary and the post-primary school, the 1960s were to see a number of important developments.[2] In 1966 it was decided that a pass in the entrance examinations to secondary schools, an examination which had been instituted in 1924/5 at the insistence of the Department of Education itself, would no longer be required for the recognition of pupils in secondary schools, and schools were urged to dispense with the examination; in 1967 the Primary Certificate examination was abolished. Around this time also work was begun on the development of a new primary-school curriculum and, following a pilot scheme, this new curriculum was fully phased into the schools in 1971. The new curriculum was different from the old one in that it allowed a greater freedom to both teacher and pupil, encouraged a greater integration of subjects, and laid greater stress on individual and group activity, with due allowances for individual differences among children. Before anyone seemed to realise it, pupils who had studied under the new curriculum began to appear at the doors of the post-primary school. In addition to having studied under a different curriculum and different methods of teaching, these pupils had neither studied for nor sat the Primary Certificate examination and, quite possibly, they would not have sat an entrance examination to secondary school either. Aged eleven or twelve, they also tended to be rather younger than their predecessors of not so many years earlier. And, consequent upon the measures taken at post-primary level to create greater participation in second-level education, such as the introduction of the free-education scheme in 1967 and the raising of the school-leaving age from fourteen to fifteen in 1972, pupils from the primary school were appearing in ever greater numbers and across a much broader spectrum of abilities, aptitudes, interests and socio-economic backgrounds than before.

It seems that only a little reflection would have suggested the need for the post-primary sector to take cognisance of such developments as these and to take appropriate action in anticipation of their likely impact; yet neither this nor seemingly any liaison between primary and post-primary authorities in matters arising out of these developments took place. Indeed, by the late 1960s and early 1970s it was the question of the coordination of the post-primary sector and third-level education that had become the centre of attention. This arose out of the necessity to make provision at third level, in line with that which had been made from the mid-1960s onwards at post-primary level, for new subjects of an applied nature in particular. Thus, as was seen already, the early 1970s saw the setting up of the National Council for Educational Awards (NCEA) and the National Institute for Higher Education (NIHE) in Limerick. It also saw continued efforts to have the more recently introduced technical subjects on the Leaving Certificate course recognised for matriculation purposes by the universities.

In the absence of advanced planning, or indeed provision of any sort, for the coordination of primary and post-primary curricula, teaching methods and examining, and in the face of a new breed of pupil, substantially enlarged enrolments and internal changes within the post-primary sector itself, the post-primary school was to face considerable difficulties from the early 1970s onwards. Much of the difficulty experienced arose out of the fundamental mismatch between traditional secondary-type curricula, teaching methods and examinations, which were now coming to dominate much of the post-primary sector, and the new type of pupil who was entering second-level education. The post-primary school had long been primed to cope with pupils of the older primary school curriculum, pupils who would have taken the Primary Certificate examination and possibly an entrance examination as well. Now post-primary schools of all types, and the secondary schools in particular, were being faced with a type of pupil for whom their programmes had not been designed and many of whom would not have sought entry a decade earlier. Shaped over the years to prepare pupils for the Intermediate and Leaving Certificate examinations and for eventual entry to the universities, the civil service and the professions, this form of secondary schooling was, by the terms of its underlying philosophy, content and methodology, quite unsuited to large numbers of the pupils now entering post-primary education. Thus, a form of schooling which originally had been designed for a select group and for entry to which various formal and informal selection procedures had existed, was now being made available — indeed compulsory — for all.

The mismatch between the offerings of the post-primary school and the pupils entering is perhaps nowhere more noticeable than in the growing demand in recent years for remedial education at the junior level of the post-primary school.[3] And while it has been said on occasions that this situation has been brought about by the new primary school curriculum, there is some reason to believe that the new curriculum is being used as a scapegoat. For example, there had always been backward pupils in such areas as reading and mathematics in the primary school, the areas of greatest concern. In the past, however, fewer of these pupils would have gone forward to a post-primary school, and fewer still would have embarked on the Intermediate Certificate course.[4] But when such pupils did begin to go forward, not only did they find themselves following courses not originally intended for them, but their teachers, both by their years of second-level teaching experience and by dent of their training, had not been adequately prepared to cope with the difficulties which ensued. It was a situation which was exacerbated by the fact that these pupils were leaving behind the relatively free and uninhibited learning atmosphere of the new primary school environment for the examination-conscious ethos of the post-primary school, be it secondary, vocational, comprehensive or community school. And since nothing that had been done during the curriculum changes of the 1960s at post-primary level succeeded very well in improving matters in this regard, cumbersome and inflexible examination courses and curriculum patterns saw to it that all pupils, be they bright or remedial, were being provided with what were substantially the same examination courses and examinations.

In the concern from the mid-1960s onwards with shaping the curriculum and organisation of post-primary education to meet the emerging economic needs of the country, little or no attention had been given to the matter of the pedagogy of the curriculum. Little or no account was taken of the need for different forms and approaches to post-primary schooling which would be needed for the greater number and greater variety of pupils which were about to embark on it. But finally in the early 1970s, in the face of mounting concern with problems of the kind I have referred to, the Minister for Education was forced into taking some action in respect of pedagogical issues affecting curriculum and examinations. Addressing the UNESCO General Conference in September 1970, Pádraig Faulkner, the then Minister for Education, spoke as follows: 'The emphasis,' he said, 'is now passing from that of quantity to quality — from concentration on an expansion in the number of students in attendance at educational institutions to particular concern with the diversity of opportunity provided, the suitability of curricula, and long-term planning for the future.'[5]

In the Minister's address to the UNESCO General Conference, and in the actions which followed, one sees some of the first signs of official recognition and attention to those aspects of the challenge to post-primary education of the 1960s which hitherto had been overlooked and neglected. And while it might be argued that what was to be done would be too little and very late, it was at least a beginning. The action which was taken took basically two forms. The first had to do with examinations reform. In September of 1970 Pádraig Faulkner set up a committee to evaluate the form and function of the Intermediate Certificate examination and to advise on new types of public examinations. In particular, the committee was asked to consider the question of the aims of education in the junior cycle of the post-primary school and the extent to which the attainment of these aims was being evaluated by the Intermediate Certificate examination. The committee was asked to consider the role of the Intermediate Certificate examination in relation to the senior cycle of post-primary education, to part-time education, and to those leaving school. And it was asked to consider the effect of the examination on the curricula and syllabuses in the junior cycle, with particular emphasis on its effect on innovative practices. In September 1974 the committee presented its report to the Minister for Education, and the report was published in March 1975.[6]

The chief recommendation contained in the report was that the existing system of external examining at the junior level should be abolished and replaced by 'an on-going service of school-based assessment, supported by external moderation and nationally normed objective tests'.[7] This recommendation of the committee will receive attention later on and so I shall not dwell upon it here. What ought to be pointed out, however, is that to date no action has been taken on the recommendations of the committee. A sub-project, known as the Public Examinations Evaluation Project, which the committee had initiated with a view to training teachers in new methods of examining, has also been terminated.[8]

The second innovation affecting the pedagogy of the curriculum was in the area of curriculum development projects, centred on the junior cycle of the post-primary school.[9] Thus during the early 1970s a number of curriculum projects modelled in a general way upon projects which had been underway in other countries, especially in the United States and England, began to be set up. Notable among these were the Social and Environmental Studies Project (SESP) which was based in St Patrick's Comprehensive School in Shannon and two curriculum projects carried out under the joint auspices of the City of Dublin Vocational Education Committee and the School of Education, Trinity College, Dublin. One of these, the Dublin Humanities Project, was, as the title indicates, concerned with humanistic studies and the other, the Integrated Science Studies Project (ISCIP) was concerned with science. In the course of these projects considerable pilot work in schools was undertaken and some curriculum materials for teaching in the schools were produced. It was hoped that the courses developed by such projects might eventually be recognised as constituting subjects for examination at Intermediate Certificate level and in some cases this has occurred. The future of all projects of this sort has now become somewhat uncertain, however; departmental funding for such projects has been facing difficulties, and in 1977 a separate curriculum development unit was established within the Department of Education itself. Another project, much heralded at the time of its introduction by the then Minister for Education, Richard Burke, and which was aimed at the development of a new course in Irish Studies, has come to nothing.

Aside from curriculum projects of this kind, a new emphasis was to emerge in the area of new programmes in Irish post-primary education from about the mid-1970s onwards, one to which reference has been made already — transition-year programmes and work-preparatory programmes of one type or another. This development was to give rise to a number of related curriculum projects. Recently an EEC-sponsored project on the relationship between school and work has been initiated at the Curriculum Development Centre in St Patrick's Comprehensive School in Shannon; a similar project, the North Mayo Project, is funded by the EEC and the Foundation for Human Development; another, based in Dublin, is sponsored by the City of Dublin Vocational Education Committee and the School of Education in Trinity College.

At this point it is impossible to say what impact any of these measures, be they in the area of examinations reform or curriculum reform, will have on the present course of post-primary education in Ireland. What can be said, however, is that to date, with the possible exception of the work-preparatory programmes, the impact of such measures on the day-to-day conduct of post-primary education in Ireland has been very slight. Thus, ten years after the Minister for Education took initial measures to come to grips with the pedagogical problems arising out of the increased numbers and greater variety of pupils entering post-primary education, little has been done to co-ordinate the primary and post-primary sectors. As if to bear testimony to this, in June 1978 the Minister for Education, John Wilson, set up yet another committee, this one to investigate the transfer from primary to post-primary school. At best, or perhaps at worst, post-primary schools, in the meantime, have begun to adapt more or less satisfactorily along the lines of traditional secondary education to the quite extra-ordinary demands being made upon them.

If the post-primary sector was slow to react to or anticipate demands being made upon it from the primary sector, it must be borne in mind that demands were also being made on it from the third-level sector; and it was to these demands that it paid its first allegiance. This is particularly true of secondary education which had always been largely conceived and developed in terms of the university preparatory. The interests of the third-level sector in the post-primary curriculum, moreover, had always been in the area of curriculum content rather than curriculum pedagogy. And to this day its chief concern remains with the content of various subject syllabuses and the standard of achievement in the Leaving Certificate examination. Choosing the areas of content and standards as those upon which it would concentrate, it was to show a certain disregard for many educational and pedagogical aspects of the post-primary curriculum. In more recent years it has become the architect and prime user of the controversial points system for gaining entrance to third-level education.[10]

The points system is operated by means of assigning different numbers of points to different levels of performance in the subjects presented for matriculation or third-level entry.[11] In general, the greater the number of points that a third-level applicant receives in the university matriculation or Leaving Certificate examination the greater the chances of his gaining a third-level place and of gaining entry to the degree course of his first choice. Accordingly, level of performance in the examinations is the main determinant of whether an applicant will gain university admission or not, and to what degree programme. In addition to the points system, the universities and other third-level institutions may operate other qualifying requirements as well; thus, some specific subjects may be required for entry to certain faculties or degree courses and some subjects may be weighted more heavily than others. Thus, for matriculation in the faculties of science, dairy science, medicine, engineering, architecture, veterinary medicine and general agriculture in the National University of Ireland, applicants were required to present the following subjects in 1981: Irish; English; mathematics; another language from the matriculation programme; a laboratory science subject; and any other subject of the matriculation programme which was not already chosen. Furthermore, the three-language requirement applied to matriculation in all faculties.[12] In the three constituent colleges of the National University of Ireland there has also been provision to give additional weighting to the subject mathematics in the Leaving Certificate examination.

While the points system of selection has been the object of many criticisms in recent years, one issue stands out as a particular grievance. In the conclusion of their study 'The Leaving Certificate and First Year University Performance', Moran and Crowley expressed the view that 'the most telling criticism of the points system is, in our opinion, the manner in which it magnifies the influence of the university and indeed the third-level sector in general on the schools'.[13] It was this same influence that Séan O'Connor was criticising in his celebrated article of 1968 when he wrote that 'there is little point in encouraging a potential university student to develop his interests and aptitudes if the subjects of his interest do not tally with university requirements'.[14] This view is shared by the headmasters and teachers as well, with good reason.

There may be much to be said for the subject requirements of matriculation as they stand. Already I have suggested that they can have the effect of regulating the choice of subjects at post-primary level, thereby ensuring some breadth of studies at that level; thus, one might argue that any influence which encourages a pupil in the study of a language subject, mathematics and a science subject at post-primary level is beneficial. This is not the entire picture, however. Only a relatively small proportion of school leavers go forward to third-level education yet, such is the traditional orientation, organisation and size of many post-primary schools that the matriculation requirements largely shape the programmes of study for pupils who do not intend to go into third-level education as well as for those who do. Moreover, since the arrangements were introduced whereby the subjects on the Leaving Certificate course may qualify for purposes of university matriculation or third-level entry, third-level institutions have a more direct influence than before in shaping the syllabuses of subjects at post-primary level. But can the criterion of suitability of a subject for purposes of matriculation or third-level entry be justified as a requirement which is to be met by subjects on the Leaving Certificate programme?

Pupils who do not have the interests or aptitudes suited to third-level education should have available to them the full range of post-primary school subjects, drawn up and developed with a view to meeting their particular educational requirements; certainly, they should not be limited to those subjects which are drawn up with the intention of being acceptable for matriculation or third-level entry purposes. This is where the real weight of third-level entry requirements on the curriculum of the post-primary school becomes evident, for as long as third-level entry requirements specify particular subjects as acceptable for meeting the entry requirements, those subjects not so specified stand in danger of being neglected. As a consequence of this, universities are very understandably brought under pressure to have a change of heart on the question of the subjects recognised for matriculation and on the question of the points system. But is it the universities who are to carry the responsibility for the non-availability of non-matriculation subjects on the Leaving Certificate course?

There are a number of inter-related factors at work here. In discussing the question of curriculum provision for meeting the practical demands of living earlier on I adverted to the constraints imposed on second-level education in attempting to promote practical subjects. It is the kind of constraint which points to the care which ought to be taken by the universities and other third-level authorities in framing their entry requirements. To judge by recent developments in other countries coping with the problem of selection for higher education, a problem which by no means is unique to Ireland, Irish universities might perhaps have adopted too conservative and insufficiently discriminating an approach in some respects in the past. Yet while one would wish them to be open to the kinds of practices coming into use in some European countries and the United States, practices such as giving a specific and positive weighting to work experience,[15] it would be a mistake to think that the responsibility for the nature and range of subjects available in post-primary education in Ireland lies solely or even largely on the universities. But where it does lie exactly is difficult to say.

To an extent the responsibility lies with the universities and to an extent it lies with those who are charged with the shaping and conduct of second-level education. (And here again the failure to develop a philosophy of post-primary education in line with the aspirations and reform moves of the mid-1960s must be mentioned: it would be a philosophy in which second-level education would not necessarily be so closely tied to the requirements of third-level education as was secondary education in earlier times.) To an extent, also, societal and parental demand for subjects which qualify for third-level entry undoubtedly militate against the fortunes of any non-matriculation subjects which might be introduced at second level. It may be, in fact, that this is where the main support for the present arrangement is actually rooted and, if this is so, then both second-level and third-level authorities may be more tightly bound in this matter than anyone thinks.

Before leaving this issue, one or two other points might be mentioned. Inertia within the post-primary sector, and possibly even its willingness to use the third-level sector as a scapegoat, has been suggested as being part of the problem.[16] Furthermore, there are increasingly other non-third level forces which bear on post-primary schooling also. These include such pressures as the growing demand to establish a much stronger link between school and work than has existed in the past and care ought to be taken that pressure such as this, no less than pressures from third-level institutions, does not come to dictate to the post-primary sector in the future.

In discussing the matriculation requirements and entry requirements of third-level institutions, and in discussion of the relationship between the second-level and the third-level sectors generally, the points system of selection and its alleged impact on second-level schooling has tended to monopolise. While this is an issue of major importance there is also a second major point and one which, in many ways, is the more fundamental question. And this is none other than the question of what constitutes a general education and the related question of whether the requirements of entry to third level do or ought necessarily tally with those of general education understood as a preparation for life.

Increasingly the view is being expressed in regard to post-primary education in Ireland, and it is a view which earlier chapters have attempted to articulate more fully, that the requirements of general education at post-primary level and the present entry requirements to third-level education in Ireland are not one and the same. By the standards of the preceding chapter, curriculum provision in Irish post-primary education is, in general, considerably too restricted to provide a reasonable opportunity for general education. By this same standard, meeting the matriculation requirements of the National University of Ireland, for example, would not of itself give testimony to the satisfactory completion of a general education. Indeed such are the requirements that they militate against it because, indirectly at least, they discourage forms of education which are not in line with matriculation requirements but which may constitute an important element in general education. So much so is this the case, that one is forced to ask now if the stated aim of the Leaving Certificate course to prepare pupils for further education — at least if it is understood in the narrow sense of enabling pupils to matriculate — is not to some extent inconsistent with the idea of a broad general education as a preparation for life? This is so because not only do the entry requirements seem to encourage a narrow range of studies at post-primary level but the attainment of satisfactory standards within this narrow range seems to be a full-time educational occupation for most pupils. It is one which, in view of the strong competitive element, seems to limit the scope for other broader educational activities at post-primary level.

Curriculum organisation and the hidden curriculum

In recent years considerable attention has been devoted to the question of the hidden curriculum.[17] Essentially the hidden curriculum, as contrasted with the public curriculum, refers to those learnings which are largely the side-effects of the nature, structure and operations of institutionalised schooling. In the conduct of schooling, through the way in which schools are organised, the role of teachers *vis-à-vis* pupils, the ratio of teachers to pupils, the school timetable and the organisation of subjects, the exercise of authority, and the social composition of the teaching and pupil bodies, there is unavoidably transmitted to pupils many and varied learnings. These include principles, views of life, views of the nature and uses of knowledge, and values and attitudes on a wide range of issues including those of schooling and learning itself.

Some have spoken of the hidden curriculum as being, in a sense, more fundamental than the public curriculum, and most are in agreement that it can exercise a considerable influence on pupil learning, including the formation of attitudes and the development of social and interpersonal skills.[18] Chief among the learnings attributed to the influence of the hidden curriculum are learning to live with others; learning to be patient; learning to withstand evaluation and assessment by others; learning to get to know the ropes and the power structures, and how to please those in authority; and the learning of norms that are of relevance to society.

While these aspects of the hidden curriculum have attracted attention only in recent years, the principles governing the hidden curriculum have long been operational and, some would argue, for questionable motives. Already I have referred to the hidden curriculum and the place which it occupied in the grammar school tradition; in the Irish case, one thinks also of the religious ethos encouraged in private secondary schools and the prevalence of single-sex schools. More recently, contemporary critics of schooling such as Michael Katz and Bowles and Gintis in America, and M.F.D. Young and others in England, have argued that schools, through the hidden curriculum, have served very largely to promote the interests and the kinds of knowledge which are favoured by the dominant groups in society.[19]

Little or no study of this aspect of the curriculum has been carried out in respect of post-primary education in Ireland. In the absence of such research one must keep an open mind on the matter, while at the same time taking cognisance of what has been said with regard to schooling elsewhere. If what is said to be the case elsewhere applies in Ireland, then one might conclude that in some important respects the hidden curriculum prepares pupils for various roles in society. At the same time, there may be some respects in which such socialisation is effected through means of a curtailment of personal freedom for the benefit of those who have greatest power in the shaping of schooling rather than the pupils themselves.

There is one aspect of the hidden curriculum which has not received quite as much attention as other aspects. Since it is concerned largely with pedagogical aspects of the hidden curriculum, however, it warrants further attention here. Underlining the importance of this aspect of the curriculum, John Dewey, who was aware of the problem before there was a more general recognition of it, wrote as follows:

> Perhaps the greatest of all pedagogical fallacies is the notion that a person learns only the particular thing he is studying at the time. Collateral learning in the way of formation of enduring attitudes, of likes and dislikes, may be and often is much more important than the spelling lesson or lesson in geography or history that is learned. For these attitudes are fundamentally what count in the future.[20]

Thus while a pupil is learning history or mathematics or French, or any other subject, he may also be learning to like or dislike history, mathematics, French or whatever. He may be developing a liking for and an interest in learning generally or he may be developing a dislike for learning, for schooling and for all that is associated with it.

In any consideration of the pedagogical character of the curriculum of post-primary education in Ireland, one of its characteristics which comes most readily to notice is the organisation of curriculum content along discipline-dominated subject lines. In this arrangement curriculum content is selected and organised for teaching well in advance of its actually being taught; it is organised into various discrete subjects. Some subjects or group of subjects are required or core subjects; the great number remain elective. Frequently these subjects are co-terminous in range of content and method with an established academic discipline; in other cases some practical activity, as in the case of woodwork, becomes the delimiting focus;

other organisational foci serve as the organising centres in the case of subjects such as physical education and civics. And while considerations of logic, sequence and orderly neatness are to the fore in all cases, the selection and presentation of content is also determined by considerations of the ages and intellectual levels of pupils.[21]

Curriculum content in Irish post-primary education, as was seen earlier on, is organised into some sixty or so different subjects between the junior and senior cycles. In the case of almost all of these subjects, including all of those examinable in the public examinations, a syllabus of greater or less detail is provided.[22] In the case of all subjects, with the notable exception of religion, the syllabus is drawn up and approved by the Department of Education in conjunction with the syllabus committees. Once approved, a subject syllabus is in theory, and largely also in practice, identical for all pupils. As was seen earlier on, however, one or more syllabuses, including honours syllabuses, exist in many subjects at the different levels.

While any given syllabus within a subject is one and the same for all pupils who follow it all over the country, there is a strong likelihood that the methods of teaching it, and indeed of teaching syllabuses in many other subjects as well, will also be very much of a kind. And while this might be attributable in part to the influence of the public examinations, it is attributable in part also to the type of curriculum organisation employed which tends to emphasise expository discourse and techniques of explanation. That is to say that while the subject curriculum does allow for different kinds of teaching, including project work and laboratory work for example, it is also generally associated with a highly didactic and linguistic form of teaching in which the emphasis is upon 'lectures', questions and answers, and written exercises.[23]

The extent to which the subject organisation of curriculum dominates post-primary education in Ireland is noteworthy; it is the single subject which constitutes the basic unit of instruction at all levels and in all forms of post-primary school. To be recognised as a full-time pupil one must be enrolled in a minimum number of subjects and, although the regulation no longer holds whereby to pass an examination a pupil has to pass in a minimum number of subjects, examination success in practical terms still depends on 'passing' a certain number of subjects. Thus, for matriculation purposes on the basis of the Leaving Certificate, the National

University of Ireland demands that a pupil should have 'passed' or attained a minimum standard in at least six subjects in the Leaving Certificate examination. The much-heeded points system is also based on performance in subjects.[24] Teachers and schools, no less than pupils, are governed by subjects: thus, for a secondary school to become a recognised school it must offer a minimum number and range of subjects.[25] As for the teachers, they are teachers of subjects: thus there is the Irish teacher, the mathematics teacher, the history teacher, and so on. For the most part teachers are university graduates who are recognised by the state as teachers partly on the basis of their subject-based university degrees.

It is true, of course, that curriculum content has to be organised in some way for teaching purposes and that teachers, and indeed pupils to a lesser extent, may be expected to be more expert in some areas of the school curriculum than in others. And it may be that the popularity, if one may so call it, of the subject curriculum organisation owes much to the fact that it caters for requirements such as these. But its popularity arises from other considerations as well, particularly from the way in which it lends itself to planning and organisation at both school and national levels. And while this may be good in itself, sight must not be lost of the possible impact which it has on schooling.

In the first place, the subject curriculum is a very visible or public one. That is to say that with curriculum content organised in a predetermined and fairly orderly or logical sequence, it is possible to identify in advance of teaching, the various topics or elements of a subject — for example the concepts, theories, facts, principles, examples and illustrations — which are to be taught. Indeed, as practised in Irish post-primary education, it is often the case that an entire outline of a five-year course in a subject is set forth in the form of a reasonably detailed syllabus in the *Rules*, thereby facilitating the organisation and distribution of teaching time, and so on. With a curriculum that is as visible as this, schools are enabled to plan well in advance for purposes of teaching, space and facilities, teacher supply, and textbooks and materials, for example. And knowing precisely what lies before them, as it were, both teachers and pupils can pace themselves accordingly.

The organisation of the post-primary curriculum is significantly more influenced by subject considerations than that of the primary school. Thus there is the subject teacher in the post-primary school as opposed to the class teacher in the primary school. It is true, of course, that as a pupil moves through the primary school the more integrated approach of the infant and junior classes becomes more differentiated into a subject approach in the senior classes. This differentiation is emphasised in the post-primary school through the more systematic apportioning of teaching time to different subjects, in some cases the use of different subject rooms, and the switch to subject teachers.

Additional to this increased differentiation, however, is an increase in the specification of courses and syllabuses. No longer is one in the area of suggested approaches and more general content guidelines; now there are stipulated syllabuses and texts leading to specific examinations. There is, in practice, almost a total absence of individual teacher autonomy in the matter of syllabus or course development; this has become a more centralised function of the syllabus committees. And relevance to the subject, coverage of the subject, bringing pupils up to pre-university standards or higher at Leaving Certificate level, rather than primarily pedagogical and broader educational considerations, would appear to have become the dominant considerations of the syllabus committees. With the adoption of these subject syllabuses by the Department of Education the way is paved for centralised control of curriculum. A situation is created in which one is set firmly on the road to what Freire[26] has aptly termed 'banking education', in which the emphasis will be on passing on to pupils the sacred, chosen content, content to be reproduced at examination time.

It is difficult to assess the impact of schooling where a central feature of it is the centralised control of curricula such as one finds in the case of post-primary education in Ireland. To recognise that in such matters one is moving in the area of the hidden curriculum suggests, moreover, that one's observation may be no more than speculative. Nonetheless, it may be salutary even to speculate on the possible impact on the pupils' perceptions of knowledge and of schooling of such an approach.

When there is as much emphasis upon centralised control, organisation, quantification and standardisation of knowledge as one finds in Irish post-primary education, features supported by the system of public examinations, the view of knowledge presented to pupils is liable to be of a most distorted kind — the world of knowledge may well come to be seen in terms of a pre-packaged world of book learning and abstractions. For under existing circumstances it is difficult to see how knowledge can come to be seen as anything more than something which is 'out there' in books, highly organised, readily identifiable and quantifiable, and for others to discover in the first place. Under such circumstances there is every chance that pupils will conceive of knowledge as mere content to be committed to memory and reproduced upon request, as having little or nothing to do with action, application or the conduct of living. Accordingly, one of the more likely effects of this approach is to make a curriculum which already is very bookish even more bookish still. It is a feature of conventional schooling which, surely, has much to do with the emphasis on merely cognitive skill and verbal dexterity at the expense of other facets of the development of personality, such as a sense of initiative and responsibility, a feature to which attention has been drawn already.

To say that the curriculum is bookish is first of all to say that it is to books, to linguistic or bookish experiences, to the written word, to paper and pencil work, very largely, that it turns for its content. In an earlier chapter it was seen how the more traditional academic and literary subjects monopolise the subjects offered at post-primary level in Irish education. The more recently introduced practical subjects fare markedly less well at Leaving Certificate level in particular; it was also seen that the emphasis on practical subjects at Group Certificate level was giving way to a more literary one. Thus, while there is quite a number of practical subjects on the curriculum, both by dent of pupil choice and by dent of the didactic and linguistic emphasis encouraged by the type of curriculum organisation employed, literary or bookish studies predominate.

Yet the curriculum may be said to be bookish in another important respect as well. It is a bookishness that also originates in the organisation of content which one associates with the subject curriculum. Whitehead's observation regarding the 'fatal disconnection of subjects which kills the vitality of our modern curriculum', which I have quoted already,[27] seems eminently applicable to the Irish scene where the world of knowledge as presented in the post-primary school is, or certainly appears to be, a world of compartmentalised and separate packages of knowledge, with each bearing little or no relationship to the other. It is a feature of schooling which is effectively promoted and maintained by the strong emphasis on subject boundaries and by the separation of teacher from teacher on the basis of subjects and other organisational practices, notably the timetable.

In the preceding chapter it was argued that there may well be grounds to charge the public content of post-primary education in Ireland with a degree of irrelevancy. It may well be the case that pedagogical factors are at work in this direction too. Yet aside from the question of the impact of the highly compartmentalised curriculum of the post-primary school in Ireland on the pupils who undergo it, and the image of knowledge and learning which it creates, there is also the question of its suitability from the point of view of motivation and interest. And straight away it can be said that the subject-type curriculum has long been found wanting from a motivational point of view.[28] Knowledge as found in subjects and books, as arranged in school timetables, and taught under the shadow of examinations, cannot be for many pupils the most inspiring of propositions, a situation which is undoubtedly aggravated by contrast with more modern and appealing forms of communication, notably television. And to return to the point made above, no matter how important one might consider the chosen content to be, unless the pedagogical and motivational factors are attended to, the teaching may all be for nought, or worse still, for rejection. This is a point which the unpedagogic viewpoint, long dominant in Irish secondary education, does not acknowledge sufficiently. And until it does, until considerations regarding what should be taught are more influenced by considerations of how it can best be organised for teaching, the more fundamental values of schooling about which there is a good measure of agreement may remain in jeopardy.

To an extent not sufficiently appreciated, perhaps, considerations of the impact of the highly organised and pre-packaged nature of subject matter as presented to pupils ought to be borne in mind in developing the school curriculum. In addition sight must not be lost of the associated or collateral learnings to which the public curriculum gives rise. In these regards, and possibly others also, there is reason to believe that greater attention ought to be given to the hidden curriculum of post-primary education in Ireland.

Provision for individual differences
That attention to the factor of individual differences is of the greatest educational and pedagogical importance has come to be widely recognised. Yet, even though certain measures are taken in Irish post-primary education to provide for individual differences, in some important and fundamental respects post-primary school-

ing, inadvertently or otherwise, does much to institutionalise and perpetuate uniformity. Thus, irrespective of their individual characteristics, pupils entering post-primary school are, for the most part, faced with what are substantially the same courses, subjects and examinations.

Among the ways in which an attempt is made to provide for individualisation at the junior cycle are the provision of lower courses and higher courses in subjects like English, Irish and mathematics. And there are some differences between the require-ments to be met by junior-cycle pupils following the Group Certificate course and those following the Intermediate Certificate course. In addition to the core of subjects to be followed by all junior-cycle pupils, there is also provision for some free choice of subjects[29] and for some remedial education. At senior cycle Irish remains the only compulsory subject of study of the five subjects which must be taken. And it might be argued that at senior cycle, in particular, the range of subjects and alternative syllabuses available is not ungenerous.

Such provisions, however, do not cater adequately for individual differences and they do not introduce sufficient variety and flexibility into the existing curriculum of the post-primary school. This is so because what is in question, basically, is not the extent to which existing curriculum practice in Irish post-primary education provides for alternatives but rather the adequacy of the basic model and understandings of curriculum provision which are employed. The model is such that in a number of important respects it is at odds with the notion of providing for individual differences and for flexibility of programming and content.

A number of features cause this effect, an effect which is all the more profound when certain traditional preferences in the matter of the content and practice of post-primary education in Ireland are taken into account. A fundamental feature of the post-primary curriculum in Ireland, as has been seen already, is the adoption of the subject as the basic unit of instruction. Thus, for example, a pupil either studies English or he does not study it at all; independent sub-units of English such as the short story, the works of Shakespeare, twentieth-century Anglo-Irish literature, for example, do not exist in themselves, even at senior level. Thus, one cannot choose to study aspects of English; one must study 'all' of it, both literature and language. As a result, the basic unit of curriculum is quan-titatively enormous and not very conducive to flexibility; to study six or seven units, that is subjects, constitutes a full-time course of study for most pupils.[30] And such are the regulations that the same minimum number of subjects, at either junior level or senior level, must be taken by all pupils, irrespective of ability.

In addition to the quantitative aspect of a curriculum unit or element, there is also the question of its duration; not only are subjects comprehensive with regard to content but they are also extensive in regard to duration. Thus, the Intermediate Certificate course in English is three years long, as are all other Intermediate Certificate examination courses. This means that not only can a pupil study no more than six or seven subjects simultaneously, because of their considerable quantity, but those which he does choose he will study for a minimum of three years. A similar arrangement applies at Leaving Certificate level, though in this case the course is normally of two years' duration.

There are other restrictions of a similar kind. Since, for example, almost all subjects available at senior cycle build on subjects available at junior cycle – with junior cycle courses, in practice, usually becoming pre-requisite to senior cycle courses – a pupil at senior cycle is limited very largely to those subjects which he had taken at junior level or which are closely related to such subjects. Thus, rarely does one find a pupil beginning the study of science or foreign language subjects, for example, at senior cycle and for most pupils the basic unit of the post-primary curriculum is the subject which extends over a period of five or six years of schooling. There is little or no allowance for the changing or developing interests or aptitudes of pupils; yet the choices which are made in the early years of the post-primary school are made at an age which many would consider to be a difficult and unsuitable one.[31]

The examination system exercises an influence here also. Thus, the reason why subjects extend over such a long period of time, and why it is difficult to break into new subjects at senior level, is because for most pupils there are but two (three, if one includes the Group Certificate examination) official standards of measurable achievement in Irish post-primary education. No standards intermediate to, prior to, or consequent upon these exist. Furthermore, all subjects studied by a pupil at a given time will be studied at only one or other of these levels. Thus, a pupil taking Leaving Certificate mathematics, physics and chemistry, who might wish to take up studies in French or German at Intermediate Certificate level, would not be in a position to do so. The combined forces of curriculum organisation and the examination system militate against it. And with only two or three levels of attainment in any subject or group of subjects officially recognised, and with no provision for the recognition of different levels of study or attainment in different subjects by a given pupil at a given time — some subjects at Intermediate Certificate standard and others at Leaving Certificate standard — the rigid curriculum structure of the post-primary curriculum is maintained.

The issues under consideration above might be described as structural characteristics of the model of curriculum provision in Irish post-primary education. Other features of a non-structural nature, which are also part of the Irish post-primary education tradition, serve to complement them in the maintenance of uniformity and the minimisation of flexibility. Chief among these are the close relationship which exists between post-primary education and the demands of universities; the traditionally high status of some subjects; practical limitations on curriculum provision such as school size, costs of facilities, and availability of teachers; the centralised nature of post-primary organisation and the associated implications for textbooks, publishers, school suppliers, and so on; and the encouragement given to didactic teaching.

The Irish tradition in post-primary education, as was seen in earlier chapters, is one in which secondary rather than vocational education enjoyed the favour of status and prestige. With this went a demand for the academic and literary subjects of the secondary school over the employment-oriented and practical subjects of the vocational school. It was the traditional secondary school subjects also which, alone, were acceptable to the universities for matriculation purposes and which also found favour with powerful and prestigious employment bodies such as the civil service, the banks and others. It is hardly surprising, then, that it was those subjects also which found favour among parents and school authorities keen to set their children on the more likely success routes in life. The outcome for the curriculum of post-primary education in Ireland was a marked imbalance in the participation rates in secondary and vocational or practical subjects. This imbalance had the effect of reducing the range of curriculum options open to post-primary pupils, and it further supported uniformity. In earlier times it meant that fewer pupils sought entry to the vocational school and, more recently, it has meant a continuing disinclination towards participation in subjects of a vocational kind.

The traditional demand for certain post-primary school subjects, coupled with the fact noted earlier that the basic curriculum unit, the subject, is quantitatively large, has also served to minimise variety and the possibility of catering for a wide range of differences among pupils. To this day, Irish, English and mathematics, are still taken in senior cycle by almost all pupils. Yet of these, only Irish is a required subject. At junior cycle, however, a core of subjects is required, a core which, as was seen, varies a little depending on the type of post-primary school which a pupil attends and the course which he is following. Owing to factors discussed already, such as the difficulty of taking up for study new subjects in the senior cycle, the influence of the core requirement in junior cycle continues to be felt at senior cycle. By tradition, then, it has become almost unimaginable that a pupil studying for the Leaving Certificate examination should not study both English and mathematics, along with Irish. The widespread cognisance taken of university matriculation requirements encourages this, of course, as does the seemingly widespread belief that a Leaving Certificate without English or mathematics is seriously deficient.

Size of school is another factor in determining range of curriculum choice; the range of subjects which can be offered at a reasonable cost is considerably limited in the smaller school. And while a number of larger schools now exist, especially in the urban centres, the proportion of small secondary and vocational schools throughout the country still is, and always has been, quite high. As a consequence, a further restriction on the range of subject choice which can be offered to pupils has become built into the traditional pattern of curriculum provision in the Irish post-primary school.

But chief among the factors which perpetuate uniformity, which militate most against individualisation of programmes, is the very high degree of centralisation which is found in Irish post-primary education. Thus, by and large, only those subjects and those syllabuses approved by the Minister for Education qualify for state aid and for inclusion in the public examinations in the non-vocational sector, and to a lesser degree in the vocational sector.[32] As a consequence in very many cases, exactly the same subjects, the same syllabuses and the same prescribed and non-prescribed materials are being taught and studied throughout the entire country as pupils from one corner of the land to the other prepare to take the same examination papers, even the same examination questions. The objective, it would almost appear, is to approximate to that state of affairs castigated by Pearse under the intermediate system, of which he wrote, 'precisely the same textbooks are being read to-night in every secondary school and college in Ireland'.[33] Although such centralisation may appear to have advantages for purposes of certification and standardisation, one must question seriously, however, the educational and pedagogical impact of such a regimental approach to schooling and its disregard for the factor of individual and local or regional differences.

At a time of renewed interest in the idea of a common curriculum for all,[34] it might appear somewhat odd to be objecting to a common core of studies for all pupils. It is one thing, however, to have a common core; it is quite another to have identical courses for everyone. Thus in a previous chapter the basis was laid for arguing for a certain common core for all pupils; there it was suggested that one of the requirements of a general education as a preparation for life is to pass on certain common understandings, values and attitudes of society. But whether common studies should dominate the curriculum is another matter; and so is the question of whether the common elements should be identical and be taught or presented in an identical manner for all pupils.

While some choice of content and, to a lesser degree, of method may exist in Irish post-primary education, the likelihood is that it is far from enough. And while it may be true that there are pupils who benefit from the courses on offer, Raven's research suggests very strongly that there is considerable disenchantment with them.[35] Moreover, the fact that some pupils may benefit from the courses on offer is hardly an argument for not extending or improving the range of choice for these or any other pupils. And in the case of pupils who do not benefit, it may not be just a matter of failing to make suitable subjects available to pupils. There are those who are of the view that not only might pupils be gaining nothing worthwhile from the actual programmes and subjects on offer — irrespective of what justificatory arguments may be exhumed in support of them, they are untenable if pupils do not actually benefit from such courses — but that failure to achieve or even to maintain an interest in such offerings as exist may seriously contribute to feelings of frustration and alienation which can, in turn, manifest themselves in delinquency and even more serious forms of anti-social and criminal behaviour.[36]

In summary, while it is true that the past fifteen years have seen the introduction of some new school subjects and modifications of existing programmes, it is questionable if the changes have succeeded in providing a sufficient range of choice for pupils who, as a group, have undergone substantial change in the past two decades or for a society which has experienced major social and economic development. While the evidence which exists does not provide comparative data with earlier generations of post-primary school pupils, it does strongly suggest that the present post-primary school population does not find the post-primary school curriculum — indeed the entire post-primary school experience — as enticing or fulfilling as one might wish it to be. There is evidence, further-more, that many teachers feel likewise.[37] The failure to provide more fully for individual differences is a likely factor in causing this state of affairs.

The public examinations
No less dominating a feature of the curriculum of post-primary education in Ireland than its rigid organisational features, and no less pregnant with possibilities for the shaping of learning and teaching, are the various public examinations. Long criticised as the chief culprits in Irish post-primary education from their beginnings with the Intermediate Education Act of 1878, the public examinations still exist in substantially unchanged form and many of their ill effects would also appear to remain. The most serious of these are the control which the examinations exert over the aims of schooling, and through this, over the curriculum both public and hidden.

To a considerable degree the day-to-day aims, objectives and working philosophies of Irish post-primary education appear to be examination oriented and the pressures to be so are great. Generally speaking it is the school which pulls off the greatest number of 'honours' combined with the fewest 'failures' in the examinations that is held in highest esteem and individual teachers are accorded recognition on the same grounds. But it is the pupils who have the biggest stake in the examinations. Those who perform well have much to gain thereby in terms of educational and employment opportunities. This being so, it can hardly be a source of wonder that schools should be so heavily examination conscious. But do the examinations warrant such primacy of place? To answer this question it will be necessary, first of all, to take a closer look at how they work.

The three main public examinations share many common features. In general, each examination takes place once a year and each subject is examined usually over a two- to three-hour period under tightly supervised conditions. There are practical examinations in some subjects and some provision for taking account of a pupil's course work, but the vast majority of the examining takes the form of a year- or programme-end, written examination. The examinations are centrally organised and the correction of scripts is organised and carried out under the general supervision of the Department of Education. Ordinarily school teachers are hired for the purpose of correcting scripts, and certain guidelines and procedures are adopted with a view to standardising the marking.

In speaking of the pedagogy of the examinations it is probably more to the point to speak of them in terms of their function rather than their purpose. For, irrespective of what their purpose may be or may be considered to be, it is in terms of their function that their impact on the educational system is felt. In general the examinations function directly in three ways: they give a measure of a pupil's level of education and intelligence in relation to others; they form a basis for career choices by teachers, pupils and parents, and a basis for selection by employers, schools, institutions of third-level education and government agencies; and, allied to this, they serve as an entry qualification for many forms of employment and further studies. Additionally, external examinations, it has been found, exercise an enormous influence on what is actually taught in schools, how it is taught and what is learned.[38] Post-primary education in Ireland is no exception.

It is in the indirect functions of the examinations – their influence on curriculum, teaching and learning – that their chief pedagogical significance lies, and it is to this aspect of the Irish examinations that I wish to devote chief attention. Before doing so, however, it will be helpful to take a closer look at the technical quality of these examinations since some doubt has been cast on their adequacy in this respect in recent years.

There is a considerable demonstration of public confidence in and reliance on the examinations, and on the Leaving Certificate examination in particular, both as an index of ability and as a predictor of future performance in a career or different forms of advanced study. That this is so is not, of course, any necessary indication that the examinations merit such confidence and reliance. Indeed there may be good grounds for doubting the suitability of any one examination or kind of examination to perform the varied functions demanded of the Irish post-primary school examinations.[39] In the final analysis, any examination or form of assessment can perform a useful service only to the extent that it can assess learning, or its absence, with accuracy, validity and reliability. Yet it is in this regard that the technical adequacy of the Irish post-primary school examinations, and the Leaving Certificate examination in particular, may be suspect. Moreover, such are the demands made on the examinations, and the uses to which they are put, that unless they possess a very high degree of accuracy, validity and reliability, there is the possibility of grave injustice being done to examination candidates, institutions of further education and employment bodies.

A notable feature of the Irish post-primary school examination system is its complete dismissal of the factor of luck. Thus a pupil may be ill, or injured or excessively nervous and no account is taken of it; a pupil may have the good or bad fortune of having a particularly good or a particularly poor 'examination teacher' and no account is taken of it. The public examination system simply ignores the plain and simple fact that a pupil may be off form or unable to do as well as he might for a thousand and one reasons. And surely it can be no other way in a system where an approximately two- or three-week period at the end of a two- or three-year examination course, or of a pupil's entire post-primary career, is normally the only period of testing. Not only does such an approach to assessment introduce untold psychological factors and pressures, not only does it put a premium on luck, but it very likely severely reduces the possibility of accurately assessing actual ability and attainment.

But luck in the sense of a candidate being lucky enough to write a good examination, for whatever reason, is not the only factor that is liable to tip the balance in a pupil's favour or disfavour, as the case may be. For despite the obvious necessity of an examination to be reliable in its assessment of pupils if results are to be fair and dependable, a now widely quoted study has suggested that the Leaving Certificate examination, like other such examinations, may be unreliable.[40] Based on an investigation of the 1967 Leaving Certificate examination, the study concludes that despite the taking of measures to guard against bias or error, there was a good chance that different markers would mark the same script differently. Such were the differences that in some cases it could have meant the difference between a safe pass and a clear fail. The degree of unreliability was such, the authors concluded, as to 'cast serious doubt on the value of an overall mark in an individual subject'. In general, it was found that there was a one in twenty chance for marks to swing up and down by about 10 per cent in each direction.[41] Thus, added to the other factors of luck already identified, there was also the question of luck in who was to mark a candidate's scripts.

This study, although not reported until 1970, was actually based on the Leaving Certificate examination of 1967 and a number of changes have been made in the examination and in the marking system since 1967. One of these changes, the adoption of a letter-grade system in place of the old numerical grade system, has probably increased the possibility of error.[42] Despite the time-lag since the appearance of the study, one further aspect of the Leaving Certificate examination which has been brought to light by the study of Madaus and Macnamara should be mentioned: the Leaving Certificate examination is popularly regarded as a measure of a pupil's knowledge and general intellectual ability and the course, as was seen, is specifically said to aim at preparing pupils for further studies and for entry to open society, but Madaus and Macnamara found that the examination, at both pass and honours levels, might well be little more than largely a measure of memorised knowledge.[43] This finding supports a very long-standing criticism of the public examinations. In the absence of a similar study being made since the changes introduced after the Madaus and Macnamara study, it is not possible to say with assurance what the present-day situation is. What can be said is that the Leaving Certificate results are still used widely for a number of purposes in respect of which their predictive validity does not appear to be as high as it might be. This is certainly true in respect of selection for university.[44]

Whatever changes have been introduced into the Leaving Certificate examination since 1967, and however successful they have or have not been in resolving the difficulties mentioned, it does not alter the thrust of my argument. This is so because, one way or the other, it will be well to keep in mind the foregoing remarks on the possible limitations of the examinations as assessment devices. My main concern here, however, is with the impact of the examinations on the conduct of schooling. And this influence stands whether or not the examinations are as reliable and valid as one would wish them to be.

If the technical quality of the examinations, at least at the time of the Madaus and Macnamara study, do not appear to warrant the influence which the examinations exercise, the power which they have secured for themselves does explain it. While no detailed studies exist which show the actual effect of the public examinations on the content, teaching and kind of learning that goes on in Irish post-primary education, one may hazard a reasonable guess as to what this is likely to be, based on the sad history of these examinations. The question largely becomes what does one need to know and be able to do in order to succeed in the examination. And as this question is answered, the actual curriculum of the post-primary school is drawn up.

Madaus and Macnamara in their study argued that memorised knowledge was all that was necessary, very often, in order to pass or, indeed, to gain honours in the Leaving Certificate examination. A necessary and related characteristic of the kind of knowledge and intellectual skill demanded by the public examinations is that it should be examinable knowledge or skill. And in the case of Ireland, and most likely other countries also, this would appear to exclude learning outside of the cognitive domain. Even then, the emphasis would appear to be on convergent thinking as opposed to creativity and divergent thinking.

To say that there is something wrong with the examinations because they concentrate on examinable knowledge may be of little consequence in itself. What is of considerable consequence, however, is the likelihood that the easily examinable is of the least consequence as well, a point which gets some support in the findings of Madaus and Macnamara and from the *ICE Report* on the Inter-mediate Certificate examination.[45] But objectionable as it may be that the examinations should concentrate on examining what is of least importance, the seemingly inevitable corollary of this situation is still more objectionable, namely that that which is examinable, or likely to be examined, is what is taught and pre-sumably studied. As Ó Catháin put it grimly, it is a situation in which teachers determine to 'concentrate on the corpse, the spirit can't be examined'.[46] The consequences of this for the public examinations and courses of studies are not comforting to contem-plate, for it means that since the examinations came into existence an unerring process of sifting out the examinable has fully woven itself into the fabric of the Irish post-primary curriculum; and even though attempts at reform may have been made from time to time, the effect of these too have become diluted in time. Whatever the course or courses, the outcome is likely to be a curriculum that is not simply examination oriented but one which emphasises what would appear to be of least importance as well!

In a situation where 'passing' the examinations and amassing points for admission to third-level education, as the case may be, appears to have become the overriding objective of Irish post-primary education, the sad truth of the matter is that Irish post-primary schooling seems to have abdicated its commitment to the attainment of its espoused educational aims, however inadequately these may have been conceived and expressed. Replacing such aims with what, from an educational point of view, are in themselves largely artificial obstacles to be overcome, that is the examinations — at least to the extent that the examinations dictate the actual curriculum — has had the resultant effect of creating equally artificial curricula. And until such time as the vicious circle is broken, artificially created objectives will give rise to artificial curricula. Meanwhile, worthwhile and necessary educational experience regrettably goes abegging.

At this point the influence of the examinations on the kind of teaching engaged in in Irish schools comes into focus. As Raven's study shows, teachers are to a rather alarming degree examination oriented.[47] And it could hardly be otherwise when pressures for examination success are considerable. The effect on post-primary education is likely to be unsavoury; with success in the examination as the goal to which the teacher aspires, one cannot reasonably expect teaching to be carried on for educational reasons as much as for reasons of examination success. And with substantial amounts of material prescribed for learning, 'examination teaching' might well be the only way to cope. Hence, over the years there has been a proliferation of all sorts of 'learning aids' — notes for study, trial examinations, collections of past examination papers for study purposes, and a variety of tricks of the trade in the preparation of examination classes.

Of central importance, however, is the impact of the examinations on pupil learning. And here, again, one is back in the uncertain area of the hidden curriculum where one can only speculate on the possible effects of the examinations on learning. Nonetheless it is very likely that the methods of study and learning employed by the pupil, as well as the conceptions of the nature of study and learning which they develop, are greatly affected by the kind of teaching and learning which the examinations encourage. As a direct product of the mechanics of the examination 'method of teaching' and examination-oriented 'curriculum materials', pupils are encouraged to conceive of matters in highly systematic, categorical and unimaginative terms. Not only is one poem summarised, analysed, 'discussed' and in cases partially memorised, but dozens of them receive a similar treatment. It is the same with literary and historical figures and events, geographical phenomena and mathematical and scientific formulae, 'theories' and 'experiments'. Through its summarised form in the various 'learning aids' and teacher's notes, the world of learning takes on an unreal appearance. Everything is more or less cut and dried. Disputes do not arise in the world of science; the great decisions of history were arrived at without unnecessary debate and uncertainty as to their appropriateness; poets and popes alike were pre-ordained for office.

Debating, thinking, questioning and investigating may come to be seen as wasteful of time. Originality, which has been known to be associated with error, may be seen as a loser's strategy in the race for marks. Pupils preparing for examinations may well be advised to stick to the tested and tried 'views of your own' and 'evaluations' provided. And so, just as the teacher is encouraged to capitalise on time-saving teaching strategies, so also is the pupil encouraged to avail only of the short cuts to 'wisdom'. There is little time for the non-book or non-vicarious but time-consuming learning experiences. Most of all, there is little time for learning what real learning is, what it means, and how to go about it.

Despite these limitations, however, and despite the array of pre-packaged knowledge readily, though not always inexpensively, available to them, pupils do insist on some genuine learning experiences; and these are likely to include collateral or concomitant learnings of the kind referred to earlier in the chapter. Aside from teaching to like or dislike school and the world of learning itself, the examination system also seems fitted to create the view that one studies only for examinations, for external reward and the avoidance of punishment, in whatever form. And so it must be asked if, in the final analysis, it is in the form of collateral learnings that some of the most lasting, and yet outrageous kinds of learning, such as dislikes and disappointments, occur in Irish post-primary schools? This is a form of learning of which there has been too great a neglect in the past, yet it may well be that for many pupils it is also the most important and influential kind of learning that goes on in Irish post-primary schools. It may well be that it is learnings of this kind which cause many to look back on their schooling as a time of unreality and irrelevance, an object of some ridicule.

Conclusion

When examinations become closely bound up with the goals and motivations of those concerned, the distortions in schooling to which they can give rise are very considerable. When these distortions are commonplace they all too easily become accepted as the norm. To guard against this there must be some way of deciding what is appropriate and what is inappropriate educational procedure or practice. Earlier on I outlined a model for the evaluation and development of curriculum. There I argued that the content, teaching, examining and administration of education ought to take their starting point from some concept or idea of the aims and goals to be achieved. In a subsequent chapter on the aims of post-primary education in Ireland I argued that no such model or approach is to be found in the conduct of Irish post-primary education. It is partly through the absence of some such procedure for curriculum development and evaluation that the examinations have come to control post-primary education in Ireland to the extent that they do. Through the power vested in them, through their efficacy over the years in opening up educational and career opportunities for pupils, the examinations no longer function merely as a means of examining what a student has learned – they have come equally to dictate what he had better learn, for only in this way can the student succeed in the examination and gain entry to his chosen field. The objective conditions of this success, namely the public content of the curriculum, has become to a considerable degree tradition bound and stagnant and out of touch with the needs of the day and the needs of a general education.

But if the examinations have become a disruptive influence in respect of curriculum content, they have also interfered with the pedagogy of the curriculum, with teaching and with learning. Yet the examinations are not the only disruptive influence. Other major factors such as the uncontrolled pressures which are brought to bear on the post-primary school – pressures against which the post-primary school has allowed itself to remain defenceless in the absence of any guiding philosophy of its own — the organisation and control of knowledge in the post-primary school, and insufficient provision for individualised instruction and programmes are also at work. Lesser factors, such as the design and condition of many school buildings and the lack of adequate facilities and teaching resources have also contributed to the overall unsatisfactory position.

I have already discussed the details of this situation. It simply remains to draw attention to the fact that these are considerations which have been overlooked in the past, partly because of an unawareness of the extent of their influence. One continues to overlook them, however, only at the risk of isolating the school — through means of largely bookish and at times somewhat artificial forms of knowledge — from the actual needs of the society and the individuals which it is supposed to serve, and at the risk of the disaffection of pupils — through inappropriate pedagogical pro-vision — with the world of school learning.

It is not possible in this chapter to arrive at anything other than tentative conclusions and to raise the questions for consideration. What the investigation does raise for consideration may be sum-marised as follows. What is learned in school is a function of more than just the public curriculum; it is a function also of pedagogical factors and matters which have a pedagogical impact. Four of these are worthy of special mention. Firstly, there is the lack of coordination between the different levels of education, and indeed as between post-primary education and other non-educational institutions. As a result a number of pressures are brought on the curriculum of post-primary education which disrupt desirable curriculum practice and learning. Secondly, the structure of the curriculum gives rise to a high degree of rigidity and inflexibility with consequent limitations on and possible distortions of what is learned. Thirdly, there appears to be insufficient provision for the individualisation of instruction and programmes. And fourthly, the examination system bears heavily, and possibly with very serious negative effects, on the curriculum, teaching and learning.

Chapter 6

Curriculum Reform

Tomorrow's school will be a school without walls — a school built of doors which open to the entire community.

Tomorrow's school will reach out to the places that enrich the human spirit — to the museums, the theatres, the art galleries, to the parks and rivers and mountains.

It will ally itself with the city, its busy streets and factories, its assembly lines and laboratories — so that the world of work does not seem an alien place for the student.[1]

Introduction

Hitherto chief attention in this study of curriculum and policy in Irish post-primary education has been devoted to analysis and evaluation. Such analysis and evaluation is important as a means of understanding more fully the workings of, and the reasoning behind, the system. It also provides a means of assessing what is of lasting value in it. Such analysis and evaluation is also a necessary first step in any consideration of areas in which there might be need for improvement in the future. Accordingly, it is appropriate in this final chapter to devote some attention to what the foregoing analysis and evaluation, and the considerations upon which they are founded, suggest for the future direction and conduct of post-primary education in Ireland. I repeat, however, that the proposals which follow are of necessity both broad and tentative in nature.

Philosophy and aims in Irish post-primary education

To rectify a situation in which educational policy and practice have not had the benefit of a guiding philosophy of education, it is necessary to develop an explicit and comprehensive statement of aims and philosophy of post-primary education in Ireland. Here I propose to set forth in outline form what I consider to be essential features of any such position; the features are determined by what I consider to be the general aim of post-primary education in Ireland today, namely the provision of a general education as a preparation for life. In setting forth these features I shall be drawing upon the general position which I have presented in chapter three; there I relied upon the notion of the major demands of living as a basis for developing a broadly-based concept of general education as a preparation for life.

It is possible, I have suggested, to identify four major demands of living: the vocational, the recreational, the philosophical and the practical demands of living. To aim at preparing pupils for life is to aim at preparing them to meet successfully these various demands. Each of these demands may, of course, take many forms and it may be helpful to consider what some of these are likely to be and how they might be provided for.

Preparing pupils to meet the vocational demands of living suggests that pupils should be enabled to develop in the knowledge, attitudes and skills which are basic to a range of employment situations. Already I have referred approvingly to the stance which post-primary education in Ireland has adopted in the matter of the vocational subjects on the curriculum, a stance in which general technical knowledge and skill rather than specialised trade skills are taught. I have also drawn attention to the complexity and different kinds of knowledge demanded by the world of work, knowledge which entails skills in interpersonal relations as well as technical knowledge and skill in specific areas of work. Pupils should also become sensitive to the values and assumptions of the workplace and this should be achieved in such a way that pupils may not merely accept in a passive way dominant but possibly objectionable values and practices. In particular, I would be anxious to ensure that pupils could look objectively at the conditions of the workplace and be willing to take measures to withstand its dehumanising influences. Accordingly, the objective of preparing pupils in post-primary education to meet the vocational demands of living will entail bringing about a development in pupils of appropriate interpersonal and other knowledge, skills and attitudes of a general kind, along with more specialist knowledge and skill.

In regard to preparing pupils to meet the cultural and recreational demands of living, an enormously wide range of possibilities exist. In general, the objective would be to develop in pupils the ability to gain enjoyment, pleasure and recreation from as wide a range of sources as possible and also to develop in them an appreciation of the place and importance of leisure and the productive use of leisure time. Thus, one would envisage a range of sources including literature, art, music, sport, film, crafts, hobbies, outdoor pursuits and so on, to which pupils would be introduced as a means of enabling them to engage in as wide a range of recreational and cultural activities as possible.

The goal of preparing pupils to meet what I have called the philosophical demands of living emphasises that aspect of general education which has traditionally been regarded as the principal feature of the idea. Thus, one is speaking here of developing in pupils an awareness and appreciation of the human situation and of the nature and the complexity of the world in which we live. Such knowledge or awareness is not important for the mere factual information which it entails but rather for the perspectives on life and on living which it provides. It is, perhaps, best understood as providing a basis for judgment on a wide range of issues and as a basis for developing a set of values in ordering one's priorities in life.

In a sense, the philosophical demands of living can be seen as pervading all the demands of living. Thus, as a person thinks about his vocation in life, his dealings with others, how he will spend his leisure, he is, in a sense, philosophising. In a sense too, one's day-to-day activities and decisions are an expression of a philosophy of life, however unconscious or unarticulated it may be. And the aim of the post-primary school in this regard should be to assist pupils to heighten their awareness of this philosophy or general outlook on life, with a view to making pupils more conscious, rational, sensitive, and hence fuller human beings.

We come, finally, to what is perhaps the area of greatest difficulty. To talk of preparing pupils for meeting the practical demands of living is to talk of bringing about in pupils a growth in the knowledge, attitudes and skills needed to cope successfully with the enormously wide and varied range of everyday demands of living. Such demands include one's dealing with others in the home, at work, in places of trade and commerce, in casual and fleeting encounters with others as well as in relations with friends and loved ones. Practical demands also include attending to one's personal health and welfare, maintaining one's personal finances, dealing with consumer affairs, with advertising and the mass media, and with one's personal rights and responsibilities. The practical or personal demands of living also include the making of important decisions in life, such as whether to marry and rear a family; and they link up with the philosophical demands of living when they embrace decisions regarding moral issues of the day, issues such as abortion and contraception, violence, poverty, labour relations. Also included in the practical demands of living is a host of activities which necessitate an element of physical skill, coordination and judgment. These activities would include driving a car, cooking a meal, administering first aid.

The area of practical or personal demands of living is a difficult area for two reasons. The first difficulty has to do with effective teaching in this area; the second has to do with the question of whether the school should have any role at all in the area. And while this objection may also be raised against vocational education, one encounters it less frequently in that connection today.

Some of those who argue against the involvement of the school in practical education in the sense I am using it here, argue that the purpose of the school is strictly intellectual. Others object less on grounds of principle than on practical grounds, arguing that even if it is legitimate for the school to become involved, it cannot do so successfully. The first of these arguments is the more important, and it will be dealt with first; although the argument has had strong support, the arguments against it are more convincing.

There are several grounds for arguing in favour of the involvement of the school in preparing pupils to meet the practical demands of living. I shall begin by adverting to actual practice in this matter. Historically schools have seen it as an important part of their job to cater for the practical education of pupils — witness the continued efforts of schools in the area of civic or social education — and this has been as true of the tradition of grammar school education as of any other. Likewise, education in the 3Rs owes at least some of its justification to the fact that it provides pupils with the wherewithal to meet many of the practical demands of living of the kind which I have in mind.

The second ground for arguing for the involvement of the school in practical education is not unrelated to the first. It is difficult, if not impossible, to isolate aspects of the development of pupils for which the school should have a responsibility from aspects where it should have none. Thus, to insist that schools should not engage in practical education because the specific concern of the school is with intellectual education, is to imply that practical education is a non-intellectual affair. It is also to suggest that intellectual education can be cut off from other forms of education. The weight of present-day educational thinking, however, would be slow to accept that intellectual development can be easily cut off from other forms of development.[2]

A third reason for arguing for the involvement of the school in practical education is the fact that post-primary education in Ireland actually aims at the broad preparation of the pupil. Thus, the *Report of the Council of Education* argued for 'the organized development and equipment of all the powers of the individual person – religious, moral, intellectual, physical'.[3] To exclude provision for preparing pupils to meet the practical demands of living is to introduce an unwarranted limitation on the remit of the schools.

Finally, and most importantly perhaps, the trend of developments in society favours the involvement of the school in preparing pupils to meet the practical and personal demands of living. Changing patterns in family life in particular, changes such as the increased incidence of mothers working outside the home, strengthen greatly the case for the schools' adopting an even more important role in the practical education of youth. This is not to suggest that other agencies in society, such as the family and the church, have no role here; neither is it to deny that there may be other state agencies that might also have a role to play. It is simply to say that, as with other areas of education, this is an area where the schools have a legitimate contribution to make.

In addition to setting ends or goals to be achieved in Irish post-primary education, a broad philosophical stance must also be adopted in regard to how these goals are to be pursued. This stance will establish the values and principles which determine the choices that need to be made in the selection of curriculum content and in the adoption of pedagogical principles. For there are many different types of curriculum content and many different approaches to teaching which might be chosen with a view to achieving any particular educational goal. Accordingly, before proceeding to a consideration of the content and pedagogy of the curriculum, it may be helpful to draw attention briefly to some of these values.

The first of these principles has to do with the idea of the school itself and the notion of life-long learning. In the face of the criticisms which have been levelled against it in recent years, the school must re-assert itself. For whatever shortcomings the school may have, there is an essential job of education to be done. If the school does not do it, it will be taken over by some other agency and there is no reason to think that any other agencies will be any more successful or enlightened than the school can be.

To say this much in support of schooling, however, is not to say that schools need not change, neither is it to say that schools should not become involved in forms of education which they cannot provide at the present time. This would be to accept the charges that the schools cannot educate.[4] It is my view that the schools ought not to shrink from the task of education, whatever form it takes. What they must do, however, is to develop and adapt in such ways as are necessary for them to engage successfully in those forms of education for which, at present, they may be unsuited. This, in all likelihood, will call for a willingness to break down the walls, to open windows on the world and to see education and learning as a life-long process. It will call for greater cooperation between the schools and other institutions in the work of education. And if it is to become the responsibility of the school to re-integrate itself more fully into the wider society from which it has increasingly become cut off over the years, it may be no less a challenge and a responsibility for the wider society and its institutions to respond and adapt for their role in education, both during the years of in-school education and throughout life. This opening up and integration of the schools and other institutions will not be without its own difficulties. Yet it is the only direction which appears open if the schools are not to become even more cut off and irrelevant and if education is not to be seen as over and done with on leaving school. One area where there is a rapidly growing need for integration, and where some advances have in fact been made in the form of work-placements, is the area of pre-employment education.[5]

A second important principle which must be maintained is that of autonomy, and the autonomy of post-primary education in particular. Lacking a guiding philosophy of its own, and largely defenceless against the demands of the third-level sector and to a lesser extent against the demands of primary education and the workplace, post-primary education, particularly in recent years, has increasingly allowed itself to be at the beck and call of external forces.

To speak in this way of the demands of the workplace and of higher education is not to say that these do not have legitimate demands to make and to which the post-primary school ought to respond, but the post-primary school has other demands on its time and its attention as well. What I am saying is that the post-primary sector must itself become the chief arbiter in curriculum matters, deciding the manner and the extent to which the various demands will be responded to and the relative importance of each. To say this is to advert to the responsible role of post-primary education in the welfare of the nation. It is also to pinpoint what I mean by autonomy. It is an autonomy which ought to be guided by a clear view of the aims and philosophy of post-primary education in Ireland. It is an autonomy which should be informed by a continuous dialogue with, and sensitivity to, the interests and requirements of the individual pupil and of society at large.

The autonomy which has been established in the primary sector is founded, very largely, on a view of the nature and development of the child. It is supported also by a new curriculum and a guiding philosophy.[6] While the autonomy of the post-primary sector will also be founded on an understanding of the pupil, the picture here is perhaps more complex. For there are many demands on the post-primary school which complicate the situation. But one requirement does seem indispensable, namely the institution of appropriate curriculum structures.

When the revised programme of 1924 was introduced into the secondary schools attention was drawn to the fact that it involved the setting up of courses, one for the Intermediate Certificate and the other leading to the Leaving Certificate. Some such structural provisions, which would apply in the entire post-primary sector, are also necessary at the present time, I believe. The objective of these structures would be to protect by regulation and organisation the various elements in general education to which I have adverted already. Similarly, the proper use of structures is the mechanism by which provision would be made for the implementation of a flexible common curriculum. In particular, I would see such structures providing support for those areas of the curriculum — typically the areas of the recreational and practical studies — which tend to be neglected. Such a use of structures will, I trust, be evident in the proposals which I shall be putting forward.

Although structures are important, they must not inhibit flexibility and the individualisation of curriculum where this is necessary. And this is the next main point to which I wish to draw attention. A good deal has been done in recent years to increase variety and alternatives in Irish post-primary education, yet much more must be done to provide for the range of interests and abilities at all levels. Such provision may take the form of introducing new subjects, the provision of remedial programmes which merit greater recognition at junior level, greater provision for vocational subjects and programmes at senior level, opportunities to take up new subjects at senior level, and the like. Whatever the specific provision, however, the main point which I wish to stress here is that the principles of flexibility and alternatives must constitute an important element in the philosophy of post-primary education. Otherwise there is a danger of a rigidity which can kill the vitality and responsiveness of schooling to meet ever-changing circumstances.

Bound up closely with considerations of this kind is an organisational one. Post-primary education in Ireland is very highly centralised and nowhere is this more evident than in the curriculum and examinations. And although there is good reason to believe that some degree of centralisation is both necessary and generally beneficial, it has been excessive in Irish post-primary education. The recommendations of the *ICE Report* point a way forward towards the decentralisation of examinations. The approach of vocational education, especially in the early years of the state, and as represented in *Memo V. 40*, also gives a lead; moreover, it gives a certain assurance that not only can decentralisation be 'safe' but that it can be highly responsive to local and national needs, needs both of the economy and society at large as well as of pupils. Accordingly, when decentralisation in curriculum matters holds out the promise of improved programmes, such a move ought to be given favourable consideration.

In this section I have elaborated upon what I consider to be the main aims of post-primary education in Ireland today. I have also attempted to identify important values and priorities which I believe ought to be subscribed to in any philosophy of post-primary education in Ireland. And after many years of waiting for some 'official' philosophy of post-primary education to be developed and set forth, it is disheartening to find so little of such a philosophy emerging in the *White Paper on Educational Development*.

The public curriculum

It is possible to turn now to a consideration of the kind of curriculum provision which may be considered suitable for the preparation of pupils to meet the major demands of living. In doing so, two preliminary points must be made. Firstly, in the considerations which follow I shall be taking for granted a number of general features of post-primary education in Ireland, and I shall be working within the context which they provide. Thus, the age range with which we are dealing is the twelve to seventeen years age range, approximately; and the post-primary school is seen as being divided into a junior cycle catering for pupils up to the age of fifteen or so, and a senior cycle catering for pupils between the ages of fifteen and seventeen. The junior cycle is taken to be compulsory by and large for most pupils. The senior cycle is considered to be post-compulsory.[7] Secondly, I do not wish to suggest that special arrangements either in place of, or in addition to, the proposals which I make may not be necessary in the case of pupils who may have very special needs or very special abilities, for this may well be the case. But my concern here is with the broad thrust rather than the details of curriculum policy.

I shall begin by dealing with the practical demands of living. In doing so, it will be helpful to refer to the publication of the North Tipperary Vocational Education Committee to which I have referred already, namely *Post-Primary Education 1985-2000 and its Relevance to the Economy: A Policy Document.*[8] In this document we find a concrete example of an attempt to come to grips with the problem of preparing pupils for the varied practical demands of living. It is an attempt, moreover, which appears to be in line with the life-activities approach to general education for which I have been arguing. In particular, I wish to refer to the section of this document which is devoted to 'Education for Living – a Pastoral Care Programme', in which a tentative but coherent set of proposals for a programme in this area is set forth.

The scope of the programme is indicated in the statement of purpose which begins by stating that the purpose of the programme is 'to ensure that aspects of education for living which may not be covered in the general curriculum are adequately treated and to co-ordinate the approach of different teachers in these areas'.[9] What these areas are is set forth in the classroom content of the programme which is organised under the following main headings: school familiarisation course, courtesy and etiquette, health education, personal relationships and sex education, money, consumer education, the environment, decision making, marriage and home-making, leisure-time activities and career guidance. The content of each of these topics is further broken down. Thus, in the case of consumer education, the following sub-topics are treated: value for money, rights as a consumer, sales techniques, advertising and methods of payment.

My main interest in the suggested programme lies in its identification of the general kind and range of issues and areas of study which are taken to constitute a necessary part of 'education for living' for all pupils. It will be noted that many of the topics and issues treated are not unique to this programme; in fact many of them form elements in a number of subjects — recognised subjects like civics and home economics, and others such as religious education — which have been well-established in Irish post-primary education. Thus, health education is part of the syllabus in physical education; consumer education is included in home economics, as are also aspects of home-making and personal relationships. Increasingly, too, many schools are making provision for pastoral care programmes and programmes of guidance and counselling which deal with personal, school and career-related problems of pupils. All of these are issues of practical and immediate concern to pupils, and they are the kinds of issues with which practical education of the kind which I have in mind ought to deal.

What is important here is the fact that the need for education of this kind is already acknowledged; it has actually been granted a place in the schools. What is equally important, however, is the fact that such education occupies a very minor place. It is of uncertain status and, with the exception of home economics, it does not appear in the form of an examination subject. This is not to argue that it should become an examination subject in the way that other subjects are. It is simply to point to the degree of seriousness which is attached to it.

If greater attention is to be given to this area of the curriculum, a more explicit recognition of, and support for, the place of preparation for the practical demands of living must be provided. One concrete step in this direction would be the introduction of appropriate curriculum support structures to maintain it as a 'subject' in the curriculum. These support structures would include inspection and assessment. Curriculum time should also be expressly set aside for it.

Provision for education of this kind should run right throughout the full course of the post-primary school and it should be a requirement for all pupils. Although there should be special timetable provision for this 'subject' and although there should be specialist teachers — drawn typically from the ranks of the guidance teachers, civics teachers and religious education teachers, as well as others — this is an aspect of education which lends itself to being tied in with pastoral care education. Thus, it should have links with the pastoral care programme and with the counselling services in the school. Practical education would also benefit from a system of form masters or year tutors who would have special responsibility for a particular class in the school. Above all, it would need to be conceived and treated as an area of the school programme in which the focus of attention is squarely on the pupil — rather than on subject-matter for examination purposes — and in which there would be ample opportunity to engage in projects, discussion, debate and one-to-one exchange in an air of openness.

It is a feature of the pastoral care programme envisaged in the North Tipperary VEC *Policy Document* that it aspires to this particular approach. The proposal in the *Policy Document* has the further merit that the programme takes as its starting point a very practical issue indeed, namely the problem of the pupil finding himself in the quite new world of the post-primary school, with its range of teachers, subjects and new procedures. Some attempt to introduce the pupil to this new world would seem to constitute a good starting-point for education in the practical demands of living in the post-primary school.

One final but important general point must be made on the question of making curriculum provision for meeting the practical demands of living. I have already said that both in principle and in practice the importance of this aspect of post-primary education has been accepted — witness the pastoral care programmes, civics courses, guidance and counselling services in post-primary schools today. But there is also something lacking. There is a lack of focus. This is as a result of a failure of adequate recognition, structural support and an explicit rationale for such provision within the context of post-primary education in Ireland today. There is some agreement that education to meet the practical demands of living ought to include studies in such areas as civic, social and political education, health education, education for interpersonal relations and family-life education, consumer education, communications and media education, physical education, home economics educa-tion and religious education; these, at any rate, are the kinds of areas that I would wish to see included. Yet such provision as is made by schools in this area is at the disadvantage that it has to be fitted into a broad curriculum and examinations context, a context which is brought forward from another age, an age in which curriculum provision of the kind in question either had little place or could be dealt with in different ways. And until such time as the broader curriculum context, supported by an appropriate philosophy, is set forth and adopted officially, the approach of individual schools will, of necessity, remain tentative and limited.

All of these deficiencies, however, cannot be rectified overnight. As a first step in the right direction, provision ought to be made for more intensive research and pilot work in this area with a view to identifying and developing appropriate and successful ways of dealing with it. In doing so, attention ought to be given also to methods of assessment in the area, an area in which major technical and even ethical problems exist. This is necessary not only because assessment is necessary in any educational endeavour, but because the existing examination arrangements actually penalise effort in this area by not providing recognition for it. Later on I shall deal more fully with the question of assessment and examinations. Suffice it to say here that new assessment procedures ought to be devised which provide a satisfactory way of assessing in this area and which, at the same time, would do much to provide support, and indeed reward, for both teachers and pupils.

I wish to turn now to the area of the vocational demands of living, and in doing so there is nothing that I wish to add to the argument which I have made already in regard to the necessity of providing for education in this area.[10] I shall argue at a later point, however, that during the senior cycle of the post-primary school, education of this kind ought to constitute the major area of study. This, however, ought not normally to be the case in the early years of post-primary schooling.

It is desirable that vocational education ought to constitute a part of each pupil's programme from the beginning of post-primary education. The extent of this form of education, however, should depend on a number of factors. It ought to be included, in the first place, because quite a number of pupils leave school at or around the age of fifteen; unless education of this kind is started early on, little time may remain during the years of compulsory schooling. As will be seen, education in this area in the first year ought to be very general in character. It should give pupils their initial orientation to the world of work and its place in the life of the individual and of society; a basis should also be provided for pupils to reflect on what their own general preferences may be. And if pupils are free to leave school at fifteen, it seems unsatisfactory to me to say that pupils ought not be faced with thinking about their career preferences at this stage, even if it may not be the most suitable age for making far-reaching decisions. Far better also, surely, to have had some such experience rather than none in the first year of the post-primary school, and to have had the benefit of close observation and some initial career guidance, as a basis for subject choices in what, for many pupils, will be the final two years of schooling. These are the pupils, moreover, it is increasingly being recognised, whose position tends to be the most disadvantaged under the existing school arrangements.[11]

For those pupils who plan to remain in second-level education up until the end of the senior cycle, there is not quite the same degree of urgency. Early on in post-primary school, programmes may need to be devised — subject to revision for those pupils whose early plans or expectations change — which reflect the expectations and plans of pupils as to whether they intend to leave post-primary education on reaching the minimum school-leaving age or not.

While this consideration will have some implications for the curriculum measures intended to cater for the practical demands of living and the recreational demands of living, it has most significance for the areas of the vocational demands and the philosophical demands of living. This is so because, in general, I would see the amount of time given to education in the areas of the practical and recreational demands remaining fairly constant relative to one another throughout each year of the post-primary school. In the case of the liberal or philosophical studies and the vocational or specialist studies, however, I would see a greater commitment to the vocational studies in the middle and later years.

If programme decisions are to be made in the early years of the post-primary school which differentiate between programmes which are followed by those who plan to leave school at fifteen and those who plan to go on until later — though, as we shall see, such differentiation may be kept quite slight — it may be helpful to begin by looking at those elements of the programmes of vocational studies and liberal studies which will have most in common for all pupils. And at this point a further word as to what I mean by the vocational studies will be in order.

As it is envisaged here almost any area of study can qualify for study under the heading of vocational studies. In conventional terms vocational studies have tended to be woodwork, metalwork, technical drawing and building construction; more recently business and secretarial studies have come to be spoken of in like terms. It is also true that many conventional, so-called liberal subjects are studied, both at second level and third level, for specialist and indeed career purposes: thus the study of mathematics, science and even social, humanistic and recreational subjects are frequently studied for vocational or career purposes. The study of subjects of this kind by prospective teachers is an obvious case in point. For this reason it is confusing to talk of such studies as being only liberal studies; they may be liberal studies or they may be vocational and specialist studies. And there is good reason to think that the study of liberal subjects in second-level education has given way increasingly to the study of such subjects at pre-specialist and pre-vocational levels.

With this view of the vocational studies in mind, we can return now to the question of the place of vocational studies in the first year of the post-primary school and its relationship to the other areas of study. Organisationally, in the first year and possibly right throughout the full post-primary course, I would see vocational education as being the general responsibility of one teacher, possibly the guidance teacher, who would be charged with the overall coordination of the vocational education programme. This teacher would also probably be involved in teaching aspects of the course. In the first year the course would be arranged in such a way that the impact of guidance counselling in the form of information, discussion with pupils and testing would be supplemented by a comprehensive set of guest speakers and visits to places of work and maybe even places of further studies.

In the first year, I would see the liberal studies — with adequate provision for individual differences, remedial education and the like — consisting mainly of studies in mathematics, science and technology, and English and Irish language and literature. The recreational studies I would see as wide-ranging and 'experiential' in so far as possible and including music, art, physical education, film appreciation, outdoor pursuits and miscellaneous other recreational activities. The first year in the post-primary school programme is set out in Table 7.

Having given an overview of the type of course structure which I would envisage in the first-year of the post-primary school, there are a number of more general points which I wish to take up before

Table 7: Programme of studies for first year in post-primary school

Practical Education	Vocational Education	Philosophical/Liberal Education	Recreational Education
Aspects of:			*Aspects of:*
Civic, social and political education	Vocational information	Mathematics (3 hours weekly)	Music
Health education	Visits and guest speakers	Science and technology (3 hours weekly)	Art and crafts
Consumer education	Work-orientation		Physical education
Communications and media education	Observation and testing	Irish and English language and literature (6 hours weekly)	Miscellaneous leisure activities (e.g. film appreciation, hobbies, chess, photography)
Moral education		Remedial education where necessary	Leisure education
Home economics			
Religious education			
Average minimum of 5 hours (approx.) weekly per annum	Average minimum of 3 hours (approx.) weekly per annum	Average minimum of 12 hours (approx.) weekly per annum	Average minimum of 5 hours (approx.) weekly per annum

discussing the overall structure of courses for subsequent years. I will pay particular attention to the implications of my view of the vocational studies and their interrelations with the liberal studies.

As I have said, the range of potential vocational subjects as understood here is quite broad: it includes all those subjects which may be studied with a career or specialist goal in mind. Thus the study of history by a pupil whose goal is to enter university to study history — whether with a view to becoming a history scholar, a teacher or for some other such purpose — may be counted as a vocational or specialist subject just as much as the study of short-hand, typing and other secretarial skills and related studies may be counted as vocational or specialist studies by another pupil. (This, of course, is not to deny that different more general educational benefits might also attach to each.)

This approach to the question of vocational studies has beneficial implications for general education. It allows one to draw up alter-native syllabuses in a number of subjects which are distinguished from one another on the grounds of whether they are to be studied for vocational purposes or for practical, recreational or philosophical purposes. If no such distinction is made, then all subjects are treated in roughly the same way. This has led to a situation in Irish post-primary education where, as I have observed already, with about six or seven subjects being studied in senior cycle, the range of subjects which can be studied in a programme of so-called general education is very narrow. The subject units are so large as to call for the omission of many subjects from a pupil's course of study. The adverse effects of this situation on the study of music and art at senior cycle have already been noted; it is no less true of studies in other areas also, notably the practical area.

To implement this distinction which I am making between the vocational studies and the non-vocational studies it would be help-ful to adopt a system of 'major' and 'minor' subjects. Thus, in crude terms, one would devote more time to the study of, say, English or music as a major vocational subject than to the study of English as a minor liberal studies subject or music as a minor recreational studies subject. The minor subjects would be sufficiently small as to allow for the study of a fairly good number of such subjects. By blocking out a certain proportion of the curriculum time for vocational studies, one could distinguish the approach and the kind of depth and specialisation sought in the vocational area from that of the other areas.

This, as I see it, is possibly the only way of ensuring an exposure of the pupil to the broad range of studies which is required to prepare him to meet the broad demands of living. And although it might be argued that such treatment of the non-specialist studies might be superficial, a choice must be made between some study and none at all.[12] At the same time, provision is made in the vocational area for serious in-depth and demanding study. The vocational studies area could also be used as a means of providing the necessary opportunities and challenge to pupils of outstanding ability.

This latter point is important. The advocates of liberal education have never shown that the study of a particular subject or group of subjects which are studied for a vocational or specialist purpose is of less intellectual benefit than if they were studied for 'their own sake'. It is recognised, moreover, even by such strong advocates of liberal education as Hirst and Peters, that the amount of study in a particular form of knowledge ought to be determined by a pupil's interests and career goals. Thus, their main concern would appear to be with ensuring that some exposure ought to be given to pupils in each form of knowledge. They do not require each pupil to study each form in the same way or to the same extent.[13]

The scheme which I am proposing is one which attempts to come to grips with the very real difficulty of providing a broad general education along with in-depth and vocational studies. Firstly, it recognises the wide and varied demands on curriculum space; secondly, it recognises the need for vocational studies; and thirdly, it suggests that in-depth study in a chosen vocational or specialist group of studies is a realistic way of providing for intellectual discipline and for preparation for work. Whilst such in-depth study may have some of the advantages of the British A-level system, the approach which I am proposing avoids the drawbacks of that system by demanding, in addition to the vocational or specialist studies, courses in liberal studies, recreational studies and practical studies. Moreover, even though the specialist or vocational studies may be studied in more depth than the other areas, I would not see them as very narrowly vocational in emphasis.

In general, I see standards in the vocational or specialist studies remaining on a par with existing standards in subjects in the Intermediate and Leaving Certificate programmes. I suggest, however, that no more than three subjects should normally be required for study at vocational or specialist level. The time saved by not studying six or seven subjects at the one level, contrary to what is largely done at present, would then be given over to studies in the areas of liberal, recreational, and practical studies. At Leaving Certificate level I see the ratio, in terms of time, as something like 5 : 3 in favour of the vocational or specialist studies as opposed to all other studies combined. In the second and third years of the junior cycle I would normally expect a ratio in the region of 1 : 3 in favour of the non-vocational studies.

Even though there would be a difference between the depth in studies taken at vocational or specialist level and that in the other areas, it is important to recognise the educational value of all the areas of study and to support them accordingly. For it is only by virtue of the comprehensive nature of the programmes being proposed that one can claim to provide for the demands of a broad general education. Historically, much of this support has come through the examination system; thus, in whatever scheme is devised, it is important to ensure, whether by examination, inspection or continuous assessment, that the non-specialist subjects are not undermined in the way, for example, that one hears is true of civics on the present junior-cycle programme.

Before leaving this discussion of the possible form which the vocational and liberal or philosophical studies might take in Irish post-primary education, I will consider possible ways in which subjects in these areas might be grouped and combined with one another at different levels. Already I have suggested a general scheme of studies for the first year of the post-primary school. It is one in which a minimum of five hours weekly would be devoted to studies in the practical and the recreational studies, a minimum of three hours weekly in the vocational area and a minimum of twelve hours weekly in the liberal studies. Throughout the remainder of the post-primary school I see the time to be devoted to the recreational and practical studies remaining more or less at five hours per week at the junior level and, perhaps, dropping to four hours a week at senior level. From the second year of the post-primary school onward, however, I see increases in the amount of vocational or specialist studies in relation to the liberal studies. (In suggesting a minimum number of hours per week for each area of study I do not wish to suggest that this minimum ought to be met each week of the year. Flexible timetable arrangements could well be implemented.)

By the end of the first year of the post-primary school, and assuming that all pupils would spend a minimum of three years in the post-primary school, I see pupils opting for a range of about three vocational or specialist subjects, depending upon ability and aptitude. Depending upon these choices, the subjects of the liberal studies would then be selected. The ratio of time devoted to the study of the vocational studies relative to the liberal studies would be in the region of 50 : 50. (This would be consistent with the 1 : 3 distribution of curriculum time between vocational and other studies mentioned already for the junior cycle.) Thus, if a pupil were to choose woodwork, technical drawing and mathematics along with a general career-orientation course, as his vocational or specialist subjects, the liberal studies would be drawn largely from general science and technology, English and Irish languages and literature. Thus, in the case of a pupil who intended to leave school at fifteen and, perhaps, take up an apprenticeship, one might envisage a programme such as that set out in Table 8A. On the other hand, for a pupil choosing English, history and French as his vocational or specialist subjects with a view to a career in teaching, journalism or as an academic, the liberal studies could include, as minor subjects, studies in Irish, mathematics and either general science and technology or a 'manual' subject. Thus one would see a programme such as that set out in Table 8B.

Table 8A: **Programme of studies for second and third year in post-primary school***

Vocational Studies	Liberal Studies
1. Woodwork 2. Technical drawing 3. Mathematics 4. Career-orientation course	1. English 2. Irish 3. General science and technology
Average minimum of 8 hours (approx.) weekly per annum	Average minimum of 7 hours (approx.) weekly per annum

*Practical and recreational studies have not been included in this table.

Table 8B: **Alternative programme of studies for second and third year in post-primary school***

Vocational Studies	Liberal Studies
1. English 2. History 3. French 4. Career-orientation course	1. Mathematics 2. General science and technology *or* A manual subject 3. Irish
Average minimum of 8 hours (approx.) weekly per annum	Average minimum of 7 hours (approx.) weekly per annum

*Practical and recreational studies have not been included in this table.

As I have said, a number of constraints have to be borne in mind in drawing up the curriculum at the compulsory level of post-primary education in particular. Thus one has to provide for those who plan to leave school at fifteen and those who plan to stay on. Likewise, one has to cater for those who have a change of mind, either in regard to leaving school at fifteen or regarding their choice of vocational subjects. It is for these reasons, partly, that the amount of time and presumably the depth of studies given to vocational studies and to liberal studies should be kept on a par with one another at the junior level. It facilitates the pupil who may wish to take up as a vocational subject at senior level a subject which he might have taken as a liberal subject at junior level, and vice versa. At the same time, there are advantages for all pupils in including expressly vocational education in the junior cycle and there is also merit in the practice — and in the proposal of the *White Paper*[14] — of introducing at the senior level subjects which are not included in the junior level programmes. This practice could be extended with benefit, especially in the area of the vocational studies.

With the approach which I have been proposing in relation to the vocational studies at both the junior and the senior levels, it may be helpful to draw up two lists of subjects. One would be a list of vocational subjects and the other a list of liberal subjects. These lists would be especially helpful in devising programmes at the senior level. From one list a selection of subjects would be made for vocational or specialist study; from the second a selection would be made for liberal studies which would complement the subjects chosen for specialist purposes. In this way the idea of a broad general education would be maintained as much as possible.

Drawing heavily on the existing lists of subjects available in post-primary schools, and adding others of a kind which I have suggested already might also be included, the two lists set out in Table 9 might be considered. These lists are just examples; other subjects could be added, perhaps with a greater encouragement of applied studies, and possibly some of those included could be dropped. Or it may be that some of the subjects listed above might be more realistically seen as broader areas of study which ought to be broken down into their constituent subjects. The areas of business studies, secretarial studies and home economics may be cases in point.

Other possibilities in the area of the liberal studies exist, however, especially at senior level. An important point to bear in mind regarding the liberal studies is that they are seen as providing a means of rounding off the studies in the practical, vocational and recreational areas. They are intended to ensure a necessary breadth of curriculum which, in conjunction with all the other areas of study, would provide a basis for enabling the pupil to develop at least the beginnings of a personal philosophy, a view of life and a set of guiding values. This being so, there may be advantage to be gained from adopting a more integrated approach to the liberal studies during at least the years of the senior cycle. The purpose of these studies, and the level of maturity and educational background of the senior-level pupil, would appear to warrant attempting such an approach at senior level. The kind of course which I would have in mind – it might be entitled an Integrated Studies Course – would be akin to a course in the study of typical social problems which has been advocated by Broudy, Smith and Burnett.[15] That is to say that insofar as the purpose of the liberal studies, in line with the traditional concept of a liberal education, is to enable pupils to develop a philosophy of life, one reasonable way of attempting to set about achieving this goal with senior pupils is to select for analysis and discussion fundamental human and social issues of current interest – issues such as relations between Northern

Table 9: **Lists of vocational and liberal subjects from which programmes at senior level could be devised**

Vocational Subjects

Irish
English
Latin
Greek
Greek and Roman civilisation
Hebrew
French ⎫ Syllabus A:
German ⎬   Literary
Italian ⎬ Syllabus B:
Spanish ⎭   Commercial
Other modern languages

Mathematics
Applied mathematics
Statistics
Computer studies
Mechanics
Physics
Engineering
Building construction
Technical Drawing
Woodwork
Metalwork

Chemistry
Biology

Commerce
Business organisation
Accounting
Economics
Economic history
Secretarial studies
Agricultural economics

Home economics

Rural science
Agricultural science

Movement studies
Health education
Physical education

History
Geography
European studies
Social studies
Politics

Religion
Communications and media
        studies

Art
Music

Liberal Subjects

Irish
English
Mathematics
General science and technology
Technical subjects
Integrated studies

Ireland and the Republic of Ireland, divorce, nuclear energy. It is an approach which would have the merit of requiring pupils to draw on their discipline-based knowledge in other subjects, applying this knowledge in the discussion of everyday affairs, and facing up to and developing skills in the analysis and resolution of difficult personal, human and social issues. If such an approach were adopted it would have implications for the practical area; it might suggest a closer cooperation between the liberal studies and aspects of the practical studies at the senior level.

I hope I have given a general idea of the broad approach to providing for the public curriculum of general education throughout the post-primary school. Already I have presented some examples of possible programmes which might make up the curriculum at first-year level and during the second two years of the junior cycle. The programme outlines given in Table 10, which might be chosen by different pupils, suggest in concise terms how I would see programmes shaping up during the years of the senior cycle in the post-primary school. It will be noted that I build into the Leaving Certificate structure programmes which include substantial elements of work experience. This I do in the belief that unless such programmes are so included they may be seen as in some sense second-class programmes.

The pedagogy of the curriculum

In dealing with the question of the public curriculum in the preceding section it was impossible to avoid touching on pedagogical issues, especially that of provision for individual differences. In this section, however, a more direct consideration is given to such matters, and the four main headings under which the pedagogical aspects of the curriculum were treated in chapter five will be employed again. These are the coordination of sectors, curriculum organisation and the hidden curriculum, provision for individual differences and examinations.

It is sometimes said that what is taught at the different levels of schooling is that which is determined by the more advanced levels. Indeed there are those who feel that, to a certain extent, the requirements of university entrance in Ireland make their presence felt even in the primary school.[16] Whatever truth is to be found in such views they do, nonetheless, raise an issue which is central to any consideration of the coordination of sectors as this affects post-primary education in Ireland. Throughout this study I

Table 10: **Programmes of studies during senior cycle of post-primary schooling**

Business Studies Concentration

Practical Education	Vocational Education	Philosophical/Liberal Education	Recreational Education
Aspects of:			*Aspects of:*
Moral education	Business organisation	Irish	Music/music appreciation
Religious education	Accounting	English	Art/art appreciation
Social and political education	French B (Commercial)	General science	Film/film appreciation
Consumer education	Work-placement programme	*or*	Physical education
Health education	Career orientation	Integrated Studies	Crafts
Communications and media education			Outdoor pursuits
Interpersonal relations			Hobbies, e.g. photography, chess
			Leisure education
Average minimum of 4 hours (approx.) weekly per annum	Average minimum of 15 hours (approx.) weekly per annum	Average minimum of 3 hours (approx.) weekly per annum	Average minimum of 4 hours (approx.) weekly per annum

Humanities Concentration

Practical Education	Vocational Education	Philosophical/Liberal Education	Recreational Education
Aspects of: Moral education Religious education Social and political education Consumer education Health education Communications and media education Interpersonal relations	French A (Literary) English Social studies Career-orientation	Irish Mathematics General science *or* Integrated Studies	*Aspects of:* Music/music appreciation Art/art appreciation Film/film appreciation Physical education Crafts Outdoor pursuits Hobbies, e.g. photography, chess Leisure education
Average minimum of 4 hours (approx.) weekly per annum	Average minimum of 15 hours (approx.) weekly per annum	Average minimum of 3 hours (approx.) weekly per annum	Average minimum of 4 hours (approx.) weekly per annum

Science Concentration

Practical Education	Vocational Education	Philosophical/Liberal Education	Recreational Education
Aspects of:			*Aspects of:*
Moral education	Mathematics	Irish	Music/music appreciation
Religious education	Physics	English	Art/art appreciation
Social and political education	Chemistry	*or*	Film/film appreciation
Consumer education	Career orientation	Integrated Studies	Physical education
Health education			Crafts
Communications and media education			Outdoor pursuits
Interpersonal relations			Hobbies, e.g. photography, chess
			Leisure education
Average minimum of 4 hours (approx.) weekly per annum	Average minimum of 15 hours (approx.) weekly per annum	Average minimum of 3 hours (approx.) weekly per annum	Average minimum of 4 hours (approx.) weekly per annum

Secretarial Studies or Technical Studies Concentration

Practical Education	Vocational Education	Philosophical/Liberal Education	Recreational Education
Aspects of:	Secretarial Studies	Irish	*Aspects of:*
Moral education	*or*	English	Music/music appreciation
Religious education	Technical Studies	General science	Art/art appreciation
Social and political education	Work-placement programme	*or*	Film/film appreciation
Consumer education	Career orientation	Integrated Studies	Physical education
Health education			Crafts
Communications and media education			Outdoor pursuits
Interpersonal relations			Hobbies, e.g. photography, chess
			Leisure education
Average minimum of 4 hours (approx.) weekly per annum	Average minimum of 15 hours (approx.) weekly per annum	Average minimum of 3 hours (approx.) weekly per annum	Average minimum of 4 hours (approx.) weekly per annum

have maintained the view that if the aim of post-primary education is to provide a general education as a means of preparing pupils for life then the curriculum should be drawn up on the basis of a consideration of what constitutes the major demands of living. And so I have argued that vocational education ought to constitute an important element in post-primary education.

To argue in this way is not to suggest, however, that only considerations pertaining to the demands of living ought to determine the content and the form or pedagogy of schooling. Such demands must necessarily be regulated by a consideration of the stage of development of the pupil and his aptitudes and interests. In recent times in Ireland, as I have intimated already, considerations having to do with the nature of the child have become more influential at the primary school level. Hence there is a tendency to refer to the primary school, especially since the introduction of the new primary school curriculum, as being child-centred in its approach. The same has not been said of the post-primary school; indeed the post-primary school is sometimes said to be subject-centred in its approach by contrast with the primary school.[17]

Whether or not these characterisations of the primary school and of the post-primary school are correct, schooling must address itself to the stage of development of its pupils. This it must do from a pedagogical point of view, if its pedagogy is to be effective, and from a content point of view, if it is to prepare pupils successfully to meet the actual demands of living. It is an important principle to be also borne in mind when it comes to the question of the coordination of sectors. In a certain sense, post-primary education must be seen as an end in itself; that is to say, the post-primary school ought not to be conceived as merely preparing candidates for entry to university or employment.

A second important consideration to bear in mind in dealing with the question of the coordination of sectors is the fact that the division of formal schooling into primary and post-primary sectors is rooted in history and organisational considerations as much as anything else. Of one thing we may be quite sure: as children pass from primary to post-primary school they are not immediately changed as a result. Change may best be seen in terms of the continuous growth of the pupil. Accordingly, in attempting to come to grips with the problems of coordination of sectors, be it at the end of primary schooling or of post-primary schooling, one may best be advised to emphasise elements of continuity between sectors and a greater understanding of each sector by the other. In speaking earlier of the problem experienced by pupils and schools alike in the transfer from primary school to post-primary school, I made reference to the great lack of communication between both sectors. This lack of communication seems also to have existed between the primary and post-primary branches within the Department of Education, between the primary and the post-primary inspectorate, between primary and post-primary teachers and schools, and between the primary school and post-primary school patterns in the areas of curriculum, teaching and examinations. Such a state of affairs is surely a recipe for difficulties. But if it is, the broad approach necessary for improving matters is surely not very difficult to find: there ought to be organisational structures by which to promote communication, understanding and cooperation between both sectors in each of the above-mentioned areas. And surely the same approach is called for in regard to the coordination of second-level and third-level education. In concrete terms, I would be arguing for the setting up of joint coordinating bodies at the transition points from primary to post-primary and post-primary to third-level education. The areas of concern for such committees would include curriculum planning and coordination, approaches to teaching, inspection, validation, assessment, staff training and research and development.

I am not unaware of the traditional divisions which have been maintained between the various sectors and of the difficulties of approach in such areas as teacher education, relations with and within the Department of Education, validation, inspection, teachers' organisations and unions, independence and autonomy, subject specialisation, and so on. That differences of approach in such areas exist is, indeed, understandable and inevitable. Indeed, that such differences exist would appear to be all the more reason for a coming together of the various parties involved. This would help to ensure a greater understanding of the different perspectives of each and a greater coordination of effort. This, in turn, should help to see to it that the overall educational experience provided for pupils is not fraught with internal conflict and organisational discontinuities.

As I have mentioned already, a committee has been set up by the Minister for Education to examine the question of transition from primary to post-primary school. What I am now urging is that such a committee should not be just a once-off affair but should be appointed as a standing committee. The same provision ought to be made for the coordination of post-primary and third-level education. These committees, moreover, I would see as sub-committees in turn of a broadly based and standing advisory committee on education, a point to which I shall make reference again later on.

The next area of pedagogical import to which I wish to direct attention is the structure and organisation of the curriculum and the impact of the so-called hidden curriculum. In looking at the curriculum of post-primary education in Ireland one is impressed by the seeming lack of consideration which is given to the question of how it will all strike the pupil, yet surely this is a pedagogical point of the first importance. That is to say, schooling as perceived by the pupil must be such as to earn his respect; he must treat it as a matter of some importance in his life, not as an object of distaste. In view of the age range for which the post-primary school caters there is always the danger that it may be seen in negative terms, something against which to rebel, an aspect of the world to be rejected. It is all the more important, then, however fiercely one might argue for one kind of curriculum content or educational programme over another, that there be a willingness to yield to pedagogical and practical considerations. Every effort must be made to ensure that the overall image of schooling presented to pupils is one that casts it in favourable terms. For unless the overall image is one that inspires a sense of seriousness, rather than one of rejection or ridicule, then much may be lost in terms of pupil motivation, commitment and respect and, in the final analysis, the curriculum content and the educational values which we wish to promote. Much may also be lost by way of developing in the pupil an interest in and a positive disposition towards life-long learning, an increasingly indispensable acquisition for the school leaver.

Earlier on, in discussing the influence of the hidden curriculum, I suggested that the curriculum tended to be a very subject-dominated curriculum, that it was a very bookish curriculum, and that it suffered from undesirable collateral learnings associated with it. Earlier on also I drew attention to the increasing concern expressed by some educationists regarding the growing institutional effects of schooling, notably the extent to which it is overly protective of pupils, and as such an influence which delays the emergence of maturity and a sense of responsibility. As well as constituting significant aspects of the hidden curriculum, these features of the curriculum also constitute potent images of schooling. This being so, one must ask what measures can be taken to counteract them.

Rigorous intellectual education will always necessitate a high degree of literary studies, of subject-related or bookish learning, if one may call it that. Accordingly, when the opportunity to break out of such a pattern presents itself every effort should be made, without doing any injustice to the studies in question, to take advantage of it. And there are many aspects of the kinds of studies which I have been proposing which provide such opportunity. I am thinking of those aspects of vocational studies for example, where work-experience and visits may form a valuable integral part of career-orientation courses. In the area of practical studies, community-based projects and activities of the kind carried out in the SHARE project in Cork city suggest themselves. Recreational studies are also rich in opportunities of this kind; consider, for example, the scope for non-book-based learning in such areas as music, art, film, physical education, outdoor pursuits and so on. In the liberal studies area, an integrated humanities programme of the kind to which I have referred already would also appear to hold out excellent possibilities at senior level. Such an approach can entail a substantial element of group discussion and deliberation where pupils are exposed to the difficult intellectual problems associated with the analysis and resolution of major social problems. In this way pupils can also be exposed to the dynamics of the group decision-making process.

Part of the difficulty here has to do with the question of the timetable. But even here the kinds of departures from book-based learning which I have been discussing can be both facilitated and extended by a somewhat more adventurous approach to timetabling. It will always be necessary to rely on fairly conventional timetabling practices for substantial elements of most programmes. Nonetheless, there are many possibilities for breaking away from the unending sequence of forty-five minute sessions from 9.00 am to 4.00 pm, five days a week. Such possibilities are undoubtedly limited by the public examinations in their present-day form, including the emphasis on written examinations. But given a different approach to examinations it may be possible to devise timetabling strategies to reduce the reliance on vicarious curriculum experiences. Already I have talked of making greater use of work-placement courses; these might entail block-periods of work-experience. Two- or three-day block-periods throughout the year might also be devoted to recreational or cultural pursuits such as outdoor activities, arranging and participating in musical or drama festivals, art exhibitions and the like. Similar possibilities could be created in the areas of practical and liberal studies.

Just now I have suggested that innovative practices of the kind to which I have been adverting are not greatly encouraged by the system of public examinations and its emphasis on book-learning. It is also necessary to point out, however, that if practices of the kind I am now suggesting are to become a more prominent feature of post-primary schooling in Ireland, greater facilities in the form of in-service education of teachers, improved teacher-pupil ratios, increased support staff, and improved financing will all be necessary; there are other formidable difficulties as well such as access to work-experience, problems of insurance and logistical problems of one kind or another. Other factors such as school architecture and over-reliance on 'talk and chalk' in an age of high technology communication also have to be considered.[18] Possibilities, however, do exist which present alternatives to present-day practice and these ought to be considered in any discussion of the structure of the curriculum and its implications for the hidden curriculum.

Education of the kind implied by suggestions such as the above is, I believe, seriously under-valued today. Existing curriculum provision is probably too conceptual in emphasis for many pupils, and too deficient in valuable first-hand experience in a wide range of areas for most pupils.[19] If these weaknesses are to be overcome, and if the widespread concern which is expressed regarding the insularity and irrelevance of the school is to be acted upon, the suggestions made are at least some of the possible steps which ought to be taken. They are grounded in a view of general education which is broad and whose breadth is valued as much for the non-academic education which it attempts to promote as much as for the academic. It is a view which accepts that it is in such a broadly-based general education that the necessary intellectual and emotional flexibility, social skills and creativity, required to cope successfully with both the specialist and general demands of living in a rapidly changing world, may best be nurtured. One should probably expect, however, that the suggestions made will be seen by some as a waste of time and a lowering of standards.

I wish to turn now to a consideration of the possible measures which may be taken to increase the level of curriculum provision which is made for individual differences among pupils. It will be recalled from the earlier discussion of this point that a number of aspects of present-day practice are a hindrance to making adequate provision in this regard. These factors include the size and duration of the basic curriculum unit, i.e. the subject; the extent to which subjects studied at junior level are prerequisite for study at senior level; the lack of provision for pupils to switch into new subjects after the first year or two of the post-primary school; the traditionally high status of some subjects such as English and mathematics; the high degree of centralisation which is found in Irish post-primary education; and a number of practical limitations on curriculum provision such as school size and costs. Since many of these features derive from the high degree of centralised control of curriculum and examinations found in Irish education, it will be helpful to begin with a consideration of the question of centralisation.

To begin with, I would not wish to suggest that it is either feasible or desirable to do away completely with centralised control of post-primary education in Ireland. My concern is with reducing the extreme degree of centralisation which obtains in the area of curriculum. And in this regard there may be much to be learned from the tradition found in the vocational sector, particularly as this sector exercised its rights in the area of curriculum in the early years. While the benefits of some decentralisation are many, two in particular merit mention. The first is the benefit to the pupil: with decentralisation there is greater allowance for shaping programmes to meet the requirements of individual pupils in accordance with their needs, interests and backgrounds. The second benefit is of a more general nature: with greater regional, local and individual teacher control and autonomy in the matter of curriculum and related matters, the pupil is brought closer to the educational planner and decision maker. Teachers and school principals are likely to be more interested and involved in work where there is a greater provision for their own input. They are likely to have a fuller understanding of what is going on in terms of curriculum when what they have to say is listened to and acted upon. As a result, the entire educational process stands to become more personalised. Thus, to talk of decentralisation is not merely to seek greater diversity of curriculum and programming; it should also serve to personalise schooling and to make it more responsive to individual, local and regional needs, as well as to the needs of teachers and schools themselves.

In attempting to effect a greater degree of decentralised control of curriculum, certain national norms, standards and guidelines will be necessary if one is to maintain evenness of standards and criteria. Hence the value of the kind of approach adopted by the vocational sector in *Memo V. 40.* There broad criteria and curriculum guidelines were set forth, and it was left to the individual VECs and schools how they would settle the details. And there would appear to be no reason why the kind of position which I proposed in an earlier section of this chapter — where four areas of study which should be included in every pupil's course of study were proposed — could not be used as a basis for such an approach. In order to effect such an approach in the entire post-primary sector, it would be essential to have a greatly expanded inspectorate, one which would be devoted to the work of curriculum planning and development either with individual schools in a region or, preferably, groups of schools in a region. Such an approach would also necessitate the adoption of a more decentralised approach to public examinations, a point to which I shall give greater attention in a moment. Suffice it to say here that there would appear to be no reason why these different but related matters could not be provided for through a well-integrated and well-planned system of more local or regional control accompanied by central or national monitoring of standards, criteria, procedures and the like.

It is possible that such a proposal might meet with objection in the private secondary sector on the grounds that such a departure would amount to an invasion of privacy. In effect, it would probably have the very opposite effect. The area where I am suggesting changes is the area of curriculum and examinations, not ownership or management. And it is in the areas of examinations and curriculum that the secondary schools have least autonomy or, more correctly perhaps, where they have least exerted their autonomy.

Centralisation, however, is not the only obstacle to the greater individualisation of curriculum provision. The size or quantity and duration of the various units or subjects as constituted at the present time, the programmes on offer, and the levels or standards which are formally recognised through the system of public examinations, all pose obstacles as well. Thus, as I have suggested, one of the reasons why traditional patterns of subject choices are so strong in Irish post-primary education is because there is little room for any further subjects once six or seven of them have been chosen. Accordingly, new organisational and other devices must be contemplated if we are to be serious about having greater participation in hitherto unpopular technical, applied and recreational or cultural subjects. And it is encouraging to see that this view is also taken in the *White Paper on Educational Development.* For it is not enough simply to decry the low attendance rates in poorly subscribed subjects. It is for this reason that I have proposed a system of major subjects (in the vocational studies) and minor subjects (in the practical, liberal and recreational studies).[20]

A scheme for the public curriculum might be implemented along the following lines. One would keep approximately 35 per cent of curriculum time at junior level, and approximately 60 per cent of curriculum time at senior level, for vocational or specialist studies. The remainder would be for the liberal, recreational and practical studies. If the non-vocational studies were composed of minor subjects or units, it should be quite possible to ensure a broad range of such studies throughout the course of the junior cycle and, more importantly perhaps, the senior cycle of the post-primary school.

On a related point in this matter of individualisation of programmes, I have already suggested that it may be desirable not to have pupils tied to subjects chosen at junior level when they come to senior cycle. One way of providing for such late choices might be by making provision for individual study for those pupils who wished it during the course of the normal day. A second way, and one which could tie in with the first, would be to allow pupils at senior cycle to study junior cycle subjects in order to take up a subject not chosen at junior level. This, in turn, might be facilitated by not demanding the same minimum number of subjects for study by all pupils; thus a pupil who wishes to take up a new subject in the specialist area might be permitted to take fewer specialist studies and be given time for individual study, and attendance at junior-cycle classes, in the new subject of his choice.

Before leaving this question, one more point must be touched upon. To be able to offer a wide range of subjects it is necessary that school size be reasonably large by Irish standards. For as was seen earlier, the size of the school can be a constraint when it comes to providing for choice and flexibility. While there were very definite attempts made during the 1960s to create larger schools — whether by amalgamation of schools, cooperation among schools, or the building of new schools — a large proportion of small schools still exist in rural areas. And while there is something to be said for keeping school enrolments below 1,000 pupils, schools of 800 pupils or thereabouts, or a group of small-size schools working in cooperation, can work successfully, especially if special staffing needs and resources are attended to.

Like so many other aspects of the curriculum of post-primary education in Ireland, be they aspects pertaining to the public content of the curriculum or to the pedagogy of the curriculum, the questions of individualisation of programmes and decentralisation are bound up with the whole question of the public examinations. It is time now to see what might be said regarding the possible reform of the present-day system of public examinations.

Whatever may be the details of any new approach to the question of the public examinations, it is imperative that the overall approach is one which satisfies a number of important educational requirements which are not fully satisfied under the existing arrangement. In the first place, whatever form or system of pupil assessment or examination is devised, it must be consistent with and supportive of the aims of post-primary education. It is preposterous that a system of public examinations should threaten to undermine, as the present system appears to, the important educational goals to which post-primary education professes to aspire and to institute pseudo-educational objectives in their place. The second condition which must be met is that of technical adequacy of the system of assessment; it must be such as to be valid, reliable and accurate in its assessments. And thirdly, and related to this point, the system which is adopted must be one which will entail a substantial element of school-based and continuous assessment; for only in this way can assessment fulfil its role in guiding and shaping the pupil's course of education, an aspect of assessment largely ignored in the existing system.

It is possible that part of the difficulty which has been encountered in the reform of the examination system may be due to a failure to characterise exactly what the problem is. Accordingly, it will be helpful if we begin with a brief examination of the role of testing or examining in fields other than education. In medicine, for example, tests and examinations are standard procedure. Such tests and examinations are very largely used as a basis for diagnosis and treatment. Their basic purpose usually is to assist both doctor and patient in ensuring a speedy return to good health, or in maintaining it. In talking of tests and examinations such as these one never speaks of failing or passing them in the way that one talks of passing or failing school tests or examinations. But there are other tests in medicine where it is not uncommon to speak of passing or failing. I am referring to the so-called 'medical test' which is used to declare fitness or otherwise for employment, for travel, for insurance purposes, or whatever. In this case, however, the so-called medical test is not carried out for medical reasons as such but to certify fitness (or the lack of it) for employment purposes or whatever. If a person is declared fit he is said to have passed his test; if declared unfit he is said to have failed it.

It would appear that the public examinations in Irish post-primary education are, in many respects, much more akin to the medical test used to declare fitness than to tests and examinations in medicine whose purpose is to assist in diagnosis and treatment. That is to say that the main use to which they are put is to declare pupils qualified or fit for entry to employment, apprenticeship or higher education. As aids to guiding a pupil's progress through school, however, not only are they crude tools for this purpose but their timing is entirely inappropriate. Very often they come at the termination of a pupil's schooling and hence serve no purpose in monitoring his progress and guiding the course of his education.

One might argue that it is not the purpose of the school to certify whether pupils are fit for entry to employment, to apprenticeships or to higher education, but simply to educate. It might be left to others to decide how fit pupils may be for their particular purposes. While such a line of argument is not without merit, it would be naive perhaps to suggest that post-primary education in Ireland should disclaim all responsibility in this area. Given that schools are, at least to some extent, an agent of society, and hence partly accountable to it, it may not be unreasonable to expect the school to provide its graduates with certificates of achievement of some kind. What must be insisted upon, however, is that an educational system must give priority to its unique and particular role, that of educating pupils. And to fulfil this role satisfactorily it relies upon an adequate system of educational testing whereby to measure, monitor and guide the achievement of pupils in the course of their education. If the role of certification practised by post-primary education can be combined with this role without injury to it, there would appear to be no good reason why this function might not also be continued. As I have argued in the previous chapter, however, this does not now appear to be the case.

Where does all of this leave us in considering the possible alternatives to the present system of public examinations? It has helped, I believe, to characterise the nature of the problem. It suggests, moreover, that the following points must be borne in mind in addressing the issue. Firstly, how can a system of assessment be devised which will provide reliable feedback on pupils' progress with a view to guiding learning? Secondly, how can we devise such a system which will promote, and not undermine, the espoused aims of post-primary education? And thirdly, how might we devise a system which, while fulfilling the above-mentioned conditions, would not rule out the historical role of post-primary education in providing its graduates with certificates of educational achievement? These are not easy questions to answer, though some attempt must be made to do so. In doing so, however, I shall be concerned to sketch the broad outlines of a possible response rather than the detail. Besides, the basic thrust of what I shall have to say will be in broad agreement with the kinds of proposals put forward in the *ICE Report* which, whilst it may need modification in some respects, does constitute a very important starting point.[21]

The broad scope of the approach to assessment which I would advocate would be as follows: it would entail school-based assessment by teachers; it would be continuous in a number of respects, particularly in the sense that a teacher's views on each pupil on the basis of daily contact, and not merely contact through formal tests, would form an input into the overall assessment; it would be a form of assessment which would include a number of monitoring procedures to ensure evenness of standards on a regional and national scale; it would allow a much greater degree of flexibility than is the case in the existing system; and it would entail each pupil being awarded a certificate on leaving school, irrespective of the stage at which he left or the number and kind of subjects or programmes which he followed.

Central to the entire scheme as I envisage it would be a pupil-assessment file. Taken in conjunction with what I have just been saying regarding a combination of school-based and nationally-monitored testing, and assuming an approach to the curriculum of a general education covering the four major areas of study which I have proposed, I would see the scheme working somewhat along the following lines. A pupil-assessment file would be opened for each pupil on his entering the post-primary school; maintaining the file would be the responsibility of the school registrar; the file would be updated on a regular basis and an official return would be required in respect of each school term. While this whole system would be the responsibility of the school registrar, its contents would be drawn from a wide range of sources including subject teachers, form teachers, guidance and remedial teachers, the school principal and external agencies, including representatives of the Department of Education.

There are many possible ways in which the pupil-assessment file might be set out, and the following possibility is intended only as an example. Provision might be made in the file for entries under the headings of practical studies, vocational studies, liberal studies and recreational studies. A brief report on the pupil would be entered for each term and a ranking of the pupil in terms of the percentile (say, top 75 per cent, middle 50 per cent, bottom 25 per cent) group in the class into which he fell would also be made in respect of the four areas of study. Such ranking (in conjunction with a return of a similar kind in respect of externally monitored tests as will be detailed below) would serve as a preventative against schools issuing inflated reports in respect of all of their pupils. And while one is hesitant to introduce a competitive element here, the fact that the percentile bands are very broad may serve to reduce the impact on schooling of this element.

The statement from the school[22] would be expected to pay particular attention to aspects of the social and personal development of the pupil, and it would incorporate a cross-section of views of his teachers and of any external agencies with whom he may have contact in the form of work-placements. This section of the report would remain confidential and it would not be made available to anyone without the consent of the pupil or his parents. All other entries would be made available to interested parties.

The second major part of the file would be given over to the performance of the pupil on externally monitored examinations. Already I have suggested that there are too few recognised standards of achievement in Irish post-primary education, namely the Intermediate and Leaving Certificate examination and possibly the Group Certificate examination. It is also increasingly recognised that pupils should be given a certificate of achievement at whatever stage they leave school. Accordingly, it may be desirable to maintain at least two such externally-monitored tests in addition to the school-based ones. One of the two could be at the end of the junior cycle or compulsory school, the other at termination of second-level education. These examinations could retain the present names of Intermediate and Leaving Certificate examination or they could assume some such name as Post-Primary School Examination Part I and Part II. In this case also there may be merit in entering a pupil's result in terms of how he fared in comparison with other pupils taking the same examinations, that is in terms of the percentile group into which he fell. These examinations would all be single-subject examinations. There might be some consideration given to limiting such examinations to the specialist or vocational studies. To do this, however, it would be necessary to have a thorough system of inspection in the areas of practical, liberal and recreational studies. The verification of results in this section of the file concerned with external examinations would be a matter for the Department of Education. Provision might also be made for the senior pupil with a special interest to take one or two subjects of examination at the level of the junior-cycle examination.

At the end of each year that a pupil spent at school his termly reports would be consolidated into a yearly report. On leaving school the pupil would be issued with a yearly report for each year completed. A final school report which consolidated all previous yearly reports would also be issued. An example of the kind of yearly or final report card which I would have in mind for the pupil assessment file is shown in Table 11 on page 204.

Some final points regarding the external examinations referred to above: they would be drawn up by a consortium of schools grouped together for the purpose; they would be based on curricula drawn up by the staff of the same schools; they would be marked by the class teacher and by a teacher from one of the schools in the consortium; they would then be externally monitored by external examiners acting on behalf of the Department of Education. To assist in curriculum development and assessment, each consortium of schools would have available to it the services of curriculum specialists and specialists in educational evaluation. For purposes of general monitoring and maintaining evenness of standards each consortium of schools would be within the jurisdiction of a regional inspectorate.

As I have said, this is only intended as an outline of the possibilities which might be considered. As the *ICE Report* has shown, however, the implementation of the kind of changes called for

| YEARLY/FINAL REPORT | YEAR: | CLASS: | NAME: |

SCHOOL:

CONTINUOUS ASSESSMENT	Top 25%	Top 50%	Top 75%	Bottom 25%
Liberal Studies	e.g. √			
Vocational Studies		e.g. √		
Practical Studies			e.g. √	
Recreational Studies				e.g. √

STATEMENT FROM SCHOOL

Signed : Registrar

: Principal

: Dept. Inspector

Date : _____

PUBLIC EXAMINATIONS – SPECIALIST STUDIES

P.P.S.E. II: Subject 1 (e.g., Maths) – e.g., Top 30% in Hons/Pass

P.P.S.E. II: Subject 2 (e.g., Chemistry) – e.g., Top 40% in Hons/Pass

P.P.S.E. II: Subject 3 (e.g., Engineering) – e.g., Top 50% in Hons/Pass

P.P.S.E. I : Subject 4 (e.g., French B) – e.g., top 50% in Hons/Pass

Departmental Signature: _____

Date: _____

here would occasion detailed planning and further research and training of staff in areas such as curriculum development and assessment of pupil learning. Moreover, it might be advantageous to set up an independent examinations board to administer the examinations. The success of the National Council for Education Awards (NCEA) in its approach to the overseeing and validation of courses in a wide range of institutions in which its degrees, diplomas and certificates are awarded, and its work in combining external examining with institution-based and continuous assessment, all demonstrate that, given the appropriate guidance and support, one could expect similar success in this difficult area of post-primary education.

While the measures which I have proposed should go some way towards meeting the main conditions required for a satisfactory system of educational assessment, one serious problem still needs to be examined. This is the problem of the use of the Leaving Certificate examination in its present form as a basis for university matriculation and entry into other colleges of higher education, and the consequent influence of these institutions in shaping the programmes of the post-primary school. This influence is added to enormously through the points system of selection for universities and institutions of higher education. This is a difficult influence to overcome, and it may never be fully overcome as long as higher education retains its allure. The attitude of the *White Paper* on this matter is disappointing and misleading. The best that it can suggest is that it 'is to be hoped that expansion in other third-level [i.e. non-university] institutions and increased participation in other types of courses at school will help to moderate the pressure of university requirements on students'.[23] The issue is a difficult one to deal with to be sure, but it is naive to evade it by insinuating that the pressure of the third-level sector is exerted only by the universities as distinct from other third-level institutions. As a start, there might be something to be said for attempting to solve the problem by discontinuing the present close ties between the Leaving Certificate examination and entry to higher education. A modified open admissions scheme, whereby anyone with a final year school-leaving certificate would be eligible for entry to a pre-matriculation or foundational year would merit consideration. Such a scheme would, I believe, have considerable benefit for second-level education. The question is could it be so shaped as to win the approval of the institutions of higher education?

For some time there has been talk of adding a year to the post-primary school course.[24] If this were to mean simply more of the same, I believe it should be resisted. And if nothing can be done to change the present close link-up between the Leaving Certificate and the matriculation or other third-level entry requirements, little may change. The scheme I envisage is one whereby the institutions of higher education – and not the schools – would take this additional year and treat it as a pre-matriculation year. That is to say, at the end of a year of general academic studies (perhaps with options linked to the degree specialisations offered by the institution), the matriculation examination, or its equivalent in the non-university sector, would be taken. The scope of the examination would correspond to the course of studies of the foundational or pre-matriculation course. Only those who attained a satisfactory level of achievement would be matriculated.

While this approach would pose difficulties of its own, it would have considerable merit. The chief difficulty in adopting a scheme such as this would probably relate to the provision of the necessary resources. There might be something to be said for enlarging the existing institutions of higher education to cope with the numbers. But this scheme would relieve the schools of their present role of being third-level or university preparatory. In this way it would diminish the controlling influence of the universities over the curriculum of the post-primary school. And it would free the schools to develop programmes more responsive to what were considered to constitute the real demands of a general education rather than those of a preparation for higher education.

The broader implications

Having considered in this chapter a number of proposals for change in the areas of the aims and philosophy, the content and the pedagogy of the curriculum of post-primary education in Ireland, it is appropriate now to consider some of the possible implications of these proposals for the broader workings of the Irish educational system. The main areas to which I propose to devote attention are the education of teachers, educational research and development, and the coordination of the various sectors. I shall begin with a consideration of the question of teacher education.

I have set forth my views on the question of the preparation of second-level teachers in Ireland elsewhere, and I do not wish to depart from anything which I said on that occasion.[25] There are one or two points, however, which I would wish to emphasise in the light of what I have been saying here. The first of these has to do with the so-called subject or content preparation of teachers. At the present time there would appear to be inadequate preparation of teachers in the areas of the practical studies and out-of-school work-experience in particular. These are serious deficiencies and are surely at the basis of some of the difficulties which have been encountered in the teaching of some subjects. A second point which merits particular emphasis is the importance which ought to be devoted to the preparation of teachers in the areas of curriculum and assessment. One of the implications of the foregoing study of post-primary education is the need for teachers to assume a greater degree of involvement in and responsibility for such matters as school-based curriculum planning and development as well as the assessment of pupil learning.

This point bears on the pre-service preparation of teachers clearly, but it also bears on the in-service education of teachers. In the first place, the pre-service education of teachers, as has been well argued in the James Report on teacher education in England, ought to be seen as only a partial preparation of the teacher. Provision must also be made for proper induction facilities and for in-service education. For too long those responsible for pre-service education have been labouring alone. And they have been expected to do, through a pre-service course, what in fact can only be achieved through a combination of pre-service, induction and in-service education. At in-service level, with first-hand experience of teaching behind them, teachers are well positioned to benefit from more advanced studies in the theory and practice of education. But before in-service education can be undertaken seriously, and indeed before the kind and combination of generalist and specialist studies which one could envisage in areas such as curriculum and assessment, those responsible for the provision of post-primary education in Ireland must give the necessary lead. They must provide encouragement, funding and recognition for in-service work. And they must clearly commit themselves to a policy of greater teacher autonomy, involvement and responsibility than is the case at the present time in areas such as curriculum and assessment. For there is little attraction, and little point, in preparing teachers intensively in areas such as these if there is no policy or encouragement given in the schools to put such learning to work. And while a beginning may have been made with the setting up of the kinds of curriculum and examinations projects of recent years to which I have referred already, much greater commitment and policy direction are necessary.

The second area in need of greater attention and support than it has received in the past, if the curriculum of the post-primary school is to prosper, is the whole area of curriculum and examinations research and development. As has been noted already, the past decade or so has seen the emergence of some activity in this area. This has been an important development, yet it is imperative that funding and support on a much larger scale than before be provided. It is important also that areas of priority in terms of research and development be drawn up. Thus, for example, important work needs to be done in the areas of the aims and objectives of schooling, the selection and organisation of content, the design of materials, provision for individual differences, pre-employment programmes, testing and assessment in a wide range of areas and especially in the area of school-based assessment.

Finally, I come to the third main area of implication. There is need, I believe, for an Advisory Council on Education. This would be an independent body with powers to advise and propose policy either of its own volition or at the request of the Minister. A particular concern of this body would be the coordination of policy and practice in all areas of education. And while it would not be unduly burdened with day-to-day executive responsibilities, it would be empowered to coordinate, commission and fund educational research into matters which come under its area of responsibility.

Notes to Chapters

Notes to Introduction

1. In this connection see, for example, Raymond Ryba 'The context of curricular change in Europe at the lower secondary level', *Compare* 10/2 (1980) 101-116, and A. Harry Passow *Secondary education reform: retrospect and prospect* (New York: Teachers College, Columbia University, 1976).

2. *White Paper on Educational Development* (Dublin: The Stationery Office, 1980) p. 55.

3. As an example of a study of this kind see John Raven *Education, values and society: the objectives of education and the nature and development of competence* (London: H.K. Lewis and Co. Ltd., 1977) pp. 48-96.

4. As an example of a study of this general kind which is concerned with a wide range of educational issues see A. Harry Passow, Harold J. Noah, Max A. Eckstein, and John R. Mallea *The national case study: an empirical comparative study of twenty-one educational systems* (New York: John Wiley and Sons, 1976).

5. In this connection see, for example, William A. Reid *Thinking about the curriculum: the nature and treatment of curriculum problems* (London: Routledge and Kegan Paul, 1978) pp. 94-109, and Centre for

Educational Research and Innovation *Handbook on curriculum development* (Paris: OECD, 1975) pp. 42-6.

6. See Ralph W. Tyler *Basic principles of curriculum and instruction* (Chicago: The University of Chicago Press, 1949).

Notes to Chapter One

1. See Séamus V. Ó Súilleabháin 'Secondary Education' in Patrick J. Corish (ed.) *A history of Irish Catholicism* Vol. 5 (Dublin: Gill and Macmillan, 1971) p. 72.

2. See Ó Súilleabháin 'Secondary education' pp. 61-4.

3. For a lively discussion of the transition period see Donald H. Akenson *A mirror to Kathleen's face: education in independent Ireland, 1922-1960* (Montreal: McGill — Queen's University Press, 1975) pp. 25-34.

4. Department of Education *Report for the school year 1924-1925* (Dublin: The Stationery Office, 1926) p. 51. For the details of the new programme see Department of Education *Rules and programme for secondary schools* for the year 1924-25 (Dublin: The Stationery Office, n.d.) pp. 3-12.

5. *Rules* 1924-25, pp. 8-9.

6. *Report* 1937-38, pp. 44-49.

7. *Report of the Council of Educa-*

tion: the curriculum of the secondary school (Dublin: The Stationery Office, 1960) p. 68.

8. Department of Education, Technical Branch *Memorandum V.40: organization of whole-time continuation courses in borough, urban and county areas* (1942).

9. *Ibid.* p. 9.

10. *Report* 1952-53, p. 29.

11. Seán Ó Catháin *Secondary education in Ireland* (Dublin: The Talbot Press, 1958); J J. O'Meara *Reform in education* (Dublin: Mount Salus Press, 1958). See also Tuairim *Irish education* (London: Tuairim Pamphlet No. 9, n.d., c. 1961-2).

12. See, for example, J.H. Whyte *Church and state in modern Ireland* (Dublin: Gill and Macmillan, 1971) pp. 356-361. See also Eileen Randles *Post-primary education in Ireland 1957-1970* (Dublin: Veritas Publications, 1975) pp. 41-3, 305-310. Sister Randles pinpoints 1959 as the year in which educational expansion in accordance with national economic needs was first asserted in its new form as government policy. See also the *Second programme for economic expansion* (Dublin: The Stationery Office, 1963) Part I, p. 8.

13. In this connection see *Programme for economic expansion* (Dublin: The Stationery Office, 1958); *Second programme for economic expansion* Part I, pp. 13-15 and Part II (Dublin: The Stationery Office, 1964) pp. 193-206; *Investment in education* (Dublin: The Stationery Office, 1965; Organisation for Economic Cooperation and Development *Reviews of national policies for education: Ireland* (Paris: OECD, 1969). See also the National Economic and Social Council, Report No. 12 *Educational expenditure in Ireland* (Dublin: The Stationery Office, 1976) and

A. Dale Tussing *Irish Educational expenditures — past, present and future* (Dublin: The Economic and Social Research Institute, 1978) for more recent work which is concerned more specifically with the aspect of expenditure.

14. Interview in *Hibernia* 28/2 (February, 1964) p. 8. Quoted in Randles *Post-primary education in Ireland* p. 147.

15. There will be reason to refer again to Dr Hillery's distinction between pupils of an 'academic bent' and those of 'a technical or practical bent'. For the present it is sufficient to say that the distinction is clearly present in Dr Hillery's press conference of 20 May 1963, in which he outlined his plans for post-primary education.

16. Press Conference 20 May 1963. *Statement* by Dr P.J. Hillery, TD, Minister for Education, in regard to post-primary education. Reprinted in Randles *Post-primary education in Ireland* pp. 328-337.

17. By the time that the implementation of Dr Hillery's plan was initiated the Day Group Certificate course was also common to all post-primary schools. In time it would also be decided to drop the idea of a separate Technical Leaving Certificate examination and to have the one Leaving Certificate for all subjects and courses at senior level. From their beginnings also, the regional technical colleges offered courses other than Leaving Certificate courses. The vocational schools were also allowed to offer the Leaving Certificate course from 1968 onwards.

18. For a more detailed account of these events, see Randles *Post-primary education in Ireland* pp. 105-184.

19. For further details see Randles *Post-primary education in Ireland* pp. 182-184.

20. See Department of Education *Report on the facilities for post-primary education in each county and an estimate of requirements for 1970* (1966), and *Investment in education: annexes and appendices* pp. 610-626 where the beginnings made in this undertaking are set forth.

21. George Colley, Minister for Education, Letter to the authorities of secondary and vocational schools, January 1966. Reprinted in Randles *Post-primary education in Ireland* pp. 338-342.

22. See Department of Education *Report on facilities; Investment in education: annexes and appendices* pp. 610-626, and Randles *Post-primary education in Ireland* pp. 238-242. See also Department of Education *Structure of the Leaving Certificate course and examination* (M. 29/68) p.2.

23. See Colley, Letter. For good examples of what was intended, see Department of Education *Report on facilities* for Donegal Town and Bunclody, County Wexford.

24. According to Randles *Post-primary education in Ireland* p. 300, by 1970 some twenty-six vocational schools and nine secondary schools had been closed, there had been over twenty amalgamations of schools throughout the country, and various forms of co-operation between schools had been underway in many areas, some very successfully. For a similar view see Seán O'Connor 'Post-primary education: now and in the future' in *Studies* LVII (Autumn, 1968) pp. 238-240, 246-247. For a pessimistic view see John Horgan 'Education in the Republic of Ireland' in Robert Bell, Gerald Fowler and Ken Little (eds.) *Education in Great Britain and Ireland* (London: Routledge and Kegan Paul, 1973) p. 41. For the latest official information on this see *Report* 1978-9, p.37: it was reported that in that year eight schools operated a system of common enrolment.

25. See O'Connor *Post-primary education* pp. 240, 244, 246-7; Randles *Post-primary education in Ireland* pp. 238-242; and *White paper on educational development* (Dublin: The Stationery Office, 1980) pp. 66-69.

26. See Randles *Post-primary education in Ireland* pp. 41-43.

27. See *Investment in Education* pp. 34-43; Colley, Letter; Department of Education *Report on facilities*; Department of Education *Structure of the Leaving Certificate* p. 3; Randles *Post-primary education in Ireland* p. 242; O'Connor 'Post-primary education' p. 240.

28. See Colley, Letter; Department of Education *Structure of the Leaving Certificate* pp. 2, 4-7; O'Connor 'Post-primary education', p. 235; Randles *Post-primary education in Ireland* pp. 281-282; National Economic and Social Council *Educational Expenditure in Ireland* pp. 64-69. See also *Investment in education: annexes and appendices* pp. 610-626. It might also be pointed out that projections made in *Investment in education* p. 36, for numbers of pupils in second-level education for 1970/71 were considerably below what the actual figure was. The projected figure was 172,600. The actual figure was 197,142. See *Report* 1968/9-1971/2, p. 4.

29. See O'Connor 'Post-primary education' p. 235; Department of Education *Structure of the Leaving Certificate* pp. 1-2.

30. See Denis Donoghue's comments on O'Connor 'Post-primary education' in *Studies* LVII (Autumn, 1968) pp. 284-288.

31. O'Connor 'Post-primary educa-

tion' pp. 233-249.

32. *Ibid.* pp. 244-246.

33. *Ibid.* p. 244.

34. The article itself was dated June 1968. The publication date of the issue of *Studies* in which it appeared was Autumn 1968.

35. In fairness it might be pointed out that the universities were probably not that well informed on developments in post-primary schools themselves.

36. The Higher Education Authority *A council for national awards and a college for higher education at Limerick* (Dublin: The Higher Education Authority, 1969) (reprinted 1974) p. 5.

37. *Ibid.* pp. 9, 12.

38. *Ibid.* p. 6.

39. See *The Irish Times* 17 December 1974. While the new Government's proposals to create a so-called comprehensive system of higher education were to be modified subsequently, the decision to remove degree-granting power from the NCEA and give it to the universities stood until changed by John Wilson, Minister for Education in the Fianna Fáil Government which took office in 1977.

40. *Rules* 1924-5, pp. 9-10; *Rules* 1962-3, p. 15; *Rules* 1980-1, pp. 15-17.

41. See *Rules* 1962-3, pp. 50-109, and *Rules* 1980-1, pp. 48-335. For the current list of subjects available in the Day Group Certificate course see Department of Education *Rules and programme for the Day Vocational Certificate examinations* V.50, 80/81 (Dublin: The Stationery Office) p.xi. This reference is abbreviated below to *Memo V.50* (revised 80/81). For the current list of subjects available in Intermediate and Leaving Certificate courses, see *Rules* 1980-1, pp. 15-17. It should also be pointed out that other changes which took place, largely on a transitional basis, between 1962/3 and the present day, are not reflected in these lists.

In the case of the list of subjects for the Intermediate Certificate examination, agricultural science and manual training have been abolished, and music and drawing have undergone substantial alteration. Woodwork and metalwork have been introduced along with mechanical drawing, and there are now two syllabuses in music and musicianship. In the case of other subjects, such as history and geography, multiple syllabuses have also been introduced. In the case of science, exclusive of domestic science, two syllabuses now exist as opposed to four in 1962/3. Domestic science has been re-titled home economics, the content has been changed somewhat, and the course re-organised. And while civics is a non-examination subject, it has been introduced as a compulsory subject for all pupils up to the Intermediate Certificate level. In 1980 a new subject, classical studies, was introduced for the first time. In the case of the list of subjects for the Leaving Certificate examination, general science, botany, physiology and hygiene, domestic science, drawing, music and commerce have been either substantially altered or omitted entirely. The following subjects have been introduced: biology, agricultural economics, engineering workshop theory and practice, technical drawing, building construction, mechanics, home economics (scientific and social), home economics (general), accounting, business organisation, economics, economic history and music and musicianship.

42. See *Report* 1962-3, p. 147, and

Memo V. 50 (revised 80/81), pp. vii, xi. The 1962-3 list in turn differs in only minor respects from the list introduced for the first Group Certificate examination in 1947 and from the revised list introduced for examination in 1954. See *Report* 1946-7, pp. 30-33, and *Report* 1953-4, pp. 23-26.

43. *Report* 1946-7, pp. 30-33; *Memo V. 50* (revised 80/81), pp. vii, xi; and *Rules* 1980-1, p. 15. See also Committee on the form and function of the Intermediate Certificate Examination, the *ICE Report* (Dublin: The Stationery Office, 1975), pp. 43-47. There it is pointed out that the Day Group Certificate examination syllabuses are considered to be equal to two thirds of those for the Intermediate Certificate examination. At present the following subjects are common to both the Intermediate and Day Group Certificate lists of examination subjects: art, commerce, English, French, geography, German, history, Irish, Italian, mathematics, mechanical drawing, metalwork, science (syllabus A), Spanish, woodwork.

44. For a detailed account see Daniel C. O'Connor *Curriculum development at second level in the Republic of Ireland* (unpublished PhD Thesis, Maynooth, 1976) pp. 272-371. It is O'Connor's view that at the time of his writing curriculum innovation in Irish post-primary education since the mid-1960s had been confined largely to what might at best be described as syllabus modification. See *ibid.* p. 372.

45. See *Report* 1962-3, p. 147.

46. See *Rules* 1980-1, and *Memo V. 50* (revised 80/81).

47. *Rules* 1967-8, p. 25; *Rules* 1980-1, p. 23.

48. *Rules* 1980-1, pp. 13, 17, 29.

49. In this connection attention must

be drawn to the discussions which took place with a view to introducing other changes into the long-standing practices in respect of the post-primary school examinations in the form of an Advanced Certificate course and examination, subject groupings at senior level, and other changes. See Department of Education *Structure of the Leaving Certificate*. As it turned out the major recommendations of this report were never implemented.

50. *Memo V. 50* (revised 80/81) p. vi.

51. *Ibid.*

52. *Rules* 1980-81, pp. 23, 29; *Memo V. 50* (revised 80/81), p. vi.

53. *Rules* 1968-9, pp. 23, 27.

54. *Ibid.*; *Rules* 1975-6, pp. 25, 29. See also *Report* 1976-7, p. 55.

55. See *Rules* 1968-9, pp. 21-25; *Rules* 1970-71, pp. 29-31. While the notions of 'fail', 'pass', and 'honours' have been abolished officially, other criteria, notably the points system for university entrance, have taken their place for purposes of entry to employment and further education.

56. See, for example, *Rules* 1980-81, pp. 75, 81.

57. See *Rules* 1980-81, pp. 96, 162, 178-179; *Memo V. 50* (revised 80/81), pp. 2, 5. Considerable controversy has surrounded the conduct of the oral examinations since their introduction, and it has been argued that much more should and could be done to give greater attention to this aspect of modern languages teaching.

58. See also the numbers of pupils studying the various subjects in the Intermediate and Leaving Certificate programme. No comparable figures are given for the Group Certificate programmes, however. These figures also have the disadvantage of including pupils who may not complete

the programmes for which they are enrolled. See *Report* 1978-9, pp. 49-52.
59. *Rules* 1980-81, p. 29.
60. *Report* 1978-9, p. 56.
61. *Ibid*. pp. 58-59.
62. *Ibid*. p.56-57.
63. *Ibid*. p. 60.
64. *Report* 1976-7, p. 52; *Report* 1978-9, pp. 57-59. The same trend exists for all years since the subjects in question were introduced into the Leaving Certificate examination in 1971. See also the *White Paper on educational development* pp. 78-79. Technical drawing is the only technical subject for which the special grant will apply.
65. *Report* 1962-3, p. 147.
66. See *Investment in Education* pp. 35-36, and *Report* 1972-3-1973-4, p. 3.
67. See Hillery *Statement* in Randles *Post-primary education in Ireland* pp. 328-337. A similar distinction is found in the *Second programme for economic expansion* Part I, p. 14 and Part II, p. 200, and in Department of Education *Report on Facilities*.
68. See Tussing *Irish educational expenditures* pp. 63-64, 71. See also A. Dale Tussing 'The coming explosion in school enrolments and expenditures' in *The Secondary Teacher* 6 (Winter, 1976) 12-14. Tussing's view that the arts component is declining and the technical component is increasing is, I believe, based on a somewhat selective treatment of the figures available for numbers studying the various post-primary school subjects. To get the best picture possible, figures for all subjects must be considered. A similar criticism can be levelled against the *White Paper on educational development* p. 44.
69. Hillery *Statement* in Randles *Post-primary education in Ireland* pp. 328-337.

70. *ICE Report* p. 45.
71. Other factors aside from what might be considered specifically educational ones, factors such as the effects of home and socio-economic background on school attainment, also have an important bearing on this matter. On this point see Liam Ryan 'Social dynamite: a study of early school-leavers' in *Christus Rex* xxi (January, February, March, 1967) 7-44.
72. On this point see Organisation for Economic Co-operation and Development *Reviews of national policies* pp. 47-48, 83-84; Centre for Educational Research and Innovation *Handbook on curriculum development* (Paris: OECD 1975) pp. 119-121, 170-172; Ivor Morrish *Aspects of educational change* (London: George Allen and Unwin Ltd., 1976); and Donald E. Orlosky and B. Othanel Smith *Curriculum development: issues and insights* (Chicago: Rand McNally, 1978) pp. 287-363. It is a consistent theme throughout Randles *Post-primary education in Ireland* though one feels that she overstates the case, that the Department of Education and successive Ministers for Education did not sufficiently involve school principals and other educational interest groups in the activities of the 1960s.
73. See O'Connor *Curriculum development at second level in the Republic of Ireland* pp. 304-306.

Notes to Chapter Two

1. Press Conference, 20 May 1963. *Statement* by Dr P.J. Hillery, TD, Minister for Education, in regard to post-primary education. Reprinted in Randles *Post-primary education in Ireland 1957-1970* (Dublin: Veritas Publications, 1976) pp. 328-337.

2. See The Irish National Teachers' Organisation *A plan for education* (Dublin: The Irish National Teachers' Organisation, 1947), pp. 10-15, 73-79; Seán Ó Catháin *Secondary education in Ireland* (Dublin: The Talbot Press, 1958) pp. 25-37; and John Raven *Education, values and society: the objectives of education and the nature and development of competence* (London: H.K. Lewis and Co. Ltd., 1977). In this connection one might also refer again to J.J. O'Meara *Reform in education* (Dublin: Mount Salus Press, 1958) and Tuairim *Irish education* (London: Tuairim Pamphlet No. 9, n.d., *c.* 1961-1962).

3. Department of Education, Technical Instruction Branch *Memorandum V. 40: organization of whole-time continuation courses in borough, urban and county areas* (n.d., *c.* 1942) pp. 2-3, 21-24; *Report of the Council of Education: the curriculum of the secondary school* (Dublin: The Stationery Office, 1960) pp. 88-93.

4. Department of Education *Rules and programme for secondary schools* (Dublin: The Stationery Office, n.d., 1924) pp. 8-9.

5. *Rules* 1980-81, p. 23.

6. *Ibid.* p. 29.

7. *Rules* 1924-5, p. 8.

8. *Ibid.* p. 9.

9. *Rules* 1980-81, p. 258.

10. See *Rules* 1974-5, pp. 78-94, and *Rules* 1980-81, pp. 74-77.

11. See *Rules* 1980-81, pp. 295-296. Compare also the relatively extensive syllabus in economic history, *ibid.* pp. 291-295.

12. There are some grounds for thinking that Leaving Certificate English might be somewhat of an exception on this point. *Rules* 1980-81, pp. 164-165.

13. Some exceptions include mathematics and classical studies at junior cycle and English and building construction at Leaving Certificate level.

14. *Report of the Council of Education: the curriculum of the secondary school* p. 88.

15. *Ibid.* p. 90.

16. *Ibid.*

17. *Ibid.* p. 92.

18. *Ibid.* pp. 90-92.

19. *Ibid.* pp. 178-180, 192-198.

20. *Ibid.* pp. 178, 194.

21. *Ibid.* p. 196.

22. *Ibid.* p. 192.

23. *Ibid.* pp. 178-180.

24. *Report of the Council of Education: the curriculum of the secondary school* p. 88.

25. As was pointed out already in chapter one, the term 'vocational education' as used in the Vocational Education Act of 1930 referred to both continuation and technical education. In its everyday usage, however, 'vocational education' has come to be used interchangeably with 'continuation education' to refer to courses offered towards the Day Vocational or Day Group Certificate examinations in the vocational schools. It is in this sense of the word that I use the term 'vocational education' interchangeably with 'continuation education', and I do so because it reflects normal usage.

26. See Department of Education *Rules and programme for the Day Vocational Certificate examinations* V. 50, 80/81 (Dublin: The Stationery Office).

27. *Memo V. 40* pp. 21-22.

28. *Ibid.* p. 3.

29. *Ibid.* pp. 3-21.

30. On this point see also the Committee on the form and function of the Intermediate Certificate Examination *The ICE Report* (Dublin: The Stationery Office, 1975) pp. 43-46.

31. Seán O'Connor 'Post-primary education: now and in the

future' in *Studies* LVII (Autumn, 1968) 238.

32. Department of Education 'Community schools' October, 1970. Reprinted in Randles *Post-primary education in Ireland* pp. 347-349. The document is also reprinted and discussed by P.M. Troddyn in *Studies* LIX (Winter, 1970) 341-376.

33. In this connection see Organisation for Economic Co-operation and Development *Reviews of national policies for education: Ireland* (Paris: OECD, 1969) especially pp. 77-78.

Notes to Chapter Three

1. See John Coolahan (ed.) *University entrance requirements and their effect on second level curricula* (Dublin: Irish Federation of University Teachers, 1979); AIM Group *Education is everybody's business* (Dublin: Kincora Press, 1979); Pat Holmes 'School system makes vandals' *The Sunday Press* 18 December 1977.

2. Torsten Husén *The school in question* (Oxford: Oxford University Press, 1979) p. xiii.

3. For a good account see A. Harry Passow *Secondary education reform: retrospect and prospect* (New York: Teachers College, Columbia University, 1976).

4. As recent examples see Department of Education and Science *A view of the curriculum* HMI series: Matters for Discussion, 11 (London: HMSO, 1980); Department of Education and Science *A framework for the school curriculum* (1980); Department of Education and Science *Curriculum 11-16* A working paper by HMI (December, 1977).

5. See, for example, *From education to working life* Bulletin of the European Communities, Supplement 12/76, and Tim McMullen *Innovative practices in secondary education* (Paris: OECD, 1978).

6. For two general accounts of the development of the idea see A.D.C. Peterson 'Conclusion' in Michael Yudkin (ed.) *General education* (Harmondsworth, Middlesex: Penguin Books Ltd., 1969), pp. 187-215, and Lionel Elvin *The place of commonsense in educational thought* (London: George Allen and Unwin Ltd., 1977) pp. 46-61.

7. On this point see, for example, R.M. Hutchins *The higher learning in America* (New Haven: Yale University Press, 1936), especially pp. 59-87.

8. Jacques Maritain 'Thomist views on education' in Nelson B. Henry (ed.) *Modern philosophies and education* (Chicago: The National Society for the Study of Education, 1955) p. 77.

9. See, for example, Paul H. Hirst *Knowledge and the curriculum* (London: Routledge and Kegan Paul, 1974), especially pp. 30-53.

10. Hutchins, *The higher learning in America* p. 63.

11. See B. Othanel Smith and Milton O. Meux *A study of the logic of teaching* (Urbana, Ill.: University of Illinois Press, 1970) pp. 29-55; Harry S. Broudy, B. Othanel Smith and Joe R. Burnett *Democracy and excellence in American secondary education* (Chicago: Rand McNally & Company, 1964) pp. 118-120.

12. See, for example, G.H. Bantock *Education and values* (London: Faber and Faber, 1965) pp. 33-52; G.H. Bantock *Education, culture and the emotions* (London: Faber and Faber, 1967) pp. 65-86; Yudkin (ed.) *General education*; and Philip H. Phenix *Realms of meaning* (New York: McGraw-Hill, 1964).

13. On this point see D.G. Mulcahy 'Cardinal Newman's concept of a

liberal education' in *Educational theory* 22 (Winter, 1972) 87-98.

14. G.H. Bantock 'Towards a theory of popular education' in Richard Hooper (ed.) *The curriculum: context, design and development* (Edinburgh: Oliver and Boyd, 1971) pp. 251-264.

15. See, for example, Lawrence Stenhouse *Culture and education* (London: Thomas Nelson and Sons Ltd., 1971), especially pp. 108-147.

16. In this connection see also a publication of more recent origin: County Tipperary (NR) Vocational Education Committee *Post-primary education 1985-2000 and its relevance to the economy: a policy document* (Nenagh: Co. Tipperary (NR) VEC, 1979). In this connection see also Mary Warnock *Education: a way ahead* (Oxford: Basil Blackwell, 1979), especially pp. 1-54.

17. Herbert Spencer *Education: intellectual, moral and physical* (Totowa, N.J.: Littlefield, Adams and Co., 1969).

18. *Ibid.* p. 32.

19. *Ibid.* pp. 31-36.

20. Franklin Bobbitt *How to make a curriculum* (Boston: Houghton Mifflin Company, 1924) pp. 8-9.

21. See Hazel Whitman Hertzberg, 'Competency-based teacher education: does it have a past or a future?' in *Teachers college record* 78 (September, 1976) 1-21. On this point see also John Raven *Education, values and society: the objectives of education and the nature and development of competence* (London: H.K. Lewis and Co. Ltd., 1977) pp. 98-105. Raven also favours an approach which is based on the analysis of life activities.

22. In this connection see Abraham Maslow *Motivation and personality* (New York: Harper and Row, 1954).

23. *From Education to Working Life* p. 20.

24. For an elaboration on this point see Thomas F. Green 'Career education and the pathologies of work' in Kenneth A. Strike and Kieran Egan (eds.) *Ethics and educational policy* (London: Routledge and Kegan Paul, 1978) pp. 211-222.

25. Ciarán Benson *The place of the arts in Irish education: report of the Arts Council's working party on the arts in education* (Dublin: The Arts Council, 1979).

26. Richard Pring *Knowledge and schooling* (London: Open Books, 1976), especially pp. 18-19 and 92-94; see also L.R. Perry 'Commonsense thought, knowledge and judgement and their importance for education' in Jane R. Martin (ed.) *Readings in the philosophy of education: a study of curriculum* (Boston: Allyn and Bacon Inc., 1970) pp. 187-200.

27. Pring *Knowledge and schooling* p. 92.

28. *Ibid.* p. 94. Elsewhere I have argued that Cardinal Newman, of all people, has stressed the limitations of theoretical knowledge in dealing with practical matters. See D.G. Mulcahy 'Newman's retreat from a liberal education' in *The Irish journal of education* vii (Summer, 1973) 11-22. In this connection see also Jonas F. Soltis *Education and the concept of knowledge* (New York: Teachers College, Columbia University, 1979), especially pp. 11-16.

29. D.A. MacIver 'A question of aims and assumptions in Canadian education' in *The journal of educational thought* 13/1 (1979) 13; see also Husén *The school in question* p. 133.

30. Husén *The school in question* pp. 17-18.

31. *Ibid.* pp. 134, 143-148.

32. Raven *Education, values and*

society p. 95.

33. For a fuller discussion on the place of the practical in education see, for example, David Carr 'Practical pursuits and the curriculum' in *Journal of philosophy of education* 12 (1978) 69-80; Patrick D. Walsh 'The upgrading of practical subjects' in *Journal of further and higher education* 2 (Autumn, 1978) pp. 58-71; and David Carr 'Practical reasoning and knowing how' in *Journal of human movement studies* 4 (March, 1978) pp. 3-20.

34. Hutchins *The higher learning in America* p. 61. In this connection see also Jacques Maritain *Education at the crossroads* (New Haven: Yale University Press, 1943) p. 66 where he writes: 'I advance the opinion, incidentally, that, in the general educational scheme, it would be advantageous to hurry the four years of College, so that the period of under-graduate studies would extend from sixteen to nineteen.'

35. John Dewey *Experience and education* (London: Collier-Macmillan, 1963) **pp. 46**-47. See also John Dewey *The child and the curriculum* (Chicago: The University of Chicago Press, 1956) pp. 22-24. Much of Dewey's thinking in this matter is now reflected in a number of present-day philosophers of education. See, for example, Pring *Knowledge and schooling*.

36. Raven *Education, values and society* especially pp. 48-96. See also AIM Group *Education is everybody's business* especially pp. 45-67.

37. Husén *The school in question* pp. 13-14, 17-18, 130-131, 145-148.

Notes to Chapter Four

1. See, for example, J.P. White *Towards a compulsory curriculum* (London: Routledge and Kegan Paul, 1973); P.H. Hirst *Knowledge and the curriculum* (London: Routledge and Kegan Paul, 1974); and Denis Lawton *Class, culture and curriculum* (London: Routledge and Kegan Paul, 1975). Similar views are found in the work of American writers: see Harry S. Broudy, B. Othanel Smith and Joe R. Burnett *Democracy and excellence in American secondary education* (Chicago: Rand McNally, 1964) and Philip H. Phenix *Realms of meaning* (New York: McGraw Hill, 1964).

2. Seán O'Connor 'Are we serving the system instead of the scholar?' in *Irish broadcasting review* (Spring, 1979) p. 11.

3. County Tipperary (NR) Vocational Education Committee *Post-primary education 1985-2000 and its relevance to the economy: a policy document* (Nenagh: Co. Tipperary (NR) VEC, 1979); AIM Group *Education is everybody's business* (Dublin: Kincora Press Ltd., 1979).

4. County Tipperary (NR) VEC, *Post-primary education 1985-2000* pp. 22-37.

5. Department of Education *Rules and programme for secondary schools* 1980-81 (Dublin: The Stationery Office, 1980) pp. 273-279.

6. *Ibid.* p. 277.

7. *Ibid.* p. 278.

8. *Ibid.* pp. 267-273.

9. In this connection see Richard Johnston 'The Irish senior English course: coping with varying linguistic abilities' in *Proceedings of the Education Conference, 1976* (Galway: Education Department, University College, Galway, n.d.) pp. 30-34, and Richard Johnston *An analysis of the*

Leaving Certificate English course (Unpublished MEd thesis, University College, Cork, 1975).

10. Department of Education *Rules 1980-81*, p. 56; Department of Education *Rules and programme for the Day Vocational Certificate examinations* V.50, 80/81 (Dublin: The Stationery Office) p. 3.

11. See, for example, P.D. Walsh 'The upgrading of practical subjects' in *Journal of further and higher education* 2 (Autumn, 1978) 58-71.

12. *Report of the Council of Education: the curriculum of the secondary school* (Dublin: The Stationery Office, 1960) pp. 178-180, 194-198; *Rules* 1980-81, pp. 145-147.

13. *Rules* 1980-81, p. 252. *The white paper on educational development* (Dublin: The Stationery Office, 1980) pp. 49-50, would appear to support this view also.

14. In this connection see 'We Say' in *The Sunday Independent* 16 December 1979.

15. County Tipperary (NR) VEC, *Post-primary education 1985-2000* pp. 5-10.

16. See Mícheál Ó Lionáin 'Pre-employment courses — an overview' in *Compass* 7/2 (1978) pp. 3-9; Department of Education *Pre-employment courses* (1980); O. Egan and J. O'Reilly *The transition year project* (Dublin: The Educational Research Centre, St Patrick's College, 1977).

17. County Tipperary (NR) VEC, *Post-primary education 1985-2000*, p. 13; Irish Vocational Education Association *Official Report* 1979, pp. 32-33.

18. Egan and O'Reilly *The Transition year project*.

19. *Rules* 1980-81, p. 156.

20. See *From education to working life* Bulletin of the European Communities, Supplement 12/76.

21. Ó Lionáin 'Pre-employment courses — an overview' p. 6.

22. Department of Education *Statistical report* 1978-9 (Dublin: The Stationery Office, n.d.) pp. 56-60.

23. *Ibid.* See also *Rules* 1980-81, pp. 332-335.

24. Ciarán Benson *The place of the arts in Irish education: report of the Arts Council's working party on the arts in education* (Dublin: The Arts Council, 1979) pp. 57-58. See also Thomas G. Mullins *Literature as play* (Unpublished MEd Thesis, University College, Cork, 1980).

25. Benson *The place of the arts in Irish education* pp. 42-64.

26. P.H. Hirst and R.S. Peters *The logic of education* (London: Routledge and Kegan Paul, 1970) pp. 62-66. For an elaboration on this, see Hirst *Knowledge and the curriculum*, especially pp. 43-46, 84-100.

27. Hirst and Peters *The logic of education* p. 67.

28. Hirst *Knowledge and the curriculum* pp. 38-43.

29. Broudy, Smith and Burnett *Democracy and excellence in American secondary education* p. 45. See also Harry S. Broudy *Building a philosophy of education* (Englewood Cliffs, N.J.: Prentice Hall, Inc., 1961).

30. Broudy, Smith and Burnett *Democracy and excellence in American secondary education* pp. 71-73.

31. *Ibid.* p. 245.

32. *Ibid.* pp. 245-246.

33. *Ibid.* p. 247. It is interesting to note that Hirst and Peters appear to agree on the importance of educational experiences of the kind Broudy has in mind when he includes the study of molar problems in the curriculum. See Hirst and Peters *The logic of education* p. 72.

34. See, for example, Department of

Education and Science *A view of the curriculum* HMI Series: Matters for Discussion, 11 (London: HMSO, 1980); Department of Education and Science *A framework for the school curriculum* (1980).

35. See above, chapter one, and *Rules* 1980-81, pp. 13-15, 23.

36. Hirst and Peters *The logic of education* pp. 66-67.

37. In this connection see F.X. Russo 'Irish and the social studies: Irish eyes aren't smiling — they're closed' in *Compass* 2 (May, 1973) 5-16.

38. Alfred North Whitehead *The aims of education* (New York: The Free Press, 1967), pp. 6-7.

39. Herbert Spencer *Education: intellectual, moral and physical* (Totowa, N.J.: Littlefield, Adams and Co., 1969) pp. 54-55.

40. To be more specific: if a liberal education must meet, for example, Hirst's forms of knowledge, what I am saying is that the specific content within these forms may have to be selected against practical criteria such as the degree of preparation given for democratic decision-making, for health education, for household budgeting, etc. This, to some extent, is what Broudy succeeds in doing in his provision for the study of molar problems. See also Hirst and Peters *The logic of education* p. 72.

41. In this connection see, for example, Douglas Barnes *From Communication to curriculum* (Harmondsworth, Middlesex: Penguin Books, 1976) pp. 147-149.

Notes to Chapter Five

1. See Dewey's interesting remarks on the uncomfortable situation experienced by second-level education arising out of its middle-ground position between primary and third-level education in John Dewey *The educational situation* (Chicago: University of Chicago Press, 1904; reprinted by Arno Press and the New York Times, New York, 1969) pp. 50-79.

2. In this connection see Seán P. Ó Conchuir 'Transition from primary to post-primary school' in *The secondary teacher* 8 (Autumn and Winter, 1978) 18-19.

3. See T. Desmond Swan *Reading standards in Irish schools* (Dublin: The Educational Company of Ireland, 1978); see also *White paper on educational development* (Dublin: The Stationery Office, 1980) pp. 56-57 and *Compass* 6 (February, 1977) 1-80.

4. See, for example, Swan *Reading standards in Irish schools* pp. 2-3, 8-9.

5. Pádraig Faulkner, TD, Minister for Education, addressing the UNESCO General Conference, Sixteenth Session, Paris, September, 1970, in Randles *Post-primary education in Ireland, 1957-1970* (Dublin: Veritas Publications, 1975) p. 323.

6. See Committee on the form and function of the Intermediate Certificate Examination *The ICE Report* (Dublin: The Stationery Office, 1975).

7. *Ibid.* p. 87.

8. For further information on the project see J. Heywood (ed.) *Assessment in history* Report No 1 of the Public Examinations Evaluation Project (Dublin: School of Education, Trinity Colledge, 1974); J. Heywood, *Assessment in mathematics* Report No 2 of the Public Examinations Evaluation Project (Dublin: School of Education, Trinity College, 1976); J. Heywood, S. McGuinness and D. Murphy *The public examinations evaluation project: a progress report* Report No 3 of

the Public Examinations Evaluation Project (Dublin: School of Education, Trinity College, 1977); and J. Heywood, S. McGuinness and D. Murphy *The public examinations evaluation project: the final report* (Dublin: The School of Education, Trinity College, 1980).

9. For a brief account of the work of these and other projects at the post-primary level in Ireland during the period being considered, as well as a most useful and comprehensive bibliography, see Tony Crooks 'Research and development in curriculum and examinations at second level in the Republic of Ireland' *Compass* 6/2 (1977) 26-46. A five-week series on new curriculum projects in second-level schools is also to be found in *The Irish Times* commencing on 19 January 1981.

10. On this question of the points system, see John Coolahan (ed.) *University entrance requirements and their effect on second-level curricula* (Dublin: Irish Federation of University Teachers, 1979). See also M.A. Moran and M.J. Crowley 'The Leaving Certificate and first-year university performance' paper presented to the Statistical and Social Inquiry Society of Ireland, Dublin, 24 May 1979; and Seán O'Connor 'Post-primary education: now and in the future' *Studies* LVII (Autumn, 1968) 244-246.

11. For details of how the points system for entry to higher education operates, and information on the complicated and intricate criteria which are applied by the various participating institutions of higher education, see the Central Applications Office *Handbook 1978* (Dublin: Central Applications Office n.d.).

12. National University of Ireland *Matriculation regulations and courses for 1981* (Dublin: National University of Ireland, n.d.) p. 9.

13. Moran and Crowley 'The Leaving Certificate and first-year university performance' p. 42.

14. O'Connor 'Post-primary education' p. 246.

15. See Dorothea Furth 'International trends in selection for university' in Coolahan (ed.) *University entrance requirements* p. 4-12, and Irish Federation of University Teachers 'University selection procedures' unpublished position paper, n.d., c. 1979.

16. See Patrick O'Connor 'The effect of the present selection procedures as seen from the community school' in Coolahan (ed.) *University entrance requirements* p. 45.

17. Two important early studies in this area are Philip W. Jackson *Life in classrooms* (New York: Holt Rinehart and Winston, 1968), and Robert Dreeben *On what is learned in school* (Reading, Mass.: Addison-Wesley Publishing Co., 1968); see also John Eggleston *The sociology of the school curriculum* (London: Routledge and Kegan Paul, 1977) pp. 109-118; John Holt *How children fail* (New York: Pitman Publishing Corporation, 1964). For an older-style treatment of the same topics see W.A.L. Blyth *English primary education: A sociological description* 2 vols. (London: Routledge and Kegan Paul, 1967). For accounts which highlight some particularly Irish features see John Horgan 'Education and community' in Michael W. Murphy (ed.) *Education in Ireland III: to unleash the potential* (Cork: The Mercier Press, 1972) pp. 19-33, and Patrick Clancy 'The hidden curriculum' in AIM Group *Education is everybody's business* (Dublin: Kincora Press Ltd.,

1979) pp. 36-44.

18. Eggleston *The Sociology of the school curriculum* pp. 109-118.

19. See Michael B. Katz *The irony of early school reform: educational innovation in mid-nineteenth century Massachusetts* (Cambridge, Mass.: Harvard University Press, 1968); Samuel Bowles and Herbert Gintis *Schooling in capitalist America: educational reform and the contradictions of economic life* (London: Routledge and Kegan Paul, 1967; and M.F.D. Young (ed.) *Knowledge and control* (London: Collier-Macmillan, 1971).

20. John Dewey *Experience and education* (London: Collier-Macmillan, 1963) p. 48.

21. For a fuller account of the subject curriculum see, for example, B. Othanel Smith, William O. Stanley and J. Harlan Shores *Fundamentals of curriculum development* (New York: Harcourt, Brace and World, Inc., 1957) pp. 229-263. For an interesting discussion of the subject curriculum, some criticisms of it, and a consideration of alternative approaches, see Harry S. Broudy *Building a philosophy of education* (Englewood Cliffs, N.J.: Prentice-Hall, Inc., 1961) pp. 283-310.

22. Department of Education *Rules and programme for secondary schools, 1980/81* (Dublin: The Stationery Office, 1978), and Department of Education *Rules and programme for the Day Vocational Certificate examinations* V. 50, 80/81 (Dublin: The Stationery Office).

23. See Smith, Stanley, Shores *Fundamentals of curriculum development* pp. 231-234.

24. See *Rules, 1980/81* pp. 9-21, and National University of Ireland *Matriculation regulations and courses for 1981* pp. 7-10.

25. *Rules* 1980/81, pp. 9, 13.

26. See Paulo Freire *Pedagogy of the oppressed* (New York: Herder and Herder, 1970) pp. 57-74.

27. A.N. Whitehead *The aims of education* (New York: The Free Press, 1967) pp. 6-7.

28. See, for example, Broudy *Building a philosophy of education* p. 285.

29. In this regard it must be acknowledged that a number of the new comprehensive and community schools in particular have taken measures to provide all first-year post-primary pupils with a particularly wide range of subjects as a basis for making an informed selection of subjects subsequently.

30. In this connection it is noteworthy that there once was serious consideration given in the Department of Education to the idea of introducing 'major' and 'minor' subjects into the Leaving Certificate course. See Department of Education 'Structure of the Leaving Certificate course and examination' (M.29/68) pp. 4-7.

31. See, for example, Tim McMullen *Innovative practices in secondary education* (Paris: Centre for Educational Research and Innovation, OECD, 1978) p. 23.

32. Religion may be considered somewhat of an exception in this regard in that, in practice, a teacher may teach religion for up to nine hours per week and be paid for it, even though religion is not a subject on the Minister's programme.

33. P.H. Pearse 'The murder machine' in P.H. Pearse *Political writings and speeches* (Dublin: The Talbot Press Ltd., 1966) pp. 34-35.

34. See, for example, J.P. White *Towards a compulsory curriculum* (London: Routledge and Kegan Paul, 1973); Denis Lawton *Class, culture and the curriculum* (London: Routledge and Kegan Paul,

1975); and Maurice Holt *The common curriculum: its structure and style in the comprehensive school* (London: Routledge and Kegan Paul, 1978).

35. John Raven *Education, values and society: the objectives of education and the nature and development of competence* (London: H.K. Lewis and Co. Ltd., 1977) pp. 47-88.

36. See Pat Holmes 'School system makes vandals' in *The Sunday Press* 18 December 1977.

37. Raven *Education, values and society* pp. 47-88.

38. For further details see George F. Madaus and John Macnamara *Public examinations: a study of the Irish Leaving Certificate* (Dublin: Educational Research Centre, St Patrick's College, 1970), pp. 123-135. Despite my critical remarks in this and following pages, it must be acknowledged that, poor though it may be, the Leaving Certificate examination may still be the best predictor of university performance which exists in Ireland. See also Monica Nevin *School Performance and university achievement* (Dublin: Higher Education Authority, 1974) pp. 23-24; Monica Nevin, 'University Selection based on school performance' in Coolahan (ed.) *University entrance requirements* pp. 87-93; and Vincent Greaney 'The predictive validity of the Irish Leaving Certificate examination' in Coolahan (ed.) *University entrance requirements* pp. 70-86.

39. In this connection see Madaus and Macnamara *Public examinations* pp. 10-11 and the *ICE Report* pp. 50-51. See also Department of Education 'Structure of the Leaving Certificate' p. 7.

40. See Madaus and Macnamara *Public examinations*; see also John Macnamara and George F. Madaus 'Marker reliability in the Irish Leaving Certificate' in *The Irish journal of education* III (Summer, 1969) 5-21.

41. Madaus and Macnamara *Public examinations* pp. 16-17.

42. Greaney 'The predictive validity of the Irish Leaving Certificate examination' p. 71.

43. Madaus and Macnamara *Public examinations* and George F. Madaus and John Macnamara 'The quality of the Irish Leaving Certificate examination' in *The Irish journal of education* IV (Summer, 1970) 5-18.

44. Greaney 'The predictive validity of the Irish Leaving Certificate examination'.

45. Madaus and Macnamara 'The quality of the Irish Leaving Certificate examination' and *Public examinations*; see also the *ICE Report* p. 34.

46. Seán Ó Catháin *Secondary Education in Ireland* (Dublin: The Talbot Press, 1958) p. 61; see also Madaus and Macnamara *Public examinations* pp. 123-135.

47. Raven *Education, values and society* pp. 58-60.

Notes to Chapter Six

1. President Lyndon Baines Johnson, quoted in Donald William Cox *The City as a schoolhouse* (Valley Forge, Pa.: Judson Press, 1972) p. 179.

2. In this connection the shift of position by R.S. Peters from his earlier and 'more differentiated' concept of education to an 'undifferentiated' concept is noteworthy. See R.S. Peters *Ethics and education* (London: George Allen and Unwin Ltd., 1966), especially pp. 23-62, and P.H. Hirst and R.S. Peters *The logic of education* (London: Routledge and Kegan Paul, 1970), especially pp. 17-28.

3. *Report of the Council of Education: the curriculum of the*

secondary school (Dublin: The Stationery Office, 1960) p. 88. The stance adopted in the *White paper on educational development* (Dublin: The Stationery Office, 1980) pp. 45-46 is consistent with this.

4. Ivan Illich *Deschooling society* (New York: Harper and Row, 1971) is probably the best-known work of criticism of recent years.

5. In this connection see, for example, Department of Education *Pre-employment courses* (1980).

6. See Department of Education *Primary school curriculum: teacher's handbook* Parts I and II (Dublin: Browne and Nolan, 1971).

7. See *White paper on educational development* p. 43.

8. County Tipperary (NR) VEC *Post-primary education 1985-2000 and its relevance to the economy: a policy document* (Nenagh: Co. Tipperary (NR) VEC, 1979).

9. *Ibid.* p. 22.

10. For an important document with implications for post-primary education in Ireland in this area, see *From education to working life* Bulletin of the European Communities, Supplement 12/76.

11. In themselves, the efforts of the Department of Education in the form of pre-employment courses may be valuable. I would, however, be concerned about their possible implications, and the implications of the position adopted in the *White paper on educational development* p. 49, which is in line with them. One of the achievements of the reform measures of the past fifteen years has been the bringing about of a greater unification of post-primary education in Ireland. But to talk now of introducing non-Leaving Certificate, post-inter-mediate level, vocational type courses may be to revert to a 'vocational versus a secondary' stance again. Far better, I would argue, to broaden the concept of senior-cycle second-level education so as to include pre-employment education within the framework of the school Leaving Certificate programme than to introduce potentially divisive distinctions. In the end, vocational education will be the most likely to lose out under such circumstances. Moreover, if greater provision were made for pre-employment education within the context of general education at the junior level, as I am arguing should be done, there may be less need to provide pre-employment courses to equip young school leavers for work after they have left school. And this, it must be remembered, is the aim of the existing pre-employment courses. See Department of Education *Pre-employment courses*.

12. For a different viewpoint from mine on this whole question see Gerry Gaden 'Depth of knowledge as an educational aim' in *Proceedings* of the Educational Studies Association of Ireland Conference, Dublin 1979 (Galway: Galway University Press) pp. 224-233.

13. Hirst and Peters *The logic of education* pp. 60-73.

14. *White paper on educational development* p. 46.

15. Harry S. Broudy, B. Othanel Smith, and Joe R. Burnett *Democracy and excellence in American secondary education* (Chicago: Rand McNally and Company, 1964) pp. 231-243, 272-274. This is also the general idea behind the City of Dublin Humanities Curriculum at the junior level.

16. See Paul Andrews 'The influence

of university entrance requirements on second level curricula and examinations' in John Coolahan (ed.) *University entrance requirements and their effect on second level curricula* (Dublin: Irish Federation of University Teachers, 1979) p. 57.

17. This view is quite explicit in the terms of reference for the committee set up by the Minister for Education in June 1978 to investigate the question of transfer from primary school to post-primary school. See Department of Education 'Pupil transfer Committee' (Dublin: Government Information Service, 12 June 1978) p. 1. The terms of reference read as follows: 'To report on the problems of transition from child-centered primary to subject-centered post-primary schools and to make recommendations as to changes which may be necessary in primary and post-primary curricula in order to alleviate these problems.'

18. In this connection see, for example, Cox *The city as a schoolhouse* and Thorsten Husén *The school in question* (Oxford: Oxford University Press, 1979), especially pp. 149-181.

19. There is a significant though neglected tradition in European educational thought, as represented by such a variety of writers as St Augustine, Rousseau and Cardinal Newman, which emphasises the educational value of first-hand experience of the concrete world.

20. *White paper on educational development* p. 46.

21. Committee on the form and function of the Intermediate Certificate Examination *The ICE Report* (Dublin: The Stationery Office, 1975), especially pp. 55-81; see also, however, *An Appraisal of the ICE Report* by A Working Party set up by the Irish Association for Curriculum Development; and John Heywood *Examining in second level education* (Dublin: Association of Secondary Teachers, Ireland, 1977).

22. For further discussion of current thinking and practice in this area, and of the need for further research, see Heywood *Examining in second level education* pp. 131-146, and *ICE Report* Appendix F.

23. *White paper on educational development* p. 50.

24. See, for example, Christina Murphy *School Report* (Dublin: Ward River Press, 1980) pp. 96-97.

25. D.G. Mulcahy 'The need for a rationale and alternative approaches to teacher education' in *The secondary teacher* 5 (Winter, 1975) 5-12.

Bibliography of Selected Sources

Official publications and documents

Colley, George, Minister for Education. Letter to the Authorities of Secondary and Vocational Schools, January, 1966.

Committee on the form and function of the Intermediate Certificate Examination. *The ICE Report*. Dublin: The Stationery Office, 1975.

Department of Education. *Rules and programmes for secondary schools* for the years 1924/5 to 1980/81. Dublin: The Stationery Office.

Department of Education. *Rules and programme for the Day Vocational Certificate Examinations* V. 50, 80/81. (Memo. V. 50.) Dublin: The Stationery Office, 1980.

Department of Education. *Report* for the years 1924/5 to 1978/9. Dublin: The Stationery Office.

Department of Education. *Pupil transfer committee*. Dublin: Government Information Service, 12 June 1978.

Department of Education. *Primary school curriculum: teacher's handbook* Parts I and II. Dublin: Browne and Nolan, 1971.

Department of Education 'Community schools' October 1970.

Department of Education. *Structure of the Leaving Certificate course and examination* (M. 29/68), 1968.

Department of Education. *Report on the facilities for post-primary education in each county and an estimate of requirements for 1970*, 1966.

Department of Education, Technical Branch. *Memorandum V. 40: organization of whole-time continuation courses in borough, urban and county areas* n.d., c. 1942.

Department of Education and Science. *A view of the curriculum* HMI Series: Matters for Discussion, 11. London: HMSO, 1980.

Department of Education and Science (UK). *A framework for the school curriculum,* 1980.

Department of Education and Science. *Curriculum 11-16.* A working paper by HMI (December, 1977).

Investment in education. Dublin: The Stationery Office, 1965.

National Economic and Social Council. *Educational expenditure in Ireland.* Report No 12. Dublin: The Stationery Office, 1976.

Programme for economic expansion. Dublin: The Stationery Office, 1958.

Second programme for economic expansion. Part I. Dublin: The Stationery Office, 1963.

Second programme for economic expansion. Part II. Dublin: The Stationery Office, 1964.

Statement by Dr P.J. Hillery, TD, Minister for Education, in regard to post-primary education. Press Conference, 20 May 1963.

Report of the Council of Education: the curriculum of the secondary school. Dublin: The Stationery Office, 1960.

Vocational Education Act, 1930.

White paper on educational development. Dublin: The Stationery Office, 1980.

Other works

Andrews, Paul. 'The influence of university entrance requirements on second level curricula and examinations' *University entrance requirements and their effect on second level curricula.* Edited by John Coolahan. Dublin: Irish Federation of University Teachers, 1979.

An Appraisal of the ICE Report. By a working party set by the Irish Association for Curriculum Development.

AIM Group. *Education is everybody's business.* Dublin: Kincora Press, 1979.

Akenson, Donald H. *A mirror to Kathleen's face: education in independent Ireland 1922-1960.* Montreal: McGill, Queen's University Press, 1975.

Bantock, G.H. 'Towards a theory of popular education' in *The curriculum: context, design and development.* Edited by Richard Hooper. Edinburgh: Oliver and Boyd, 1971.

    Education, culture and the emotions. London: Faber and Faber, 1967.

Education and values. London: Faber and Faber, 1965.

Barnes, Douglas. *From communication to curriculum.* Harmonds-worth, Middlesex: Penguin Books, 1976.

Benson, Ciarán. *The place of the arts in Irish education: report of the Arts Council's working party on the arts in education.* Dublin: The Arts Council, 1979.

Blyth, W.A.L. *English primary education: a sociological description.* London: Routledge and Kegan Paul, 1967.

Bobbitt, Franklin. *How to make a curriculum.* Boston: Houghton Mifflin Company, 1924.

Bowles, Samuel, and Gintis, Herbert. *Schooling in capitalist America: educational reform and the contradictions of economic life.* London: Routledge and Kegan Paul, 1967.

Broudy, Harry S. *Building a philosophy of education.* Englewood Cliffs, N.J.: Prentice-Hall, Inc., 1961.

Broudy, Harry S., Smith, B. Othanel, and Burnett, Joe R. *Democracy and excellence in American secondary education.* Chicago: Rand McNally and Company, 1964.

Carr, David. 'Practical pursuits and the curriculum' in *Journal of philosophy of education* 12 (1978) 69-80.

    'Practical reasoning and knowing how' in *Journal of human movement studies* 4 (March, 1978) 3-20.

Central Applications Office. *Handbook 1978.* Dublin: The Central Applications Office, n.d.

Centre for Educational Research and Innovation. *Handbook on curriculum development.* Paris: OECD, 1975.

Compass 6/1 (1977) 1-80.

Coolahan, John (ed.). *University entrance requirements and their effect on second level curriculum.* Dublin: Irish Federation of University Teachers, 1979.

County Tipperary (NR) Vocational Education Committee. *Post-primary education 1985-2000 and its relevance to the economy: a policy document.* Nenagh: Co.Tipperary (NR) VEC, 1979.

Cox, Donald William. *The city as a schoolhouse.* Valley Forge, Pa.: Judson Press, 1972.

Crooks, Tony. 'Research and development in curriculum and examinations at second level in the Republic of Ireland' in *Compass* 6/2 (1977) 26-46.

Dewey, John. *Experience and education*. London: Collier-Macmillan, 1963.

The child and the curriculum. Chicago: The University of Chicago Press, 1956.

The educational situation. Chicago: University of Chicago Press, 1904. (reprinted by Arno Press and the New York Times, New York, 1969.)

Donoghue, Denis. 'Comments' in *Studies* LVII (Autumn, 1968) 284-288.

Dreeben, Robert. *On what is learned in school*. Reading, Mass.: Addison-Wesley Publishing Co., 1968.

Egan, O., and O'Reilly, J. *The transition year project*. Dublin: The Educational Research Centre, St Patrick's College, 1977.

Eggleston, John. *The sociology of the school curriculum*. London: Routledge and Kegan Paul, 1977.

Elvin, Lionel. *The place of commonsense in educational thought*. London: George Allen and Unwin Ltd., 1977.

Freire, Paulo. *Pedagogy of the oppressed*. New York: Herder and Herder, 1970.

From education to working life. Bulletin of the European Communities. Supplement 12/76.

Furth, Dorothea. 'International trends in selection for university' in *University entrance requirements and their effect on second level curricula*. Edited by John Coolahan. Dublin: Irish Federation of University Teachers, 1979.

Gaden, Gerry. 'Depth of knowledge as an educational aim' in *Proceedings* of the Educational Studies Association of Ireland Conference, Dublin 1979. Galway: Galway University Press, 224-233.

Greaney, Vincent. 'The predictive validity of the Irish Leaving Certificate examination' in *University entrance requirements and their effect on second level curricula*. Edited by John Coolahan. Dublin: Irish Federation of University Teachers, 1979.

Green, Thomas F. 'Career education and the pathologies of work' in *Ethics and educational policy*. Edited by Kenneth A. Strike and Kieran Egan. London: Routledge and Kegan Paul, 1978.

Hertzberg, Hazel Whitman. 'Competency-based teacher education: does it have a past or a future?' in *Teachers college record* 78 (September, 1976) 1-21.

Heywood, John. *Examining in second level education*. Dublin: Association of Secondary Teachers, Ireland, 1977.

Assessment in mathematics. Dublin: School of Education, Trinity College, 1976.

Heywood, J. (ed.) *Assessment in history*. Dublin: School of Education, Trinity College, 1974.

Heywood, J., McGuinness, S., and Murphy, D. *The public examinations evaluation project: the final report*. Dublin: The School of Education, Trinity College, 1980.

The public examinations evaluation project: a progress report. Dublin: School of Education, Trinity College, 1977.

Higher Education Authority. A council for national awards and a college for higher education at Limerick. Dublin: The Higher Education Authority, 1969. (Reprinted 1974).

Hirst, Paul H. *Knowledge and the curriculum*. London: Routledge and Kegan Paul, 1974.

Hirst, P.H. and Peters, R.S. *The logic of education*. London: Routledge and Kegan Paul, 1970.

Holmes, Pat. 'School system makes vandals' in *The Sunday Press* 18 December 1977.

Holt, John. *How children fail*. New York: Pitman Publishing Corporation, 1964.

Holt, Maurice. *The common curriculum: its structure and style in the comprehensive school*. London: Routledge and Kegan Paul, 1978.

Horgan, John. 'Education in the Republic of Ireland' in *Education in Great Britain and Ireland*. Edited by Robert Bell, Gerald Fowler and Ken Little. London: Routledge and Kegan Paul, 1973.

'Education and community' in *Education in Ireland III: to unleash the potential*. Edited by Michael W. Murphy. Cork: The Mercier Press, 1972.

Husén, Torsten. *The school in question*. Oxford: Oxford University Press, 1979.

Hutchins, R.M. *The higher learning in America*. New Haven: Yale University Press, 1936.

Illich, Ivan. *Deschooling society*. New York: Harper and Row, 1971.

Irish Federation of University Teachers. 'University selection procedures'. Unpublished Position Paper, n.d., c. 1979.

Irish National Teachers' Organisation. *A plan for education.* Dublin: The Irish National Teachers' Organisation, 1947.

Irish Vocational Education Association. *Official Report,* 1979.

Jackson, Philip W. *Life in classrooms.* New York: Holt Rinehart and Winston, 1968.

Johnston, Richard. 'The Irish senior English course: coping with varying linguistic abilities' in *Proceedings* of the Education Conference, 1976. Galway: Education Department, University College, Galway, n.d.

  An analysis of the Leaving Certificate English course. Unpublished MEd thesis, University College, Cork, 1975.

Katz, Michael B. *The irony of early school reform: educational innovation in mid-nineteenth century Massachusetts.* Cambridge, Mass.: Harvard University Press, 1968.

Lawton, Denis. *Class, culture and curriculum.* London: Routledge and Kegan Paul, 1975.

MacIver, D.A. 'A question of aims and assumptions in Canadian education' in *The journal of educational thought* 13/1 (1979) 3-15.

Macnamara, John, and Madaus, George F. 'Marker reliability in the Irish Leaving Certificate' in *The Irish journal of education* III (Summer, 1969) 5-21.

McMullen, Tim. *Innovative practices in secondary education.* Paris: OECD, 1978.

Madaus, George, F. and Macnamara, John. 'The quality of the Irish Leaving Certificate examination' in *The Irish journal of education* IV (Summer, 1970) 5-18.

  Public examinations: a study of the Irish Leaving Certificate. Dublin: Educational Research Centre, St Patrick's College, 1970.

Maritain, Jacques. 'Thomist views on education' in *Modern philosophies and education.* Edited by Nelson B. Henry. Chicago: The National Society for the Study of Education, 1955.

  Education at the crossroads. New Haven: Yale University Press, 1943.

Maslow, Abraham. *Motivation and personality*. New York: Harper and Row, 1959.

Moran, M.A. and Crowley, M.J. 'The Leaving Certificate and first year university performance'. Paper presented to the Statistical and Social Inquiry Society of Ireland. Dublin, 24 May 1979.

Morrish, Ivor. *Aspects of educational change*. London: George Allen and Unwin Ltd., 1976.

Mulcahy, D.G. 'The need for a rationale and alternative approaches to teacher education' in *The secondary teacher* 5 (Winter, 1975) 5-12.

   'Newman's retreat from a liberal education' in *The Irish journal of education* vii (Summer, 1973) 11-22.

   'Cardinal Newman's concept of a liberal education' in *Educational theory* 22 (Winter, 1972) 87-98.

Mullins, Thomas G. *Literature as play*. Unpublished MEd Thesis, University College, Cork, 1980.

Murphy, Christina. *School Report*. Dublin: Ward River Press, 1980.

National University of Ireland. *Matriculation regulations and courses for 1981*. Dublin: The National University of Ireland, n.d.

Nevin, Monica. 'University selection based on school performance' in *University entrance requirements and their effect on second level curricula*. Edited by John Coolahan. Dublin: Irish Federation of University Teachers, 1979.

   School performance and university achievement. Dublin: Higher Education Authority, 1974.

Ó Catháin, Seán. *Secondary education in Ireland*. Dublin: The Talbot Press, 1958.

Ó Conchuir, Seán P. 'Transition from primary to post-primary school' in *The secondary teacher* 8 (Autumn and Winter, 1978) 18-19.

O'Connor, Daniel C. *Curriculum development at second level in the Republic of Ireland*. Unpublished PhD Thesis, St Patrick's College, Maynooth, 1976.

O'Connor, Patrick. 'The effect of the present selection procedures as seen from the community school' in *University entrance requirements and their effect on second level curricula*. Edited by John Coolahan. Dublin: Irish Federation of University Teachers, 1979.

O'Connor, Seán. 'Are we serving the system instead of the scholar?' in *Irish broadcasting review* (Spring 1979) 7-12.

'Post-primary education: now and in the future' in *Studies* LVII (Autumn, 1968) 233-249.

Ó Lionáin, Mícheál. 'Pre-employment courses — an overview' in *Compass* 7/2 (1978) 3-9.

O'Meara, J.J. *Reform in education.* Dublin: Mount Salus Press, 1958.

Organisation for Economic Co-operation and Development. *Reviews of national policies for education: Ireland.* Paris: OECD, 1969.

Orlosky, Donald E. and Smith, B. Othanel. *Curriculum development: issues and insights.* Chicago: Rand McNally, 1978.

Ó Súilleabháin, Séamas V. 'Secondary education' in *A history of Irish catholicism* Vol. 5. Edited by Patrick J. Corish. Dublin: Gill and Macmillan, 1971.

Passow, A. Harry. *Secondary education reform: retrospect and prospect.* New York: Teachers' College, Columbia University, 1976.

Passow, A. Harry, Noah, Harold J., Eckstein, Max A. and Mallea, John R. *The national case study: an empirical comparative study of twenty-one educational systems.* New York: John Wiley and Sons, 1976.

Pearse, P.H. *Political writings and speeches.* Dublin: The Talbot Press Ltd., 1966.

Perry, L.R. 'Commonsense thought, knowledge, and judgement and their importance for education' in *Readings in the Philosophy of education: a study of curriculum.* Edited by Jane R. Martin. Boston: Allyn and Bacon Inc., 1970.

Peters, R.S. *Ethics and education.* London: George Allen and Unwin Ltd., 1966.

Peterson, A.D.C. 'Conclusion' in *General education.* Edited by Michael Yudkin. Harmondsworth, Middlesex: Penguin Books Ltd., 1969.

Phenix, Philip H. *Realms of meaning.* New York: McGraw Hill, 1964.

Pring, Richard. *Knowledge and schooling.* London: Open Books, 1976.

Randles, Eileen. *Post-primary education in Ireland, 1957-1970.*

Dublin: Veritas Publications, 1976.

Raven, John. *Education, values and society: the objectives of education and the nature and development of competence.* London: H.K. Lewis and Co. Ltd., 1977.

Reid, William A. *Thinking about the curriculum: the nature and treatment of curriculum problems.* London: Routledge and Kegan Paul, 1978.

Russo, F.X. 'Irish and the social studies: Irish eyes aren't smiling — they're closed' in *Compass* 2 (May, 1973) 5-16.

Ryan, Liam. 'Social dynamite: a study of early school-leavers' in *Christus Rex* xxi (January, February, March, 1967) 7-44.

Ryba, Raymond. 'The context of curricular change in Europe at the lower secondary level' in *Compare* 10/2 (1980) 101-116.

Smith, B. Othanel and Meux, Milton O. *A study of the logic of teaching.* Urbana, Ill.: Bureau of Educational Research, College of Education, University of Illinois, 1962.

Smith, B.O., Stanley, W.O., and Shores, J.H. *Fundamentals of curriculum development.* New York: Harcourt, Brace and World, Inc., 1957.

Soltis, Jonas F. *Education and the concept of knowledge.* New York: Teachers' College, Columbia University, 1979.

Spencer, Herbert. *Education: intellectual, moral and physical.* Totowa, N.J.: Littlefield, Adams and Co., 1969.

Stenhouse, Lawrence. *Culture and education.* London: Thomas Nelson and Sons Ltd., 1971.

Swan, T. Desmond. *Reading standards in Irish schools.* Dublin: The Educational Company of Ireland, 1978.

Troddyn, P.M. 'The community school document: a first examination by the editor of *Studies*' in *Studies* LIX (Winter, 1970) 346-376.

Tuairim. *Irish education.* London: Tuairim Pamphlet No 9, n.d., c. 1961-62.

Tussing, A. Dale. *Irish educational expenditures — past, present and future.* Dublin: The Economic and Social Research Institute, 1978.

'The coming explosion in school enrolments and expenditures' in *The secondary teacher*, 6 (Winter, 1976) 12-14.

Tyler, Ralph A. *Basic principles of curriculum and instruction.* Chicago: The University of Chicago Press, 1949.

Walsh, Patrick D. 'The upgrading of practical subjects' in *Journal of further and higher education* 2 (Autumn, 1978) 58-71.

Warnock, Mary. *Education: a way ahead*. Oxford: Basil Blackwell, 1979.

Whitehead, A.N. *The aims of education*. New York: The Free Press, 1967.

White, J.P. *Towards a compulsory curriculum*. London: Routledge and Kegan Paul, 1973.

Whyte, J.H. *Church and state in modern Ireland*. Dublin: Gill and Macmillan, 1971.

Young, M.F.D. (ed.). *Knowledge and control*. London: Collier-Macmillan, 1971.

Index

Note: *n* after a page number signifies that the reference is to a note and the following italicised number refers to the number of the note on the page.